Peter Manley Scott

A Theology of Postnatural Right

Studies in Religion and the Environment
Studien zur Religion und Umwelt

published on behalf of the
European Forum for the Study
of Religion and the Environment
by

Sigurd Bergmann

Volume 13

LIT

Peter Manley Scott

A Theology of Postnatural Right

LIT

Cover Image: 1254929 Dandelion (Taraxacum sp) growing on
wasteland by derelict, graffiti-covered building, Bristol, UK
© Michael Hutchinson/naturepl.com.

This book is printed on acid-free paper.

Bibliographic information published by the Deutsche Nationalbibliothek
The Deutsche Nationalbibliothek lists this publication in the Deutsche
Nationalbibliografie; detailed bibliographic data are available on the Internet at
http://dnb.d-nb.de.

ISBN 978-3-643-91076-9 (pb)
ISBN 978-3-643-96076-4 (PDF)

© LIT VERLAG Dr. W. Hopf Berlin 2019
Verlagskontakt:
Fresnostr. 2   D-48159 Münster
Tel. +49 (0) 2 51-62 03 20
E-Mail: lit@lit-verlag.de   http://www.lit-verlag.de

Auslieferung:
Deutschland: LIT Verlag, Fresnostr. 2, D-48159 Münster
Tel. +49 (0) 2 51-620 32 22, E-Mail: vertrieb@lit-verlag.de

E-Books sind erhältlich unter www.litwebshop.de

To my teachers

Rex Ambler
Daniel W. Hardy
Denys Turner

CONTENTS

ACKNOWLEDGEMENTS

In what follows, I seek to develop a theological and social ethics for an ecological age. The book has been some years in the writing and extends earlier work at the intersection of ecological theology and political theology. During this long period of gestation, I have accrued many debts and I am glad to acknowledge these here.

For more than a decade, I have been honoured and proud to be the Director of the Lincoln Theological Institute, and I am deeply grateful for the confidence that the Institute's trustees have shown in me during this period. It is especially fitting, I hope, that the book appears during the Institute's 21st anniversary. I am glad to have this opportunity to thank the trustees publicly for their interest, support, and encouragement, and for their continuing commitment to the work of the Institute.

Colleagues in the Department of Religions and Theology at the University of Manchester have commented on earlier drafts. I am very grateful to David Law and Alex Samely for their advice. Furthermore, Gary Keogh and Scott Midson have read and commented on much of the book, and their feedback has been of enormous help to me. John Rodwell, co-worker in the Institute, discussed chapter 5 with me, and Alison Stone gave me a very helpful set of comments on chapter 8. Three anonymous reviews provided me with some stringent criticisms and the argument has been much strengthened by my attempt to respond to them. If there is a 'Manchester School' of social theology, I hope that this book, composed in its entirety in Manchester, can be located within it.

During the writing of this book, I joined the congregation of St John the Evangelist, Old Trafford (John Hughes, rector, to whom huge thanks), and I am profoundly grateful for my time there, and the ways in which the congregation took me in as one of their priests. Some of the ideas presented here were tested there; and some matters learned there are discussed here.

This book is no. 13 in the LIT series, Studies in Religion and the Environment. I thank series editor, Sigurd Bergmann, for his critical appraisal of the manuscript, his guidance through the publication process, and his timely suggestion of a concept that allowed me finally to knit chapter 1 together. Material in chapters 4 and 7 is adapted from P. M. Scott, "Technology in a Postnatural Condition?", in C. Deane-Drummond et. al. (eds) (2015), *Technofutures, Nature and the Sacred*, Aldershot: Ashgate, 67-80, and has been significantly expanded. It is represented with permission.

To my children, Harry Jonathan and Esther Katelyn, I owe a different, and more profound, debt. It has been a great pleasure to share a household with them for more than two decades and I am the beneficiary of their love and forgiveness in many areas. I love you both, dearly.

Finally, as an acknowledgement of another sort of debt, I would like to thank three theologians whose direct teaching has influenced my work: Rex Ambler, Daniel W. Hardy (d. 2007), and Denys Turner. To them this work is dedicated, with great respect and affection.

PREFACE

This book provides a theological and social ethics for an ecological age. It develops a concept of right for an order of creaturely life. This order consists of a "society" that encompasses humans and other creatures. The concept of right presented here is elaborated by reference to a postnatural condition, which rejects claims of a given natural order. Strong contrasts between nature and the human as well as nature and technology are also called into question. This approach – a new argument in theological ethics for ecological responsibility – will be unfamiliar. To give us some orientation, we may ask: what is the thematic basis of this argument?

Aspects of living in contemporary cities and towns of the Atlantic basin is the short answer. In other words, to live in these urban or town sites of human habitation is to live with many other creatures in a "society". These sites are not in truth places of human-only habitation. If you travel across such a town or city, you will be using the energy of oil – the sedimented residue of once-living and now long-dead organisms. The same oil provides the energy that brings millions of litres of cow's milk in from the countryside. These cows will have been cared for by humans, including the administering of antibiotics – medicines initially developed for the care of humans. You will not have to travel far to encounter road transport moving livestock of many sorts – in the UK, sheep especially. Some food production processes involve many miles of travel: for example, some Morecambe Bay brown shrimp (*Crangon crangon*) are landed from UK coastal waters and then travel by air to North Africa for preparation, then by road to the Netherlands for packing and thereafter back to Morecambe, among other places, to be eaten – a journey of over 3,400 miles. Movement is a constant: of animals, human and non-human; water and sewage; food for animals; and energy. Look up and you will see planes bringing people and fresh produce from thousands of miles away. Moreover, the shifting of the direction of light through a day, a month, and a season identifies planetary movement.[1] This living does not take place in a fully insulated techno-bubble: even in such habitation, it is possible to get a sense of human dependency on a wider nature. Parks, for example, provide the opportunity for the city or town dweller to pause, notice the sky and birds, and smell the pollution in the air. There are many activities occurring to which many creatures contribute. Evidently, this is a working social order of some sort.

To say that the social order works is not to say that it works well. Developing the concept of society is the way offered here of approaching this theme. By

---

[1] A fuller statement may be found in Scott (2010), 186-102.

encompassing creaturely life by reference to society, I am extending the meaning of the term in ways that supplement its ordinary use. Such supplementation may be counter-intuitive but it is not counter-evidential – quite the contrary. Consider the bacteria that perform a maintenance function in topsoil; such a function is required for the soil to remain productive – and not only from a human point of view. Such an asymmetrical relation between humans and bacteria is here understood by reference to an account of society both in order to maintain an account of the dependency of humans on bacteria and of the ways in which such dependencies are produced. Such dependencies are not ahistorical but are produced through specific farming practices by which needs are met. The concept of a *greater society*, I shall argue, enables a fuller identification of how these material dependencies emerge, are maintained, and may be changed.

An ethical question follows: how should this society be organised? How shall we approach the question of a right order of life? By reference to *postnatural right* is the response offered in this book. The turn to a concept of right renders possible an understanding of our current society from a perspective that is at least partially external. In other words, right – as I shall argue – permits an independent approach to the orderings of society. The term, postnatural, summarises the issues presented in the two previous paragraphs regarding a working social order.

What follows? We are faced with profound difficulties in developing a postnatural ethics because we are not used to deploying the concept of right in this extrahuman way and our concept of society requires a postnatural extension. These are unfamiliar tasks. Tropes on which we have relied – "natural order", "stewardship", technological development – are not immediately serviceable. These points are elaborated in the chapters that follow. I seek to persuade you that various ways in which we use the concepts of nature and creation are no longer convincing, that the concept of society is well placed to address the conceptual deficiencies that then arise, and that right provides us with a practical moral perspective for a postnatural condition.

The argument for postnatural right is supported by warrants from a wide range of sources. Moreover, the main resources are easily identified. My argument is in agreement with strains of ecotheology that are concerned to develop a more robust doctrine of creation, here in service to an ecosocial ethics, in which the difference between the human and the non-human is reduced by various strategies. I am cautious about the deployment of a concept of nature that commends invariant structures through time – although in what follows there is some appreciative discussion of Thomist natural law and of nature in Anglican Social Theology. In the theological consideration of technology (which works on nature), I am on the pessimistic side, and I am deeply concerned about overly triumphalist interpretations of technology. In that sense, my argument is informed by political theologies, especially feminist and liberation theologies, and their concerns regarding links be-

tween justice and technology. Last, my argument draws strength from the concept
of right, in the interpretation that stresses its social (rather than rational) basis.

The argument will be of interest to those working in ecotheological ethics and
exploring creation as the *topos* of ethical enquiry, especially those interested in
political and public dimensions. The discussion of order will, I hope, be attractive
to those interested in developing Catholic Social Thought and Anglican Social
Theology. Those concerned with theological approaches to technology and "law"
in the broadest sense will find analyses relevant to their interests.

Finally, this book is part of a larger project in Christian theological ethics.
The planned three volumes can be understood as an enquiry in a trinitarian doctrine of creation. The present argument in ethics – this volume – relates to the
source of creation. The second volume explores the material pattern or *logos* of
creation in order to identify the metaphysical foundations of the norms proposed
in this volume. The third volume appraises the politics of "spiritual community"
in a postnatural condition to discern how these aforementioned norms are formed,
promulgated and taken up. These may without difficulty be correlated to Father,
Son and Spirit. Once completed, an ethics, metaphysics and politics will be available that turn upon theological conceptions of right, matter and culture. The aim
is an ethics and theology of creation that resonate with ecological conditions.

CHAPTER 1: WHY A THEOLOGY OF POSTNATURAL RIGHT?

*We have to say that no society is too
poor to afford a right order of life. And
no society is so rich that it can afford to
dispense with a right order, or to hope
to get it merely by becoming rich.*

[Raymond Williams]

1.1 A RIGHT ORDER OF LIFE?

If every society – whether rich or poor – must make the effort to create a right order of life, what might such a right order look like at the present time? To seek after a right order of *life* is a more expansive task than seeking after a right order of society. For the latter, attention is to be paid to human society. A right order of life is a broader concept, referring us beyond the human. An order of life is an ecological concept that refers us to "nature".

The comment above by Raymond Williams is therefore especially prescient in that he refers not to a right order of *society* but to a right order of *life*. We need thereby to ponder what elsewhere I have called a *greater society*: a society that understands itself as an assembly of many participants, only some of whom are human.[2] What then is a right order of life for a greater society of creatures, and how should it be ordered? That is the fundamental question that this book tries to present and answer. The presentation and the answer are theological: a dynamic and critical articulation of the doctrine of creation. Moreover, the key issue is ecological and thereby my argument requires careful and detailed attention to concepts of nature, order and technology.

This book is thereby an argument in theological ethics. As such, my argument has two horizons. The first horizon is the doctrine of creation and the second horizon is the ecologically stressed circumstances in which we find ourselves. My argument proposes the development of a theological ethics by reference to theological anthropology on the one hand and the "natural" basis of human life on the other. Drawing on Christian doctrine, consideration of nature, theological theories of order and theories of technology, it develops a fresh line of ethical

---

[2]   Scott (2015a), 5-19.

enquiry. Differently from current discussions of ecological ethics, in this book the concept of right is discussed, the postnatural condition is articulated, and moral positions are advanced by reference to "society". In sum, I propose a creation (meta)ethics by reference to an account of postnatural right.

In this chapter, I set out the importance of creation to my argument and then explore how that relates to the postnatural condition. Thereafter, I set out how an account of right relates to nature, order and technology, before providing a fuller presentation of right and how right relates to a greater society.

1.2 BEGINNING FROM CREATION

Although not its only home, Christian ethics is traditionally placed in the doctrine of creation. There have been powerful moves in recent theological scholarship to relate ethics more fully to eschatology and the Trinity. In my argument, however, ethics is most closely related to the doctrine of creation, as theological traditions commend. It is easy to see why the doctrine of creation offers a congenial place for Christian ethics: an investigation of the relationship, if any, between divine action and human action, the possibility of the discernment of created goodness and its distortions, and the matter of the universality of said goodness are all offered by an interpretation of creation. Moreover, ecotheologians – and others – have turned to the doctrine of creation as a way of responding to the issue of whether Christianity has laid too much stress on redemption to the detriment of creation. Ernst Conradie nicely summarises the concerns regarding this stress: "an anthropological emphasis on humans as sojourners here on earth" and "a soteriology that focuses on human salvation from the earth instead of the salvation of the whole earth".[3] In response to such an anthropology and soteriology, renewed attention has been paid to the doctrine of creation. This book contributes to that effort.

Although not reducible to them, we may say that the doctrine of creation has a number of functions. Fundamental here is the way in which the ecologically attuned restatement of the doctrine requires the decentring of the human: related to *God's* purposes, human concerns are thereby denied a centrality. Rightly understood, this is not a challenge to the concept of *imago dei* but a re-working of it. Being in the image of God need not function as a way of strongly contrasting the human with the rest of nature. Instead, imaging God may be understood in relational ways: horizontally with reference to creation as well as vertically with reference to God. In this connection, Marc Cortez records the increase in importance of relational understandings of *imago dei*.[4] Jürgen Moltmann presses

---

[3]   Conradie (2005), 26.

[4]   Cortez (2010), 14-40. Cortez distinguishes the relational approach from functional and substantialist approaches.

the matter by relating *imago dei* to *imago mundi*, and insisting that these are not opposed.[5]

In displacing the centrality of human concerns, the concerns of other creatures may be moved from background to foreground. No longer does the human occlude other creatures. As an example, in Lars von Trier's 2008 film, *Anti-Christ*, a fox addresses the male character, saying, "chaos reigns". Apart from learning the welcome fact that foxes speak English, we may note that this episode – which strongly divided critics – identifies agencies in the world other than the human. (We ought to note that this encounter with the fox occurs when the married couple have retreated to their cabin, called Eden, in the woods.) Additionally, that the fox speaks suggests the perdurance of animal speech even through the cosmic fall. According to the narrative of the film, Eden is no longer edenic but instead is corrupted and corrupting.

Through such corruption, the doctrine of creation poses the perennial question: is it possible, as Lisa Sowle Cahill asks, to "defend a foundation or minimum of human morality that survives the fact of sin and that can provide a natural basis for just social life"?[6] Perhaps this way of putting the matter does not quite grasp the de-centering aspect of creation. Therefore, we might amend Cahill's analysis by asking whether the doctrine of creation can provide a basis for a just social life rooted in a common creatureliness that humans share with others. When we speak of a social life we are speaking of a society that is wider than the human. We move then from *creatio* to *creatura*: to explore the function of the doctrine of creation towards an understanding of creatures in a greater society and towards a right order of life.

Following Cahill once more, we can add further detail about the functions of the doctrine of creation. The doctrine of creation is used to note that sinful actions and structures are opposed to God's original and ongoing intentions in creation. The doctrine of creation invites the identification of that which is sinful and not aligned to God's purposes. Additionally, the doctrine of creation invites consideration of knowledge of created goodness – goodness, that is, proportioned to creatures, and the normative claims made by such goodness. Such created goodness is universal. Often, this claim is presented by reference to human nature: that all human beings share a created nature is the ontological grounding of this created goodness.[7] Others claim that goodness is presented by certain teleological structures or secures its effect through human participation in certain structures.[8] Later, I shall be arguing that such universality needs to be interpreted yet more broadly and in ways that make more difficult the discerning of intentions.

---

[5]   Moltmann (1985), 215-243; for *imago mundi*, see 51.

[6]   Cahill (2005), 7-24 (here 8).

[7]   Cahill (2005), 11-13.

[8]   For an assessment of Bonhoeffer on mandates in ecological perspective, see Scott (2010a), 25-30.

I am arguing for an account of postnatural right out of a common creatureliness and dedicated to more sustainable patterns of living. In this section, I have
turned to the doctrine of creation as an argument for a common creatureliness.
More needs to be done to defend this notion. For the present, I have shown that
my reference to creation emerges from an account of the importance of creation in
relation to ecological responsibility. In the next section, I shall explore the meanings of the neologism, postnatural.

1.3 THE POSTNATURAL CONDITION

The postnatural condition acknowledges that to act in a rightful way is to accept
that human morality emerges as part of an evolutionary development – a development that encompasses creatures other than the human. As Stephen Pope notes,
"The social institution of morality probably came into use to address certain fundamental human needs rooted in our emergent cognitive, emotional and social
capacities. Morality as such did not evolve biologically, but some human capacities that are essential to morality have evolutionary roots."[9] This careful statement
balances the emergence of morality as related to human capacities with an emphasis on a biological basis that morality contributes to surpassing. In what sense
moral capacities have evolutionary roots is debated. Pope offers a three-fold classification: morality as adaptive strategy, morality as an evolutionary by-product,
and morality as cultural.[10]

To this classification the postnatural condition brings Fredric Jameson's caution that to think about nature is to encounter a duality that is "revelatory of some
ontological rift or gap in the world itself".[11] In other words, there is a persistent
dualism in our thinking about nature. Are we in nature, or beyond nature? – that
is the question. Why this contrast persists in thought and life is a topic for chapter 2. For the present, I note that we are, so to speak, *in* a condition. For such a
postnatural condition, the evolutionary emergence of humanity identifies nature as
ground and limitation of morality and yet does not determine it. As is suggested
by Jameson's use of the term "rift", the evolutionary emergence of human morality informs the present condition but does not constitute it. An argument along
these lines is offered by Jürgen Habermas in *Communication and the Evolution of
Society* in which he argues for a logical space between *homo sapiens*' genetically
inherited characteristics and the – in effect, contingent – development of society.[12]
Following the more recent work of Elizabeth Grosz, Alison Stone has also made
the case for flexibility in the consideration of the ways in which in evolutionary
perspective humanity surpasses nature. As Stone argues, "Because nature is dy-

---

[9]   Pope (2007), 250.
[10] Pope (2007), 250.
[11] Jameson (2009), 23.
[12] Habermas (1991), 140ff.

namic, it "incites" culture to change; different cultures are different expressions of nature in its variability." The task is to find a way of "adequately accommodating the biological dimension of human life and culture" rather than opposing the biology of the human to its culture.[13] The point here then in a postnatural condition is to combine ontological boldness with epistemological caution: to affirm the relation between evolution and morality while not pressing our knowledge of that relation. What then is the postnatural condition, and what are its implications for thinking about right?

First, what is natural to the human is not to be separated from the human effort to develop its own flourishing by the transformation of its natural circumstances. More than ever before, the human mixes its labour with the non-human, even to the extent of altering the genetic code of itself and other kinds. Are humans moreover changing the conditions of planetary life to the extent that we are entering a new geological epoch called the Anthropocene, "... in which the collective imprint of human activities is so pervasive that the Earth System, most notably that associated with climate change, is destabilized"?[14] An ethical theory must therefore fully theorise the transformations by the human of its natural situatedness. This right is *post*natural. Any notion of right must therefore find some anchorage in a transforming and transformed human work – whose ensemble of social relations we refer to as human nature – and yet relate the human to other animals and a wider nature. Right is hereby *historicised*.

Second, the postnatural can be fully established only by reference to the nature that exceeds the human. Nature, in one of its meanings, transcends the human. Thus, what is natural to the human will be established by enquiring after the situation of the human in nature. A difficulty at this point is that nature is *under*-determining; it impinges too little on the concrete moral ethos or ethical life of western societies. Postnatural right seeks to address this problem of the "backgrounding" of nature in practical deliberation and the lack of thick moral experience from which to embrace the care of nature. This right is post*natural*. I argue that any theological proposal cannot fall behind this insight and proposals that seek to separate the human and the non-human must be refused. Right is hereby *contextualised*.

This means, third, that the postnatural is not a contrastive concept. I am not offering a prevenient nature, static and unchanging, with which to contrast present circumstances. In this postnatural enquiry, nature does not contrast; instead, it underlies. By postnatural, I wish to retain an emphasis on a wider creatureliness: nature here refers not to that which is contrasted with the human – although I shall be discussing this also – but how humanity is to be understood as embedded in

---

[13] Stone (2014), 105-122 (here 120).
[14] Deane-Drummond, Bergmann and Vogt (2017), 1.

a wider creatureliness. The postnatural directs us towards an understanding of a greater society. Right is hereby *socialised*.

Fourth, the interactions between humanity and other kind are to be fore-grounded. In previous work, I have explored these dynamic asymmetries by reference to the sociality of humanity and nature.[15] Yet we must also note that such an account is troubled by the postnatural condition in which western humanity finds itself. That is, the extreme mixing of humanity with nature which we find in such procedures such as genetic engineering and climate change (and proposed geo-engineering projects to combat climate change) places the human in a deeply ambiguous process in relation to other creatures and other kind. Efforts at the human mastery of nature risk the danger of considering that westerners are gods and thereby are tempted to dominating activities in relation to nature.[16] Of course, this reference to domineering activity makes it even more difficult to explore the matter of right if the relationships between humanity and nature are already deeply distorted.

A fifth and final point on the postnatural. I am also suggesting that theology, ethics and practice are conditioned by the postnatural. In its theorizing, theology confronts its own situatedness in a postnatural condition. Moreover, even the theory and practice that refuses to acknowledge this conditioning is conditioned by the postnatural. I am arguing that the circumstances in which we find ourselves today – a postnatural condition – should inform the way that theology is done. That is, in the production of theological knowledge today the postnatural as a condition must be theorised in and by theology.

So far, I have argued that the postnatural condition recommends that nature is not deployed in contrast to the human. Moreover, a static model is not helpful and a more dynamic and transformative account is preferred. Having said that, in the postnatural condition sight is never lost of the claim that nature exceeds the human. This presentation conditions the writing of theological ethics. What, then, is thinking and acting ethically in such a postnatural condition? I begin an answer to this question in the next section by reference to nature, order and technology.

1.4 NATURE, ORDER, TECHNOLOGY

A right order of life presses on us the matter of nature and its interactions with humanity ; we are concerned with life and not only human society. Additionally, a right order raises the issue of the arrangement of that order itself. Finally, given that such an order is an order of technological transformation, we are presented with the issue of what is being transformed and of the eschatological significance of that transformation.

---

[15]   Scott (2003), 43-52.
[16]   Scott (2010), 121-39.

It follows that the concept and meanings of nature are fundamental to my enquiry. There can be no theological or ethical thinking in our postnatural condition without careful and sustained engagement with nature. Two chapters of the present book are dedicated to the consideration of nature. In addition, thinking in a postnatural condition means also raising questions about order and technology. How so?

The matter of order has already been raised. At the beginning of this chapter, I set up my argument as an enquiry into a right order of life: how is a greater society to be configured? This presentation raises the matter of order and, most especially, the relation between order and nature. I have already argued that in our postnatural condition nature is not to be understood as contrastive and may not therefore be appealed to as identifying pre- or transhistorical structures. An account of order is not to be secured in such a fashion. That in turn raises the question: what order *is* identified?

These matters of nature and order are made more complex when we note that neither of these matters of nature and order – nor their interrelation – can be discussed satisfactorily except by reference to technology. For in technological practices, the natural conditions of creaturely life are changed and fresh orderings are secured. Therefore, in the postnatural condition, the transformative power of technology is also implicated. If we wish to establish a theological-ethical analysis of a right order of life, technology must be accepted as contributing to that analysis.

As crucial to understanding our postnatural condition, these matters of nature, order and technology will be carefully considered in the following chapters. In turn, these matters raise the following three trajectories that will also receive attention as my argument gathers pace. The trajectories are the *social-institutional*, the *historical-teleological*, and the *anthropological-eschatological* and they broadly correlate with nature, order and technology. How is this so?

Concerning *nature*, reference to the postnatural invites attention to the social-institutional: to the multiple ways that humanity and nature interact in a greater society. The principal sites of interaction are, broadly, institutional. In chapter 5, I discuss Ecosystem Services as practised in the UK as one example of such an institution. As regards *order*, the trajectory of the historical-teleological is raised: has nature been subsumed into history and in turn lost any interpretative force? This raises the teleological issue as to what nature is for. Is it only for humanity, and in what ways? Finally, the matter of *technology* raises a set of difficult issues regarding the anthropological-eschatological. In other words, what is being transformed in technological practices? Moreover, what is the relationship between such transformations and eschatological transformation? Does such transformation, or resistance to such transformation, have any eschatological significance?

According to the postnatural condition, we are confronted by the issues of nature, order and technology. These three issues present us, respectively, with the difficult issue of how the human relates to its ecological circumstance, to what extent our social order may be said to be "naturally" settled or given, and how our "natural" circumstances are being transformed by our technological practices. If these are the presenting issues, they may be understood theoretically as invoking the social-institutional, the historical-teleological, and the anthropological-eschatological. That is, we cannot consider fully the problems raised by nature, order and technology except by consideration of these foundational trajectories. We shall therefore consider the social-institutional interaction between creatures. We shall evaluate the place of nature in historical development, and any teleological relations. Finally, we shall come to a judgement as to the work of the human in technological practices and the related invocation of nature and the eschatological significance of transformative action.

1.5 RIGHT

Theologians propose theories. In this book, I propose a theological theory of ethics, an account of right that also invokes a wider context. What do I mean by right?

Right is a defensive or negating notion that seeks to identify and support the liberty and security of all creatures. As such, it relates to (jurisprudential) law but precedes it and enjoys a certain independence. The presentation of right is also the attempt to discern, identify and correct particular social and ecological practices. In my argument, right does not refer us to some original or primordial condition but to social patterns and arrangements that are socially useful with regard to obtaining liberty and security. Right-based arguments are opposed to a dominant or authoritative interpretation or state of affairs. As such, thinking in terms of right is a struggle against established authorities. Right is, to borrow from David G. Ritchie, antagonistic, and so related to protest.[17] As we have already noted, a previously dominant account of the human as separate from and preeminent over nature is called into question. That is, right offers an ideal commentary about the future of a society, the unity of humanity and a wider creatureliness. As already noted, I propose to explore this creatureliness along three trajectories: the social-institutional; the historical-teleological; and the anthropological-eschatological.

(i) The social-institutional trajectory refers to the constitution of modern societies and the ways in which institutions are central to this constitution. Here my central point is that institutions are the places of induction into *Sittlichkeit* and are sites of relative normativities in moral life. Too often in the consideration of nature, we are offered a zero/sum game. In other words, if nature is not authorised as an extra-social basis of human valuing, then moral relativism follows.[18] In my argument for

---

[17] Ritchie (1894), 20.
[18] For a good example, see Charles (2008).

postnatural right, I am instead arguing for the moral density and considerability of the social-institutional life of humanity-nature.

(ii) The historical-teleological trajectory secures the position that the end of nature is not humanity and neither is the end of humanity to be found in nature. Yet, neither are their respective ends not to be found there. Difficult questions now arise as to whether the postnatural subsumes the natural thereby undermining the effort to develop a postnatural *order*.

(iii) The anthropological-eschatological trajectory identifies the issue of how technological transformation is to be understood. In what sense is technological activity an humane activity and in what ways may we regard this activity as eschatological and redemptive? In turn, the matter of whether nature may be considered as redemptive is also raised.

More than this: a discussion of right proceeds to note the relation between morality and right. In this sense, it bears some similarity to natural law. As Stephen Pope argues of this relation, "The obligatory character of morality – the "law" – binds the person to moral standards that promote the well-being, or flourishing, of the person and his or her community".[19] For my discussion of right, I am concerned with both the morality and institutionality of right. That is, I concentrate on the normative good identified by the moral sense of right: what is the ideal social configuration of animals (and more)? Yet also, how is that pattern or order best produced or actualised? Whereas Pope speaks of "structures of living", I shall avoid the term "structure", preferring that of "institution". Pope and I concur that there is a constitutive relation between morality, right and order but my argument takes us to institutions (see chapter 5) rather than structures.

Care needs to be taken here in that I am not proposing a conception of right that is founded in morality. In *The Metaphysics of Morals*, Kant is often interpreted as proposing such a view. Rather, I am proposing an account of right that is based in creaturely life, social and institutional. I am not therefore proposing a "deduction" of right offered, in different ways and with different bases, by Kant and Fichte. My position is closer to Hegel: given present institutions and activities, how is right to be secured? Moreover, how is such right also *postnatural*: based in a wider creatureliness?

As regards ethical theory, there has been some acknowledgement without and within theology that ethical theories were not designed for forcefully grasping the moral considerability of the non-human. The standard concepts of value – rights, utility, duty, virtue – may of course be redesigned or extended to encompass nature. Yet, by that very action it is evident that the original home of these concepts

---

[19] Pope (2007), 272.

is the human sphere. Ethically, we are ill prepared.[20] The question is: where should repair be conducted?

There are some dead ends here. For example, as regards moral practice, the moral significance attributed to a recent understanding of human beings as embedded in nature as part of a creation story is unwarranted. This way invites us to consider ourselves – we humans – as part of a "common creation story", as late arrivals in a lengthy cosmic narrative. Often with this invitation comes a second invitation to construe together the wisdom of all religious traditions. In other words, religious traditions must respond to a scientific narrative and, chastened, should pool their resources.

My objection to this presentation is that it requires a change in thought only. In other words, to adjust to this new picture requires only an adjustment in thought and imagination in order to overcome a sense of cosmic alienation.[21] However, this is not where our difficulties – the practical difficulties of human freedom and natural agency – occur. These occur at a different level and scale, and cannot be addressed only in thought. Some will dispute this, arguing that the new story of the universe displaces humanity and chastens our hubris.[22] This may be correct but what in my view is required in addition is the re-thinking of the place of the human on a quite different – and much smaller – scale in the context of institutions.[23] Moreover, as adjustments in response will have to be made in practice, they are likely to need the virtuous practices of actual religious communities to facilitate any such changes rather than an amalgamated wisdom.

To repeat: right offers an ideal commentary about the future of a society, the unity of humanity and a wider creatureliness. Right invites us to attend to a fundamental pattern of and for the future of a greater society and a right order of life. It is also to be founded in and resourced by a doctrine of creation. For these reasons there is some overlap between my argument and Stephen Pope's presentation of an *ordo amoris*. We are both concerned by a neglect in Christian social ethics "of human beings as a part of nature" and the implications this has for thinking about order but our arguments diverge thereafter.[24] My argument pursues the matter of right rather than love. Although the fuller argument in favour of right is a matter for the final chapter, I shall say a little more about the dimensions of right here.

---

[20] For a forceful, non-theological, statement of this view, elaborated in the consideration of climate change, see Gardiner (2008).

[21] See Plant (1973), 208.

[22] For a good example, see Swimme (2014). The work of Teilhard de Chardin is foundational to this approach as is the scholarly contribution of Thomas Berry "who sought to open religions to a new story of the universe", as Willis Jenkins and Christopher Key Chapple (2011), 441-63 (here 443) argue.

[23] See my defence of this position in Scott (2014a), 108-23 (here 113-14).

[24] Pope (1994); the quotation is from 36.

As configured for a postnatural condition, right has five dimensions: universal, necessary, revolutionary, social and ideal. What do I mean by this?

Postnatural right is *universal* in that it applies to all creatures; *necessary* in the sense that it acknowledges the unsurpassibility of ecological situatedness; *social* in that creatures, human and non-human, are understood as connected through the relation of a greater society; *revolutionary* in that claims to "natural" hierarchy are herewith challenged; and *ideal* in the sense of judging the present from an ideal perspective towards a deeper sociability.[25] As such, right notes naturalness and calls it into question, affirms the desire for order but asks, which order?, and works with technological transformation but enquires after its direction. I shall now elaborate on these points.

As grounded in a doctrine of creation, postnatural right is *universal*. As Cahill notes in a discussion of the relationship between creation and ethics, the doctrine of creation "can provide a natural basis for just social life" in which "the historical order retains inherent structures of justice".[26] Such a natural basis relates to all human life. As we shall see, postnatural right leans upon the more expansive claim that right proceeds from a common creatureliness, God's gift of life, and is less concerned with structures. To think with the doctrine of creation is to attend to a general basis of creaturely living without which the conditions of life cannot be adequately grasped. Right, then, enjoys this universal basis. In turn, the divisions (including class divisions) in our societies are called into question.

As *necessary*, postnatural right identifies the human not as naked but always as living co-operatively in a determinate ecological circumstance. This dimension is contextualising: the anthropology being proposed here by reference to right understands the human as ecologically situated and thereby dependent on certain processes – of physiology, maturation, and growth (requiring food, warmth, shelter, care and so on) – to survive, develop and flourish. Human activity is always placed and locatable but needs to be understood as radically dependent on these other processes – although it is the case that there is differential access to some processes, as structured by reference to class, ethnicity, and gender.

As *social*, postnatural right understands human beings and other creatures as involved with each other in a greater society; creatures encounter each other in institutions that take us beyond only human community.[27] (I amplify these remarks in the next section.)

As *revolutionary*, postnatural right is a levelling notion: in that all creatures are found in God's regard, the matter of hierarchy is called into question. The default position of postnatural right is to be sceptical about "natural" hierarchies

---

[25] Lindsay (1925), 60-61, argues that natural right invokes negation, ideality, and revolution. I have adapted some of these ideas for my theological purposes.

[26] Cahill (2005), 10, 11.

[27] I have outlined the theological basis of this argument in Scott (2003), chapter 2.

and thereby suspicious of some of the manifestations of anthropocentrism, not least on how such anthropocentrisms impact negatively on the poor and excluded.

Finally, as *ideal*, postnatural right points towards an absolute or standard. As Cahill notes, we may appreciate that the doctrine of creation assists in "... the recognition of creation as establishing a partially lost but still recognizable ideal".[28] The ideal operative throughout this book is that of freedom, a creaturely freedom in which humans and non-humans participate in institutions, and in which the ways in which freedom is unevenly distributed are noted.

At this point, I can imagine the retort: why are we obliged to take this path? Why can we not affirm natural law, stewardship or creation care? My answer is that these responses presuppose that which our present ecological difficulties call into question. Because the nature of human/animal difference is disputed, we cannot immediately conclude that our role is unproblematically to care for other creatures. Because our societies are founded on change, and the attempt to secure freedom through such change, it remains unclear whether and/or how we may appeal to nature as the basis for a social order. We need, as Williams notes, a right order of life to flourish but that order at the very least remains obscure. To what order, then, is our care to be directed? Finally, our abilities to transform our circumstances raise the issue of the limits of our activity. So we may wish to care for creation but does that mean stepping back, so to speak, from technological change? Because we do not know the answers to these questions, we cannot simply affirm some insights from natural law, stewardship or creation care.[29]

If the argument of the previous paragraph is accepted, why is the best way of addressing these issues – of setting them out comprehensively, in a theological thought – a concept of postnatural right? What is it about postnatural right that makes it an appropriate conceptuality for addressing the issues of nature, order and technology? This book may be treated as an answer to this question. A brief answer in anticipation may be proffered here, however, and goes like this: postnatural right argues that there is a deep connection between order, morality and right. If we need a just order of life, postnatural right offers us a guide, and in offering guidance does not presuppose a strong distinction between humanity and nature. Moreover, it does not presume or require some given order and wishes to take into full account changes associated with technology. Postnatural right therefore requires the theorisation of the relationships between "givenness" (nature), order, change and morality.[30]

---

[28] Cahill (2005), 14.

[29] I have commented on stewardship in earlier work and shall not repeat that here. Certainly, there are practical drawbacks to stewardship that are amplified by recent reference to the Anthropocene. There are theological problems also in that, as I have argued, stewardship is best understood in relation to the subjective aspect of atonement. See Scott (2010b), 430-456; Scott (2003); Scott (1997), 193-202.

[30] This is an important point of overlap between my argument and Pope (1994).

Postnatural right also wishes to affirm that there are important differences between creatures as well; there may well be at times irreconcilable differences between creatures that will require humans to eradicate other creatures. Nonetheless, postnatural right does not draw a firm line between humans and other creatures. Indeed, it notes that there may be interests in common between some humans and some non-humans: the poorest and most marginalised among humans may have overlapping interests with other creatures.[31] Postnatural right is ideal: offering a critique of present societies from the perspective of the levelling universality supplied by the doctrine of creation.

I have suggested that postnatural right be understood in five dimensions. These dimensions – universal, necessary, social, revolutionary, and ideal – honour the theological commitments of the doctrine of creation out of which the concept comes and address the complexity of relationships between "givenness", order, change and morality.

1.6 A GREATER SOCIETY

To speak of right as social requires some elaboration, not least because "social" in my usage refers to a creatureliness that is wider than the human. In common parlance, "social" refers to the intrahuman sphere. In my usage, however, the social extends to the extrahuman and therefore encompasses a wider-than-human creatureliness. In other words, my position takes a definition such as that provided by Tom Campbell – "A society . . . is a form of order: it involves regularly repeated patterns of interactions between human beings"[32] – and subjects it to a postnatural extension. This, then, is the definition of a greater society: a society of creatures. The remainder of this section offers a description of a greater society.

There are warrants for a postnatural extension. In book I of *The Prelude* by William Wordsworth, the poem's speaker reports an experience on a ridge when assailed by a strong wind. We read that the "discordant elements" – the darkness of the human spirit and the weather conditions – "cling together/In one society".[33] Therefore, there is a precedent for using a term traditionally associated with the intrahuman in an extrahuman fashion. Although this may seem jarring at first, the dissonance may be reduced further if we recall, with Raymond Williams, that the first meaning of society was "companionship or fellowship".[34] We are then concerned with a fellowship or company of creatures – an active sense that we need to hold onto – and thereby we move into a doctrine of creation, as we have already seen.

---

[31] See Scott (2010a), 69.
[32] Campbell (1991), 26.
[33] Wordsworth (1995), 1850 version, Book I, l. 343-44.
[34] Williams (1983), 291.

Furthermore, Williams notes two uses of the term, "society": general and abstract. The first Williams amplifies as "the body of institutions and relationships"; the second refers to "the condition in which such institutions and relationships are formed". (We may immediately appreciate that by the title, *The Condition of the Working Class in England*, Friedrich Engels in different terms also presents the general and the abstract: an enquiry into the *society* of 1840s Manchester and an enquiry after its *condition*.) To investigate the company of creatures is thereby to understand how it is constituted by institutions and relationships and enquire after the conditions of their formation.

I shall return to the matters of institution and relationships shortly. For now, I note that there is also a converging theological warrant from the doctrine of creation. Daniel W. Hardy argues that in the doctrine of creation *two* emphases are present: (1) "... creation as the field of relevant preconditions for life ... " and (2) "normative states or processes ... ".[35] In other words, there are in the doctrine of creation emphases towards description and judgement. The first seeks universal or general descriptions whereas the second is concerned with why certain states or structures persist. Thus, in the discussion of society, we are concerned with institutions and relationships and yet always in a double sense: to enquire after *what* is socially, and *why* it is (and whether some other form is preferable). In a society, creatures associate with one another; we seek to understand that association and ask after its ethical basis. The meanings of society and creation may thus be understood as converging: both are concerned with the descriptive and the normative.

Nonetheless, there will be no easy agreement on this matter, and I do not expect such. In the social ecology of Murray Bookchin, for example, "social" is a term restricted to the intrahuman whereas "community" is used as a term to describe non-human animal arrangements: a "community of ants", for example.[36] Some contributors to the theology-science dialogue, by contrast, apply the term "social" to the non-human. This is from Simon Conway Morris: "... for example, the intriguing similarities in social organization of bacteria when compared with higher organisms".[37] Others regard this language as going back to the beginnings of western philosophical thought: for Larry Arnhart, "... in explaining the political nature of human beings, he [Aristotle, in the *Politics*] compares them with other political animals such as the social insects".[38]

The warrant for my own position is as follows. In *A Political Theology of Nature*, I argued for an ecological doctrine of creation under the rubric of a common realm of God, nature and humanity.[39] As such, the common realm had three dis-

---

[35]   Hardy (1996a), 189.

[36]   See the presentation in Scott (2003), 110-13.

[37]   Conway Morris (2010), 155.

[38]   Arnhart (1998), 2.

[39]   Scott (2003), 30-60.

tinctive features. First, it acknowledged that the modern period is to be understood as a period of the *disgracing* of nature: the understanding of nature had become separated from humanity and God. Second, that nature and humanity are best understood in mutual co-explication with the concept of God. Third, and to which the common realm is an antidote, a certain abstraction has entered theological enquiry. As I argued, human industrial activity does "not assault nature all along the line".[40] There is here, against such abstraction and generality, the matter of an appropriate *scale*. The concept of postnatural right is an ethical contribution to creating a way of life consonant with such an understanding of the common realm.

To elaborate practically on this common realm, speaking of a greater society of institutions and relationships is helpful. How do we establish such a concept, however? In a programmatic statement from the entry on "Political theology" in *Sacramentum Mundi*, Johann Baptist Metz argues that "Human society is seen primarily as an essential medium for the discovery of theological truth and Christian preaching in general".[41] The point I am highlighting here is the identification of *society* as a medium of theological truth. Much has changed since this entry's publication in 1970 so the presentation of society as a vehicle for Christian truth is important but incomplete. Not least, the reporting of and engagement with the crisis in our understanding of life and the negative feedback from the ontological rift between humanity and nature was only in its infancy. Since then, theological engagement with our "ecologic crisis" (Lynn White) has deepened as the crisis itself has deepened. In response, as Jürgen Moltmann has recently noted, "there has arisen a new political theology of nature ... which links human culture and the nature of the earth differently ... ".[42] Such a new political theology of nature takes up the concept of society as a way of pursuing this theological engagement. Yet a political theology of nature cannot do this, as we shall see, without also developing the meanings of "society" and its cognates.

Although Metz provides an encouraging warrant, the deployment of "society" and its cognates will meet theological resistance, especially from those who consider that theological attention should be paid to political authority rather than to society. Oliver O'Donovan has pressed the case for political authority vigorously and argued that society is politically shaped and thereby has resisted what he terms an "acephalous idea of society". Indeed, O'Donovan has challenged Latin American liberation theology on this ground. Elaborating this point, O'Donovan writes: "Yet the societies we actually inhabit are *politically formed*. They depend upon the art of government; they are interested in the very questions from which the study of society abstracts. ... The epithet "social", however, forecloses the

---

[40]   Scott (2003), 40.
[41]   Metz (1970), 34-38 (here 35).
[42]   Moltmann (2015), 3-22 (here 15).

agenda against such questions, often narrowing it to economic matters which are only a fraction of what a living society cares about."[43]

Three considerations count against O'Donovan's argument. First, it trades upon one meaning of the term, society, which seems restrictive; the concept of society is patient of other interpretations. Following Williams, a recovery of the active and normative senses is pertinent but not attended to here. Second, O'Donovan concedes that the approach he defends has been inattentive to ecological issues. The tradition of political theology in which he situates his own work, O'Donovan notes, does not attend to the issue of "the creaturely co-habitation of human and non-human-species in a common world".[44] Given our topic, this is a significant concession and suggests that attention needs to be paid to more than political authority. Third, as David Schindler notes, the claim that the political should be given priority is a metaphysical claim and so requires a metaphysical defence.[45] In that such a defence is not provided, the way to a theological interpretation of a greater society remains open.

"Society" is a way of speaking of institutions and relationships. In the context of a discussion of a greater society, how might its meaning be developed? In considering the term "society", we may note three closely related terms: "social", "societal" and "sociality". The resonance between these four terms renders "society" a generative term. When associated with the term "society", the concept of "social" has resonances of the processes of a particular society – a general and impersonal sense of institutions and relationships. "Societal" has the sense of the quality of social relationships. It refers to a qualitative, indeed normative, judgement on a society, although abstractly: "the overall quality of a society which at its best has a supportive and enabling culture, a culture whose root paradigms are intact and capable of comprehending both differentiation into particularities and universals which hold the human together in the ancestral sense of a *religio*, a mutual binding informed by a gospel of grace and truth".[46] Finally, when we refer to "sociality", we are referring to the for-one-another structure of creaturely living: fellowship is a dynamic of creation.[47]

Although understanding creatureliness by reference to society is unfamiliar, we can now begin to elaborate its contours. A *greater society* identifies institutions and relationships in which humanity and nature associate, so to speak. We might then speak of a *plurality of social orders*[48] – and I shall return to this point in the discussion of institutions in chapter 5. Thus, the term "society" is supplemented by a postnatural extension. Identifying the relational yet asymmetrical

---

43   O'Donovan (1996), 16.
44   O'Donovan (1996), 262.
45   Schindler (2011), 12.
46   See Roberts (1996), 179-195 (here 179).
47   See Scott (2017), 170-71.
48   I owe this suggestion to Sigurd Bergmann.

interaction of creatureliness, (the transcendental of) *sociality* provides the basis for this extension and supplementation. The common realm is secured by sociality. As we refer societies to their *societal* quality, we may explore the ways in which societies flourish, in which humanity and nature are held together. In turn, the concept of the *social* is aerated: the reference to abstract and impersonal laws that determine social institutions is not lost but the resonance of fellowship and association is retained. We are then reminded of what Raymond Williams called the active sense of society. Right is the effort to recover the active sense of social; sometimes I shall use the term "*sociability*" to capture this.

So far, I have made the case for understanding relationships between humanity and nature by reference to "society", "social", and its cognates. This is preparation for a fuller discussion of the theme of the "social-institutional" in chapters 2 and 5. Before pressing on to the end of this chapter, however, I want to review some additional arguments in support of my position and consider some objections. My first task is to reprise the argument made in *A Political Theology of Nature* that "sociality" is a transcendental concept, by which I intended to identify sociality as one of the basic or fundamental features of reality and commend its Christological root, foundation and rationale.[49] In making this case, I argued that the concepts of God, humanity and nature are, as social concepts, intelligible fully only if their social intention is drawn out. In retrospect, I regret the term "intention" and shall speak here of a social *horizon*, especially in chapter 2. Nonetheless, I affirm that sociality "specifies exchanges, transactions, interdependencies and interactions" between humanity and nature, not least because the sociality of nature is its own sociality and is not imputed to it. I do not intend to defend this argument here – interested readers may consult it if they so wish – but instead note that it is sociality-as-transcendental that functions as the epistemological warrant that allows analogy by reference to the social between humanity and nature, and thereby provides the warrant for the concept of a greater society. Such an analogy drawing on the social is new, but, as Eric Gregory has shown,[50] the matter of analogising from the social is not.[51] I accept that there are certain epistemic limitations to this position – as Pope notes, "human history cannot be usefully analogized to natural history"[52]. Nonetheless, I shall argue in chapter 2 that working with the concept of the "social" reduces the dangers involved in such analogising.

Of such a greater society, finally, the question may be asked: why is this not a problematic anthropocentrism? To which I respond that I am not proposing an anthropocentric account of value. As we shall see, postnatural right does not subscribe to a key tenet of anthropocentrism that nature is a function of humanity. Yet

---

[49] Scott (2003), 43-52.

[50] Gregory (2010), 21.

[51] I suggest that the demand for analogy goes back into Scripture and the matter of relating familial and group relationships to the cosmos.

[52] Pope (2007), 254.

neither does postnatural right wish to follow narrowly ecocentric approaches that locate value, good and worth in nature in which this nature is seen as primary.[53] Postnatural right resists the binary structuring of this debate in favour of the dynamic interactions of a greater society. In the first coinage of the phrase "greater society", I argued that the concept criticises the view of nature as prior to society and functioning as a kind of platform on which the allegedly interesting human dramatics takes place.[54] Such an understanding of a platform furnishes an anthropocentrism and the greater society was developed to resist such a view. As such, it offers a compelling alternative: decisions about value are to be made from the human side – where else could I work from? – but one of the tasks of postnatural right is nonetheless to query the assignment of value *as if only* from the human side. The greater society contributes to that query by challenging a view of nature as external, as platform.

Through this section, I have provided a definition and a description of a greater society. In the next chapter, I explain the concept by taking the unusual route of exploring the multiple meanings of the concept of nature.[55] As a justification for the approach adopted here, I shall take Raymond Williams' maxim – "in the idea of nature is the idea of man ... the idea of man in society, indeed the idea of kinds of societies"[56] – with full seriousness and seek to show that a fruitful way of considering society is through the concept of nature.

1.7 AN OUTLINE OF THE ARGUMENT:

To render my case persuasive will require both analysis and argument.

In Part 1, I seek to persuade you that our present condition is best characterised as postnatural. We must make the postnatural turn! This requires an account of how concepts of nature operate in theology in relation to right. Of special importance is giving an account of how nature is not a contrastive notion and instead underlies or underpins human action. I also explore a range of interpretations of natural order, with which my position might but should not be confused. Lastly, drawing on discussions of technology, I show how such interpretations influence theological understandings of anthropology.

What is the terminus of my argument? A theology of postnatural order is the answer. To this topic, Part 2 is dedicated. I develop the institutional aspect of the social relations between humanity and nature through a discussion of publicness. Further consideration of what is called postnatural order is now offered by attention to Paul Tillich's concept of life through the consideration of "ecstatic life":

---

[53]   On anthropocentrism and ecocentrism, see Scott (2003), 63-66.

[54]   Scott (2015a), 5-19.

[55]   I have taken the triumvirate of definition, description and explanation from Campbell (1991), 17.

[56]   Williams (1980), 71.

that life is self-transcending. Following through on the ideality of postnatural order, I explore the theme of the redemption of nature by technology.

After that, I offer in Part 3 a more detailed exploration of postnatural right
which is ideal in its orientation, radically extensive in its effort to relate humans
to a wider creatureliness, and affirming of a sociable pattern, as yet unrealised.
Additionally, I give some hints of the transformative, will-based anthropology that
I am advancing. Finally, I seek to explore the revolutionary impulse of postnatural
right, with special reference to freedom and its cognates. If, as I contend, right
is fundamentally levelling, what are the ethical implications of this conclusion?
Postnatural right is, I conclude, universal, necessary, social, revolutionary, and
ideal.

1.8 EMPIRICAL JUDGEMENTS

A theology of postnatural right is not a "dilemma ethics". I am not concerned immediately to address particular ecological issues. As the argument unfolds through
the following seven chapters, I hope it will become clearer why: how we think ethically needs rethinking for a postnatural condition and as part of that rethinking
we need to find ways of rendering ecological issues amenable for ethical consideration. The matter is not the extension of moral consideration to the non-human.
I think that theological traditions already have resources for that task. Instead, the
issue is how to produce such concerns as matters of right. That is the key question:
the *production* of ethical matters as matters of right.

With such production comes the task of making empirical judgements. Any
theological ethics turns upon empirical judgements, however hidden. Responses to
my argument that ask: what difference does thinking ethically in this way make? –
fail to grasp that all ethical approaches presuppose empirical judgements. It is a
serious mistake to conclude that because an ethical theory privileges case studies and attention to selected moral decisions that it has thereby made the correct
empirical judgements.

Empirical judgements are also a risk. In other words, if ethical matters must
be produced then empirical judgements are part of the process of production. Such
judgements are not given but instead must be risked. Thus, any ethical theory is
a risk in a double sense: it risks empirical judgements and risks an ethical interpretation. The following seven chapters are a risk of ethical interpretation. What
empirical judgements are also being risked, however?

A theology of postnatural right judges that humans with their machines interact more vigorously with the non-human than is usually accepted. Most of us
most of the time live in built environments whereby this judgement is rendered
obscure. Nonetheless, severe ecological distress – including a warming climate –
are confirmation of this judgement: such negative feedback confirms the dynamic
and (inter)dependent asymmetries between the human animal and the non-human

animal (and more widely). Although postnatural right establishes this position on other grounds, it never resiles from it. Postnatural right understands this judgement by reference to the social and the institutional.

Here is a second empirical judgement: ethical issues of postnatural right are produced by reference to the interaction in institutions of the human and the non-human. Thus we are always referred – here is a third judgement – to a social order. An ethical response at this time should not focus on the individual but with the nature of the social order which, as social animals, humans discover, produce, participate in, and change.

At this point, I stress that a theology of postnatural right is not built on a foundation of these empirical judgements. It is, however, built on an account of order – an order of life. There are, however, profound ambiguities in play here, as we shall see. For example, the concept of nature is itself ambiguous: the environment supports the human *and* threatens it. How should human beings in their societies respond to this? Any effort to *liberate* ourselves from nature seems impractical and yet to seek to *reconcile* ourselves to nature seems equally implausible. Presented as a theological argument and judgement, interpreting right as universal, necessary, revolutionary, social, and ideal is offered as a way of articulating a right order of life. As theological, postnatural right has an independence: a location for critique and ethical production in that its five aspects are informed by a doctrine of creation. By (new) creation is order found, critiqued and re-founded; by (new) creation are nature and humanity interpreted together; by (new) creation is technological change tested. To these matters we now turn.

Part I

Making the Postnatural Turn

CHAPTER 2: NATURE(S)

2.1 INTRODUCTION

Now we enter part 1. I have gathered the three chapters in this part under the heading, "Making the Postnatural Turn". Making this turn will involve three separate movements: critical theological assessments of concepts and meanings of (i) nature, (ii) order and (iii) technology. Only after this critical assessment can we in part 2 explore what it is to act postnaturally by developing a theology of postnatural order. This in turn will lead to the fuller theological statement of postnatural right in part 3.

In the previous chapter, I set out what I mean by the term "postnatural condition" and the demand placed on theology to do its work in such a condition. This chapter presents an exploration of the concept of nature and its amplification as *social-institutional*. (Chapter 5 offers a continuation of this exploration.) It is important to recall the details of the postnatural condition under which nature is to be considered theologically. I have argued that nature is not a contrastive notion: in the postnatural condition, nature underpins or underlies. I suggested that the postnatural invites us to understand the practices of the human as embedded in a wider creatureliness: the life of human lives within the lives of other creatures; humankind is always accompanied by other kinds. In sum, the postnatural argues for the privileging of the social as the key concept for interpreting human-nature relations. What does this mean?

Here are the vital steps in my argument. In *A Political Theology of Nature*, I argued for the *sociality* of human-nature relations. Humanity and nature are best understood as social humanity and social nature and can only be understood in their interactions.[57] As such, I was drawing on the meaning of one of the terms related to "social" – as I explained in chapter 1, *sociality* refers to the for-one-another aspect of creatureliness. Elaborating this point in *A Political Theology of Nature*, I suggested that we approach nature and humanity through an ontology of social relations. Moreover, I drew on Michael Welker's *Creation and Reality* to affirm that creation is to be understood as a collection of interacting realms.[58] More recently, I have deployed the phrase "greater society" as a way of elaborating on this claim, including a refusal to see nature as stable, external to and available for human society.[59] Instead, a greater society invites the thought that true society exceeds human society and that such "exceeding" may be more plural than

---

[57] Scott (2003), 180-82.
[58] See Welker (1999).
[59] Scott (2015a), 5-19 (here 6, 17, 18).

we usually consider. What requires consideration is the surpassing of human society into nature and the surpassing of nature into human society. This lead to the
conclusion that nature and humanity are best understood in terms of overlapping
societies, a plurality of social orders.

In this chapter, I extend this analysis by reference to the *social-institutional*.
Recall that at section 1.6 I presented four terms: *social, society, sociality*, and
societal. In this chapter, attention is being paid to "social" and its relationship
to "society". In other words, what is required is further elaboration of social as
it relates to the human and nature, and the organisation of humanity-nature as a
greater society, as a context for thinking about right.

In the next section, I explore ways in which nature is a theological issue. In
the third section, I explore in considerable detail the meanings of nature. In the
fourth section, I revisit theological issues raised by the concept of nature. In a fifth
section, I show how the concept of nature cannot be converted straightforwardly
into the doctrine of creation. In a final section, I argue that in the postnatural condition, nature is always in interaction with the human: as that which underlies
rather than contrasts. Throughout the analysis, the aim is to consider the concept
of nature by attention to the trajectory of the social-institutional as a way of elaborating a greater society. Alternatively, we can only properly arrive at the concept
of the social through an analysis of the concept of nature. Thinking theologically
and ethically in a postnatural condition, I am arguing, requires a reworking of the
concept of nature with reference to the social-institutional.[60] In this chapter, the
emphasis is on the social; I shall attend to the institutional more fully in chapter 5.

2.2 NATURE AS A THEOLOGICAL ISSUE

Required to do a great deal of work, "nature" is a complex and perplexing term.
As Raymond Williams puts it, "The real complexity of natural processes has been
rendered by a complexity within the singular term".[61] In exploring critically the
concept of nature, we are attending to an abiding difficulty: a single term has been
pressed into the service of identifying and assessing complex relationships and
processes. (Williams writes of "natural processes" and we shall have reason to
appraise but not reject the adjective.) In what follows, I shall untangle some of
this complexity, draw out the implications for theology, and relate these to the
trajectory of the social-institutional. How shall we do that?

Although Lynn White's 1967 essay that accuses Christianity of ecological ir-
responsibility is perhaps the best-known English-language discussion of nature

---

[60] It may be worth adding at this stage that my approach is not what we might call "sociological":
      I am not concerned *directly* with whether nature is a socially determined notion or whether it
      represents social reality in some way and nor whether it has social consequences. These are all
      important issues but detract from the focus of this chapter, the methodology of which is not
      sociological.

[61] Williams (2014 [1976, 1983]), 219.

in theology,[62] the discussion by Gordon D. Kaufman in "A Problem for Theology: The Concept of Nature", published in 1972, is in my view more important in the precision and directness of the questions that it poses. On his own admission, Kaufman accepts that he does not furnish answers to the theological challenges that he makes. Yet the questions he poses are vitally important. The questions are: "What do we mean by "nature"? What is theologically at stake in the alleged contrast of "nature" with "history"? How is the present theological interest in the "natural" related to the long tradition of "natural theology"? Are there connotations of the concept of nature which makes its theological employment questionable or even risky?"[63] These questions are important to my study for the following reasons.

First, as will shortly be presented, I agree with Kaufman that there is a basic ambivalence in the concept of nature that cannot be resolved by stipulation of a meaning. The basic ambivalence refers to a duality in the concept of nature: does nature refer to that which includes the human or does it identify that which is other than the human? (We are once more at Jameson's rift.) Of course, as the etymology will demonstrate, it refers to both and in that double referral offers the rationale for the contrast between the natural and the artificial. Yet, second, this duality and double referral do not mean that we should be sceptical of the concept of nature and so declare it redundant. The direction of my analysis is to show how approaching this issue in social categories is fruitful.

2.3 WHAT IS NATURE?

It is true that the concept of nature has come to renewed attention in theology recently partly because of ecological issues.[64] For some time, theology has been attentive to nature in terms of its moral considerability. In other words, nature has been attended to as the environment of the human that needs appropriate care; at issue is the value of nature, as we shall see in chapter 5.[65] Additionally, nature has been enquired after as that which is produced and investigated by modern science. The human is placed within science's nature yet the human is at the centre as the observer. Third, nature has also been explored as a moral concept as a means of identifying that which is by nature human. Nature here has a double meaning: as the essence of the human and how that essence is known (that is, by reason). These views present a number of the senses of nature that we are exploring in this section. Given the breadth of the concept, such a presentation is nonetheless incomplete, as I hope to show. In what follows, I shall set out the concept of nature systematically, drawing on three different terms: *natura*, *phusis*, and *kind*.

---

[62]   White (1967), pp. 1203-07. See also Todd LeVasseur and Anna Peterson (eds) (2016).
[63]   Kaufman (1972), 337-366 (here 338).
[64]   Deane-Drummond (2004).
[65]   Ellis (2016).

The etymology of the word "nature" is complex. As previously noted, the concept of nature has been understood in a variety of ways: as that which includes the human and the non-human (*natura naturata*; the concept of "world" is synonymous); as the active spirit of the world (*natura naturans*) as in expressions such as "Mother Nature" – the first two senses are closely related; as the non-human; and, finally, the "essence" of a thing.[66] How has such a range of meanings come about?

The English word *nature* stems from the Latin, *natura*. (In Greek, we also have *phusis* and in Anglo Saxon, *kind*, and I shall discuss these shortly.) According to the OED, its etymon is to be found in classical Latin where its meanings include "birth, constitution, character, the genitals, the creative power governing the world, the physical world, the natural course of things, naturalness in art".[67] Moreover, *nat-* is the "past participial stem of *nasci*, to be born". We may at this point appreciate in a preliminary way how nature refers to the shape or constitution of a thing – that which is "born". Moreover, in that things that are born also develop, we may also appreciate why nature comes to refer to the development of the essence of a thing. Finally, in its givenness as born, we glimpse the beginnings of the distinction between the natural and the artificial: naked we come into the world and naked we go out. The word "nature" has a similar range of meanings in Anglo-Norman, Old and Middle French. Moreover, according to the OED, the term exists also in Spanish, Italian and Portuguese by the 13th century.

By the early modern period, two meanings of importance to this study are in existence: the sense of what the OED terms "innate character" may refer to, for example, "human nature": "the basic character or disposition of mankind; humanity, humanness" (OED, 7a), initially understood as "given by God and arising out of his creation" but later as "innate or shaped by experience, but with no reference to divine origin or purpose" (OED, 7a). During the same period, senses of nature that relate to the material world emerge. Moreover, the OED notes the distinctions that I have already alluded to: a "creative regulative power which is conceived of as operating in the material world and as the immediate cause of its phenomena" (OED, 10a), which is often personified as female (OED, 10b). With this meaning, further meanings associated with the material world arise: "the physical world . . . as opposed to humans and human creations" (OED, 11a) and "the whole natural world, including human beings; the cosmos" (OED, 11b). These senses of nature – regulative force, essence and material world (within which the human may or may not be included) – will recur throughout this study.

Theological issues follow, which may be put like this: if creation may be seen as "born of" God, then we may appreciate that one sense of material world refers to all that is created: human beings, other creatures, and their environments. Na-

---

[66]   Lewis (1967).
[67]   OED, nature, n., p. 1 [accessed 12 December 2015].

ture, as created, relates to *universal*, as we have already seen. If, however, human beings are understood for theological reasons to be distinctive in creation – bearing the image of God, rational and voluntary, as destined to be friends of God, etc. – then a *difference* emerges in creation, and the nature and destiny of the human are seen to be distinct from that of other creatures. What is given by the essence of the human – its nature – distinguishes the human from the rest of creation. Moreover, the concept of nature in its sense of duality may support such a reading: the question as to whether humanity is essentially different from or essentially similar to other creatures is raised in the development of the concept itself.[68] Much of the theological discussion of the term "natural" slides between these senses: the claim that (1) the essence of the human can be known elides into a claim about (2) knowing what that essence is, and that (3) the essence is given (procreative heterosexuality, for example). We may grasp this through a consideration of the term *unnatural* as employed in the Christian debates on homosexuality: does unnatural here mean that which is not shared with other non-human creatures or that which goes against what is by nature human? We may also appreciate that the interpretation of *natural law* is now made more difficult: does the reference to "natural" refer to that which is essentially human (and knowable) or that which the human shares – in being born – with other creatures? Once more, the concept of nature plays the role of trickster. So now, we need to explore more fully the emergence of the meanings of nature in order to appreciate how this is the case.

There is overlap between the OED's presentation of the definitions of nature and the widely known "keyword" presentation offered by Raymond Williams. Having said that, Williams additionally makes the valuable point that nature becomes established as a term through a process of abstraction. Not only are natural processes of great variety grasped by the term but also nature itself changes from referring to a process – being born – to the more abstract matter of characterising that which is born/in existence. It is my contention that "society" and its cognates do well in their ability to re-capture this matter of process, and I shall return to it in the final section of this chapter. What is required is the recovery of the independent noun, nature, as *process* – and it is my argument that "society" and its cognates assist in this effort, not least by implicating humanity in that same process.

Williams calls the move from process to noun the emergence of nature as a "specific singular": the "essential quality and character of some*thing*" is being asserted. This gives us the *first* meaning of nature, which we might call "essence" or "character". What is the essence or character of a thing? – this question is answered by referring to its "nature". This specific sense, Williams notes, develops into a *second* sense, an "inherent force which directs either the world or human beings or both". The development is easy to grasp: the essence of a specific sin-

---

[68]   Kaufman forcefully makes this point: see my presentation in (2003), 37.

gular is applied to what Williams calls an "abstract singular". (We might note, to list Williams' examples, that nature has been understood *abstractly* as goddess/Gaia, minister, monarch, lawyer, gardener and selective breeder.) The *third* sense also operates at the logical level of the abstract singular: "the material world itself, taken as including or not including human beings". How shall we understand the relation between essence and world? According to Williams, as we have seen, nature as essence is a "specific singular" whereas the term "abstract singular" better describes senses referring to the material world, whether in the sense of power/force or material reality. Yet, argues Williams, the specific singular leads to the abstract singular: "Sense (ii) [nature as a force or principle] developed from sense (i) [nature as essence], and became abstract, because what was being sought was a single universal 'essential quality or character'".[69]

Moreover, Williams continues, "This is structurally and historically cognate with the emergence of *God* from *a god* or *the gods*. Abstract Nature, the essential inherent force, was thus formed by the assumption of a single prime cause, even when it was counterposed, in controversy, to the more explicitly abstract singular cause or force *God.*"[70] That is, and saying more than Williams himself says, the emergence and consolidation of the meaning of nature as force or power (*natura naturans*) is related to a religious development that sees the world as caused by this abstract, singular cause.[71] We may conclude that there is some contestation here between the concepts of God and nature.

Finally, Williams argues that the emergence of *natura naturans* from nature as essence also has an effect on a third sense of nature as material reality (*natura naturata*). Thus, " ... when reference to the whole material world, and therefore to a multiplicity of things and creatures, can carry an assumption of something common to all of them: either (a) the bare fact of their existence, which is neutral, or, at least as commonly, (b) the generalization of a common quality which is drawn upon for statements of the type, usually explicitly sense (iii) [material reality], 'Nature shows us that ... '".[72] In practice, therefore, we should expect slippage between the meanings of nature: from a generalization of a singular common quality or essence to that which is essentially and abstractly the case with the material world – its force or power, sometimes traced back to an extra-worldly source – and thereby to an appreciation of the material world as a type of singularity, that may or may not include the human.

Yet, if Williams is correct, the matter of a noun representing multiple processes cannot be obscured fully. For the third sense – the material world, with or without human beings – can be understood as an "assertion of a common quality",

---

[69] Williams (2014 [1976, 1983]), 217.
[70] Williams (2014 [1976, 1983]), 217.
[71] Of course, pantheism and monotheism dispute whether the abstract singular of nature requires the further explanation of a source in God – but that is another matter.
[72] Williams (2014 [1976, 1983]), 217.

and thereby be resourced by nature, sense two; or the phrase "material world" may direct us to "multiplicities and differences" in a way that denies a common quality – and yet this is also presented by the term, "nature"! That is, the complexity of the natural processes being referenced breaks through. This third sense – material world – becomes the dominant sense through the seventeenth century and has been in the ascendancy since. One more time, we must note the third sense's semantic capaciousness: a neutral description, an assertion of a universal quality (e.g. Gaia, sociobiology), and an account of a range and variety of natural processes.

The last of these meanings has steadily become more powerful. Nature now refers to "an accumulation and classification of cases", although how these cases relate to scientific laws of nature is not always clear. For, as Francis Oakley notes, laws of nature do not carry the implication of command and duty associated with natural moral law.[73] So now, we may appreciate one more time that for these scientific laws to have any normative weight, sense 2 of nature must be drawn upon to give some authority to a scientific rendition of sense 3, a point that sociobiologists might do well to remember. The contrast "artificial" emerges with greater strength at this point as these cases are understood not to be human works. In other words, the material world is increasingly seen as that which excludes the human. (Here are three examples: a term like "natural world" becomes popular; the focus of, say, the BBC TV Blue Planet II series presents this point in terms of its content, and by its concluding reference to plastic as an intrusive, artificial human product; and a recent proposal suggests restricting the human presence to 50% of the earth's land surface.[74])

Under this variety of senses, human society could be characterised as corrupt or obsolete from the perspective of "nature". In other words, a version of sense 3 could be related to sense 2 and, in combination, be offered in contrast to human society. The appeal by Hobbes to a "state of nature" is exemplary here. The point made by Hobbes is an invitation to move from this state of nature towards an ideal society of the social contract. What is most striking, nonetheless, is how social the state of nature is for Hobbes: comprised of distrustful individuals exposed to the ill will of their neighbours.[75] Alternatively, in a different approach, human society could be characterised as artificial or mechanical – a malaise that could be met only by nature's cure that either offers a source of social and moral regeneration or a resource for imagining and anticipating an alternative society.[76] A natural "society" could then be contrasted with human society, in criticism and opposition.

Although both approaches – the Hobbesian and the Romantic – suggest nature in contrast with existing society, I heed Williams' caution about the concept of na-

---

[73] Oakley (2005).

[74] Wilson (2016).

[75] For further discussion, see Scott (2011a), 57-75.

[76] Williams (2014 [1976, 1983]), 219.

ture as an abstraction from the complexity of natural processes to note that we are not being offered a contrast in any simple sense. Once reinserted back into a social process, both approaches may be seen as differing reactions to the emergence of capitalist societies in Europe, which in turn draw upon different emphases in the concept of nature. Was it possible to envision an ideal society that was based on law and contract and to which the laws of nature gave witness? Or, drawing on an older meaning (effectively the second meaning of nature), could the rapidly developing industrial society be criticised from the perspective of the regenerative power of nature? In both cases, the reference to "society" permits us to see an important link. The society of industrialism is also the society of a new sort of individual, and thereby of a new sort of society, requiring in turn the development of law and contract.[77] The society of industrialism – those dark, satanic mills – may also be understood as opposed by the regenerative powers of nature. These approaches are thereby linked through concepts of nature. The notion of "society" both respects the complexity of natural processes that the concept of nature seeks to capture and invites a reinsertion of the concept of nature into an account of social processes. When nature is offered as a contrast to society, we should ask: "which nature, whose society?" I conclude that nature has a *social horizon* and I shall comment more fully on this judgement in the next section.

So far, I have been discussing the concept of nature by reference to its origins in the Latin, *natura*. According to C.S. Lewis, the Greek *phusis* secures the major conceptual breakthrough on which *natura* and *kind* depend. (More on *kind* in a moment.) Like nature and kind, it seems that *phusis* also meant "sort or character or 'description'".[78] For Lewis, however, an astonishing innovation was achieved by pre-Socratic Greek philosophers who "had had the idea of taking all things they knew or believed in ... and impounding them under a single name" – and the name they chose was *phusis*. (In arguing for a formal concept of nature – "... in which I can conceive of the whole as nature"[79] – Heidegger makes the same point.) Importantly for this study, Lewis argues that such an abstractive use of *phusis* permits the thought: is there anything other than all there is? That is, is there anything that transcends material reality? Thinking of the whole of material reality permits the thought as to whether there is only this whole.

The last of our trio of terms to emerge is *kind*, an Anglo-Saxon term that dates from as early as AD 1000 and is in widespread use in a variety of senses, to which we are coming, by the 13th century. For Lewis, its meanings are similar to *natura* and refer to a "'kind' or sort". Moreover, it received from *natura* the innovation achieved by *phusis*: reference to the material world. Again, according to the OED, the association with birth or origin is evident certainly by the 13th century, and then by association comes to mean a person's position by birth. This

---

[77] MacPherson (1964).

[78] Lewis (1967), 34.

[79] Heidegger (2013), 21.

is interesting for my study in that this meaning carries the sense of station or office: of an objective position by birth, that which is given. (Some account of social order is not far behind.) Thereafter, of course, it can mean that to which one has a right "naturally", so to speak, because of one's position given by heritage or birth. Once more, nature has a social horizon. One may speak therefore of natural right in this sense because what one speaks of belongs to the person naturally or befittingly. As we have seen, this sense of givenness by birth is extended also to mean the nature of a thing and thereafter to identify the action of a thing after its nature; that is, to act "naturally".

Without the definite article, *kind* is close to the meaning of nature in the abstract, especially with reference to law or order. In addition, from here it is possible to see the given order or regularity as an appropriate state: precisely a natural state or condition (sense 5a). A rather different meaning of the word is also available early and that brings us to *kind* as a class or group of things (sense 10a). According to the OED, this sense is initially related to the word, kin, before acquiring its primary sense today as a genus or species, and thereby identifies a group as kin: human*kind*, for example. Marvellously (sense 13b), kind may also refer to the bread and wine at the Eucharist: "Whether it be necessary that al men should be communicate with both kindes or no" (1539). Finally, we may note the use of the adjective, kind, not in the modern sense – although the two are undoubtedly related – but in the older sense of meaning that which is fitting or suitable, appropriate to the particular kind of the agent. To act unkindly is thereby to act against one's givenness or "nature".

If nature is a trickster concept, then we should be cautious about attempts to assign a single meaning to it. The history of its senses presented above commends such caution. Certainly, the term is complex not least because of the complexity of the relationships and processes referred to in the concept. In this chapter's first section, I suggested that we could only properly arrive at the concept of the social through an analysis of the concept of nature. The analysis above supports this judgement. In and through its processes and relationships, nature contributes to the order of a greater society. Alert to the senses of nature, we may enquire how it does this and thereafter consider the condition of a greater society.

In developing this argument, I have promoted a postnatural condition in which a sharp boundary between humanity and nature is called into question. Paradoxically perhaps, the analysis of the concept of nature confirms this stance and thereby provides a warrant for my overarching argument that a right order of life encompasses human and non-human creatures. (A concept of right in turn relates to such a general creatureliness, as we shall see.) That nature supports a plurality of social orders is not in doubt. That nature is easily recruited in support of a particular social order, however, is one of the lessons of this section. How this happens is easily grasped. Nature refers us to a "givenness" – and if such a givenness is widely accepted, it can be used to reinforce or buttress a social order. This sense of "givenness" can also be generalised by reference to a common quality, and that quality can be referred to as a type of external wisdom. Notions of regulative force can also be appealed to in support of a social order – in chapter 3 we shall consider the example of vitalism in this regard. Nature can also mean the material world with a variety of emphases, one of which is the exclusion of the human.

In face of such a trickster, the conceptuality of "society" and "social" ensures that the complexity of natural processes and relationships is foregrounded and that attention is always being paid to the ways in which nature is understood as contributing to an order. How so? I have argued that the concept of society refers us to relationships and an order. Of a greater society, we may pose a further question: *whose society* is this: who benefits from it and who pays? Moreover, given the emphasis on "greater", this question is not restricted to human members of a society. Furthermore, we can ask: *which nature* is under consideration, given the dangers of the concept in securing givenness and its perceived authority as a regulative force? In that reference to society invites us to consider an order of relationships and institutions, *and their condition*, we may ask a greater society of its senses of nature and whether the institutional construal of nature is persuasive. Finally, from the perspective of the doctrine of creation, we can ask a critical question: what difference does it make to think of "all that is", and associated notions of givenness, from the perspective of a Creator active in a common realm?

2.4 IS NATURE A POSTNATURAL CONCEPT?

It looks as if nature was always a postnatural concept! How is this so? I answer this question by revisiting three aspects of the postnatural condition set out in chapter 1. There I argued that the postnatural condition is to be understood as socialised, historicised and contextualised. Put in different terms, the condition identifies a wide creatureliness, the dynamism of human activity, and a non-human nature that exceeds the human. Within the tensions generated by these three aspects the concept of nature is articulated: as relational, as transformed, and as beyond the human. We may now appreciate the sense here of nature as at least dual. As we have seen, in Williams' discussion of the third sense, and in the OED's report, there is an ambivalence in the meaning of nature as material world. Should humanity be understood as included in nature (as in the term "world", and more recently, "planet") or seen as apart from it (as in "environment")? This is the tension between the *post*natural and the post*natural*.

In light of the consideration of the meanings of nature and its cognates, it is now easier to appreciate the significance of "society" and "social" as a conceptual way of linking humanity and nature. Although the concept of nature covers a multiplicity of natural processes, some of which are independent of the human, the postnatural condition also identifies the depth of the interaction between humanity and nature in relationships and institutions and that these activities are transformative for both parties. In this connection, Jan Patočka writes of "manifold reactions".[80] In and through activities there are manifold reactions by which nature and humanity change, are changed, and will change. In their capacity to transform, technological practices are significant here but so also are the ways in which nature is active through its own dynamics and also in response to human activity. Secured by the transcendental of sociality, the use of social as an analogy is designed to comprehend this aspect of change in multiple directions for, as Williams notes, nature is a single term representing a multitude of complex processes. Moreover, such multiplicities may operate at a range of scales, from a town to a bioregion to the planet.

There may then be a number of multiplicities or "societies" of nature, interactive and overlapping and at a variety of levels. Some of these will interact with human activities in a greater society. The analysis of the concept of nature indicates that nature in sense 3 is always relational and occurs in sets of relationships, a plurality of orders. This is the case whatever terms are used to capture nature as material world: from "law" to "web" to "system", the point is constant. As concept and actuality, nature functions in complex ways therefore and I have recommended speaking of its function and activity by reference to "social" and speaking of nature as a society. In the light of this conclusion, I am not persuaded that understanding nature *only* as a society is wise. A certain agnosticism here seems wise: even if nature has a social horizon there may be occasions when non-social analogies may be helpful in illuminating that. Nonetheless, reference to society enables me to make the point that human societies are working orders that always incorporate natural multiplicities in some fashion. Moreover, as we have seen, concepts of nature are related to concepts of society. Indeed, human societies are not functional without some such interaction. Understanding a greater society will therefore require attention to both humanity and nature. As we have seen, there is variety in this incorporation and in the interpretation of nature.

Whether nature offers any guidance or authority regarding this reactive process is also central to the concept of nature, especially in relation to its second sense. So to enquire after postnatural right – that is, to enquire after some guidance for the right ordering of the creaturely life of a greater society – trades upon some notion of nature as an inherent or directive force or authority. Therefore, this aspect of nature is more than description and may be more fully understood with reference to its *social horizon*. I develop this analysis further in this section.

There seem to be two tendencies operative in this discussion. The *first tendency* concerns the complexity and range of natural processes that the term nature is required to convey together with differing reactions to that complexity. Karl Rahner, for example, records two reactions to nature, characterising them as re-

---

[80] Patočka (2016), 53.

sponses to nature as beauty and nature as threat.[81] This ambiguity is to be accepted, he argues, because to deny the ambiguity is to opt for either spirit or matter. We should not seek to flee from nature nor abandon ourselves to it. The first option might lead to a transhumanism whereas the second might lead to a rejection of individuality and the personal. Therefore, in the ambiguity we encounter once more the social horizon of nature: in its ambiguity, nature informs different social forms – different societies, we might say, with different social visions.

Rahner argues that a unity must be posited between spirit and matter. As a way of addressing the complexity of such unity, in chapter 6 we shall relate the social to the spiritual in ways that maintain the unity of humanity and nature. Such a unity points in the direction of the concept of God, Rahner argues. In chapter 1, I have already indicated my agreement with this proposal: postnatural right is a creation ethic. In my argument we may also give a preliminary and penultimate specification to the unity by reference to the social. Although such unity lies in God, so to speak, we are not invited to defer this work to an eschatological omega point. Whatever the risks, and they are not negligible as our later discussion of social order will reveal, we may enquire after the authority of unity for a postnatural order. A social horizon, we might say.

The *second tendency* is the abstractive move from specific singular to abstract singular: the identification of a generalised essence or quality. This move has social implications. Perhaps this point is easiest to draw out in relation to *kind*; the social horizon of this concept is perhaps the clearest of the three. For in one of its meanings, kind refers to social position by birth, and so carries the sense of social station. Accounts of social station presuppose and require an account of social order. We see here, in a specific society, the interaction between humanity and nature: social position related to birth requires a preceding order. Even when the meaning is extended – as in human*kind* – to all humans who are born, a social order is still required that acknowledges the equal station of each, even if the social order is only ideal. Either way, in this society, humanity and kind are related and inform each other, by reference to an abstract singular, the privileged "givenness" of kind. Thus we have a further example of the social horizon of the term.

Therefore, we have two tendencies: complexity and abstraction. The two tendencies point towards the term, social. How so? In the first meaning, nature is involved in the ensemble of social relations; indeed, human society is not possible without such social interaction. I have proposed the term, greater society, as a way of exploring this social aspect. In the second meaning, the number of examples of this directive force suggests accounts of different social orders. The first point is synthetic, and relates to the three senses within which nature is articulated; the second is analytic in that nature and social order accompany each other.

---

[81]   Rahner (1993), 82-84.

The *social horizon* of *natura* can also be drawn out. Indeed, *natura*'s social horizon is perhaps deeper than *kind* although less easily to identify. Therefore, we shall have to dig a little. Recall that for *natura* the third and final meaning of nature is material world. An important issue here is the matter of the complexity of the processes presented, of which human beings are a part and yet also re-directive of these processes. A recurring question: does nature refer to that which includes the human or does not include the human? We may appreciate the concerns here by noting that the dispute between anthropocentrism and ecocentrism is caught up in this duality and contrast. The social horizon of nature emerges clearly for the decision between anthropocentrism and ecocentrism does not turn upon a stipulation regarding nature's meaning. Other factors are involved, including an assessment of the differences between humanity and the rest of nature, human preparedness for ecological responsibility, and so on. Such undecidability is part of the *social horizon* of the concept of nature.

We can see this problematic regarding the duality of the third meaning of nature in the recent interest by humanities' scholars in Astrobiology. One definition of Astrobiology is "the study of life in a cosmic context".[82] I am not concerned here with the issue of how life might be identified. Instead, I am concerned with the deep, conceptual implications of the concept of life. I propose that life has some similarities with the term "nature". What do I mean by this claim, and how might reference to "nature" help us understand it? A tension in the concept of nature has already been noted: put briefly, does nature refer to that which includes the human or that which is other than the human?[83] In comparison, what is the range of reference of "life"? One way of understanding "life" would be to see it as including the human and as such it performs a welcome critique of anthropocentrism. "Life", we might say, encompasses the human and thereby decentres it. Yet that may be too hasty a conclusion. For if one of the reasons that we are concerned with planetary life is on account of the damage that humanity is doing to the conditions of its sustainability, "life" seems to refer to that which needs redirecting by humanity – an earth in our hands, to coin a phrase[84] – and so to that which is other than humanity. In this context, life, and nature in its third meaning, seem similar: functioning in a duality. It is not clear to me that a response to the duality can be established *from within the concept of nature itself*. Although the duality arises from within the concept, it is not clear that it can be resolved from within the concept. Once more, we arrive at the *social horizon* of the concept of nature.

There is yet a further reference to the social when interpretations of nature are presented, in relation to an understanding of nature as power or force (sense 2). My first example is evolution. For us today the theme of natural selection is im-

---

[82] Catling (2013), 2.

[83] Scott (2010a), 1-4.

[84] Grinspoon (2016).

portant in characterising this world – a notion that stresses the historicity of nature
in that change occurs through practices of selection over time. Yet the numbers of
ways of understanding this directive force is surprising. Resisting the evolution-
as-competition trope associated with Darwin and his followers, Murray Bookchin
draws on Kropotkin's emphasis on evolution-as-mutual-cooperation.[85] From a theological perspective, Jürgen Moltmann notes that social Darwinism presented "as
natural events of selection" the following: "capitalist competitive struggle, European colonialism, white racism and patriarchialism ... and class struggle"; and
he notes furthermore that "new socialist forms of community" were deduced in
a similar fashion.[86] Also from a theological perspective, Stephen Pope presents
reductive tendencies in interpretations of evolution and helpfully sets out how
the meaning of evolution gets shaped in ways that draw on nature as a directive
force.[87] Finally, no account of the uses of evolution would be complete without
reference to Teilhard de Chardin: in a fresh interpretation, Michael Burdett argues
that Teilhard relates evolution to cosmogenesis, biogenesis and anthropogenesis:
"Reality is in a state of flux, but it also has a *telos*. It is because of this directionality that evolution provides the greatest amount of meaning for today".[88] To
borrow once more from Williams, these comments provide further evidence that
with ideas of nature come ideas of society.

A second example of this issue is transhumanism. Here the material world
may once more be understood in evolutionary development. Yet there is a sense
of an inherent force that directs this evolutionary development upwards, often
into a sort of rational or mental culmination such as a disembodied existence in
cyberspace. Above all, it is optimistic. There is more than one variety of transhumanism but, as Scott Midson points out, there is also commonality: "a sense of
directionality with regards to technological changes and augmentations of the human".[89] Once more, we see the interaction between social horizon and meanings
of nature. In other words, interpretations of nature perform a function in a specific
society, on this occasion one concerned with the longevity and survival of "the
human". Nature is a post*natural* concept: open to the ensemble of social relations
including human society; nature is also patient of a range of interpretations and is
thereby a *post*natural concept.

The concept of a greater society comprehends these emphases. In that a greater
society expands the meaning of what is social to include the non-human, it is
able to take up the sense of nature as a regenerative force or an emancipatory
resource. In that a greater society requires an account of a social order, it is able to
propose an ideal society by reference to right. (In what this order consists we shall

---

[85] For an introduction to and evaluation of Bookchin's work for theology, see Scott (2003), 109-35.
[86] Moltmann (1985), 191.
[87] Pope (2007), especially chapters 3 and 4.
[88] Burdett (2015), 114.
[89] Midson (2018), 77.

explore in chapters 3 and 6.) That is, a greater society undertakes combinatory work: it explores our present society by developing these two independent yet linked perspectives that both invoke a concept of nature. To the effort to render nature external to society, a greater society specifies the surpassing of humanity into nature and nature into humanity; on this account, and in the perspective of the human, there is only a greater society that is the configuration of a social humanity and a social nature. Yet a greater society also explores the matter of *reconfiguration*: what sort of postnatural order might resource a right order of life?

As a term of complexification, "greater society" is able to perform this double conceptual task by taking up the matter of the convergence of humanity and nature *and* positing a notion of order that depends on an interpretation of nature. That is, society, as we saw in the previous chapter, requires attention to be paid to relationships and institutions. At the same time, these relationships and institutions are extrahuman as well as intrahuman: exploring the surpassing of nature and humanity in multiple reactions in institutions. More dynamic than *system* and *constitution*, "society" also has the advantage of not trading upon organic images such as *web* or *body* that are less able to present an account of the relationships of an order related to human activity.[90]

The warrants for this position can be reinforced by an example. Consider the following from J. S. Mill: "The proposition that air and food are necessary to animal life, if it be as we have good reason to believe, true without exception is also a law of nature, though the phenomenon of which it is the law is special, and not, like gravitation, universal."[91] Perhaps we might reword this as follows: for any instance of animal life, the conditions of air and food must be met, and these are not universal in the sense of laws of physics but nonetheless they are universal in the sense of being laws of life. Additionally, we might notice that although the conditions of air and food are both vital, one is met directly and immediately (or is not met at all) whereas the other – food as a law of life – can be met in a variety of ways. To say that such a law of life is universally required to be met does not mean that there is only one way in which it can be met. To make a distinction: whereas the law of gravity is universally *applicable*, the law of life is universally *operative*; and that operation may vary across cultures.[92] My concept of a greater society comprehends this presentation: a greater society both acknowledges the

---

[90] Nor I am here relying on efforts in social theory to understand society by reference to an organism. On these attempts, see Dickens (1992), 19-44.

[91] Mill (2008), 6.

[92] As Soper notes, although there may be a form of universal activity that secures human livelihood does it follow that there are universal forms of response to or appreciation of nature? Procreation, for example, may be a universal activity in the sense that all cultures must procreate or perish but does that commend that we appreciate only heterosexuality or can our response to such givenness offer a greater diversity? Soper (1995), 217.

way that "animal" needs are met and yet the ways in which these are society-specific productions.

The presentation of nature as a social concept in chapter 1 was explored by reference to the term "society" and a number of cognates. That is, nature was explored by *external* reference; we might call this an extrinsic supplementation in which the openness to analogy of the concept of society was pressed into service. I also suggested, with examples and other context, that such extrinsic supplementation was not that strange and that there have been some efforts to explore nature by reference to the social. By way of a discussion of the concept of nature in this chapter, I have concluded that nature is a postnatural concept. That is, by way this time of *internal* reference – an analysis of the term, nature, itself – we have uncovered a social horizon to the concept of nature. We may understand this social horizon in two ways. First, the reference to being born has been used to associate the term, and its cognates, with social station or position, and so some version of a social order follows. Second, and of greater importance, nature acquires its power through a process of abstraction. What essentially is with reference to a specific thing is transferred in a general way to characterise what governs or directs nature (all that is or human nature). How that power is understood is clearly related, as we have seen, to social arrangements – sometimes in criticism, sometimes not. Moreover, as we shall see later, I shall be deploying that process of abstraction as a way of giving content to postnatural right (see chapters 3, 5 and 6).

I propose to use this social horizon of the concept of nature explicitly in the concept of a greater society. The work that a concept of a greater society does supplements what we ordinarily mean by society. For a greater society enables the identification of a wider-than-usual-set of relationships: of human society opening out onto a social nature and a social nature opening out onto a human society. In chapter 6, I shall explore this matter further by elaborating on the concept of "ecstatic life", which captures more precisely this sense of movement. My concept of *societas maior* does not *replace* other ways of speaking of nature. Instead, it allows for a supplementation of meaning: a way of expanding the meaning of society that stretches from the intrahuman to the extrahuman, and thereby offers a fresh way of speaking of nature. *Society* is a term of complication, denoting an order of relationships and institutions, and consideration of their condition. A *greater society* is a term of further complication that introduces nature in the sense of material world into the relationships and institutions of a society, and the consideration of their condition. Part of the warrant for this expansion lies, as we have seen, in the concept of nature itself. Nature is a postnatural concept.

2.5 THINKING THEOLOGICALLY ABOUT NATURE

Identified as a postnatural concept, we have learned also that nature is a theological concept. *Phusis*, if Lewis is correct, provided the conceptual means for thinking about everything, and thereby opened the conceptual space for asking whether there is anything beyond something. That is, to ask: why is there something rather than nothing? Moreover, as Aquinas will say, God is the answer to this question, even if we do not know what we mean by the answer.[93] Thinking with nature, and so thinking about all that there is, is therefore a theological achievement, and opens up a conceptual path for thinking about creation. Williams also comments on this innovation to "think the whole" although he does not recognise it as a theological achievement. Reference to nature as a "single prime cause", as Williams phrases the matter, was related, historically and structurally, to the emergence of God as "abstract singular case or force". An implication of thinking abstractly about the singularity of "all that is" implicates creation: the making of all that is by a transcendent maker or giver. However much in practice the question is set aside, to consider nature is therefore to have a theological question rendered explicit. It is certainly possible to take the theoretical achievement and pay no attention to how the achievement was secured; the ladder may be pushed away after the climb has been completed. Yet the theological issue remains, fully or residually: how is the relation between God and creation to be characterised?

There is a further reason why we should attend in theology to the concept of nature. That reason may be traced to the deep tension in the theological concept of nature. As Rahner notes, an account of the contingency of the incarnation – that the triune God had created and yet that there was no incarnation (perhaps also that there was no preceding Fall) – means that a world without grace is at least thinkable. Thereby, the theological concept of nature is founded.[94] To affirm creation only – and exclude nature – as a workable concept in theology is to deny this contingency.[95] Yet, in theological perspective, there was and is incarnation, and so now the concept of nature must at least be qualified. Not only can we think the whole but must also understand the whole-that-is-not-God as related to God, and thereby as graced.[96] Here is to be found the theological desire to relate nature to creation, natural law to creation ethics that we have seen in Cahill's work and will see again in Oliver O'Donovan's. Relation, yes; substitution, no: grace does not displace nature.

Nonetheless, in privileging "society", "social" and its cognates in this way, there is also an epistemic limitation to my approach that emerges from this theological discussion. If I am, transcendentally speaking, developing an argument

---

[93] Aquinas (2006), I 2 a3. See also McCabe (2002); Turner (2008).

[94] Rahner (1975a), 1029.

[95] There remains the issue as to whether such contingency – the non-necessity of the incarnation – is theologically convincing. A minority report in western theological traditions – Barth, Jenson – wish to affirm that God always intended to be "with us" in Jesus Christ; the Fall is a complication to this account but does not function as a requirement (so to speak) of the incarnation. Nonetheless my point is: once contingency is thought, the theological concept of nature exists.

[96] Balthasar (1993) makes a similar point.

from an ontology of social being in which all entities participate, then we may note that such participation is by reference to difference. As David L. Schindler puts the matter: "... each shares in this unity differently, in terms of the ever greater difference (*maior dissimilitudo*) proper to each kind of being, from non-living to living to human".[97] Thus an epistemology of a creation ethics, constructed out of such differences, will be increasingly cautious about the analogical deployment of the term society as the discussion moves through various dimensions of life. This affirms the use of the analogy, but cautiously. We shall see in chapter 5 how this caution leads to the conclusion that the term "institution" applies in a restricted way to nature.

Yet, the contingency of incarnation is also to be linked to the contingency of creation. As Robert Jenson notes, "The question is usually posed about the motive of the Incarnation ... but of course it is about the motive of creation also".[98] If incarnation is contingent, then the condition of that contingency is the prior contingency of creation itself. Such creation contingency is often referred to as *creatio ex nihilo* : that God not only creates out of nothing but also creates *freely* out of nothing. A difficulty for my argument is that the protocol of *creatio ex nihilo* has been charged by, for example, Whitney Bauman with being the source of dualisms between history and nature, between culture and nature.[99] Such dualisms are of course precisely denied by the theology of postnatural right presented so far. After the manner of political theology, Bauman argues that theology is a discourse that organises bodies in time and space; it is a discourse of the ligaments of power. In addition, a theology founded on *ex nihilo* is radically non-liberative and non-emancipatory in the contribution it perforce makes to colonial thought and practice. If sustained, clearly such an objection damages postnatural right in that, as we recall, postnatural right does not trade in such dualisms and affirms liberty and security for creatures.

I shall not repeat the details of Bauman's critique here.[100] Instead, I wish to say that *creatio ex nihilo* does not need to function in the way that Bauman claims. Bauman interprets *creatio ex nihilo* expansively, consistently arguing that it offers what I can only call a positive account of transcendence – that is, transcendence with content, as a source of a system of thought – and then as a foundation to which no questions can be posed, a foundation to which there can be no answering-back. This is unconvincing. It is possible to interpret *creatio ex nihilo* in a more low-key fashion, as a protocol or grammatical rule.[101] As such, I think it guards against a tendency in Bauman's analysis to treat the development of *ex nihilo* as a way of widening the gap between Creator and creation. Instead, it is

---

[97] Schindler (2011), 4.
[98] Jenson (1999), 17.
[99] Bauman (2009).
[100] My full response to the critique may be found in Scott (2014b), 125-130.
[101] See Scott (1994); Burrell et al (eds) (2010).

possible to interpret *ex nihilo* as figuring the relation between Creator and creation as *qualitatively different*; there is no gap to be widened. Transcendence does not need to be used to separate the human from the animal; an *ex nihilo* transcendence affirms the sociality of all creatures.[102]

2.6 HOW IS THE RELATIONSHIP BETWEEN NATURE AND CREATION TO BE UNDERSTOOD?

How indeed! Here is part of Hans Urs von Balthasar's reading of Vatican I: "*The Church requires* first of all that we recognise an authentic *ordo* of nature and reason that is relatively independent of the *ordo* of grace. Secondly, the Church calls on us to recognise an authentic, though relative, priority of the former over the latter."[103] Is it possible for the theologian to set aside such a judgement and sidestep nature's range of meanings and history of complexities by working directly with the concept of creation? Alister McGrath has posed this question to writings on the theology of nature by Wolfhart Pannenberg. For Pannenberg, the concept of nature cannot be abandoned by theology whereas McGrath argues that nature may be interpreted by theology as creation.[104] Although McGrath concedes that nature is a public concept, there is no reason why theology should have one particular meaning of "publicness" forced upon it. Thus, McGrath in effect disagrees with Gordon Kaufman's premise – "If we are to make theological use of the modern notion of nature – and how can we any longer avoid it, since all our thinking and experience is so heavily shaped by it?" – and so is in a position to dispute Kaufman's conclusion, that "we shall have to engage in theological reconstruction going down to the deepest roots of Western religious sensibility and vocabulary."[105] Instead, theology may decide, from within its own traditioned criteria of interpretation, what counts as *public*.[106]

It is worth pausing to consider why this argument by McGrath is attractive. It leaves theology in charge of its own meanings and allows the transposing of the concept of nature into the doctrine of creation. As Kaufman notes, "If "nature" is understood to refer to "creation," cannot these problems all be resolved, provided appropriate adjustments are made to bring the interpretation of creation into accord with our modern knowledge of nature?"[107] Yet, we may pause for thought if

---

[102] Scott (2003), 20-25, 43-52.

[103] Balthasar (1993), 382.

[104] McGrath (2001), 135-37, 300-04; he repeats the criticism in McGrath (2004), 44-45, 90. For McGrath, this does not rule out exploring analogies between Christian doctrine and, for example, evolution: see McGrath (2006), 117-68. For Pannenberg's position, see Pannenberg (1993) and Pannenberg (2007).

[105] Kaufman (1972), 355.

[106] As Bergmann recommends in his review of their work, an alternative and more creative approach may be available: see Bergmann (2016), 211–214.

[107] Kaufman (1972), 356.

we consider the relation between theory and praxis that is secreted implicitly by McGrath's proposal. For McGrath's argument to be successful, a particular understanding of the relation of theory and practice is presupposed. Put briefly, this understanding recommends that one concept may be converted into another concept without any implications or consequences for practice. It is of course logically possible for this to be true and when it works successfully we call such an operation, translation. Yet in the work of McGrath and others, the concept of nature is not being directly translated into the concept of creation. Instead, it is being *transposed*. For such a transposition to be successful we need to be clear about which practices are associated with the concept, and whether or not it may successfully undergo an analogising process such as transposition. For many movements between concepts, this may not be of concern: for example, if I decide to move from the concept of "the country" to that of "the rural", we may agree that the practices that accompany these two concepts are broadly similar. Can we say the same in moving from the concept of nature to creation? To indicate why this question must be answered in the negative, I make two points.

First, there is the obvious matter that nature is an ambivalent concept. Moreover, that ambivalence identifies the difficult problem of whether or not the human is to be included in nature or not. Out of this ambivalence, western civilisation has built a whole way of life. A sense of the separateness of the human from (non-human) nature is a condition of the attempted manipulation of the non-human by the human. Additionally, if one of the demands of environmentalism is that humans act towards nature with greater respect then, in a wonderful paradox, the separateness of the human is still required. In the flex of the dialectic, the separateness of the human from the non-human is a condition of the human transformation of nature by the human. It follows logically that this single condition is the condition both for ecologically destructive and ecologically restorative actions. If those practices – the practices by which the human seeks to secure itself against the contingencies of life – are embedded in a particular construal of the meaning of the word, nature, then these practices are not easily transposed. Moreover, this conclusion suggests that *additional* considerations will have to be introduced to secure ecologically restorative actions. Presumably, the point here is that creation provides these additional considerations. What are these considerations, however, and do they address nature's ambivalence?

Second, there remains a deep tension between the discourses of creation and nature, as we may appreciate from tensions in the papal encyclical, *Laudato Si'*.[108] Methodologically there is a clear statement that nature and creation are not the same (¶155) and yet this is worked out through *Laudato Si'* in somewhat unhelpful ways. That is, reference to ecosystems, webs, etc. clearly derives from the study of nature. Terms like mystery and communion clearly stem from the theological

---

[108] Francis (2015) – references are to paragraphs in the encyclical.

side. A welcome emphasis on creaturely teleologies reinforces this sense of the intrinsic value of the non-human but does not assist in developing a consistent vocabulary. If the aim is to develop an integral ecology, the task proves to be difficult. Moreover, the sense that we are dealing with two different spheres, the human and the natural, runs deep in the text. Much of the theological material is directed towards the consideration of the human. The reference to natural law is based on a discussion of human nature and downplays those aspects of natural law that relate human beings more closely to other animals. The Encyclical is clear on the difference between humans and other creatures by reference to personhood and *imago dei* as well as by reference to human responsibility. Creation and nature are not easily brought together.

In *From Nature to Creation*, Norman Wirzba also provides an argument that encourages theologians to pay greater attention to the doctrine of creation, especially the theme of creatureliness. Arguing that nature is idolatrous, Wirzba urges great caution in theological engagement with the concept of nature. In a brief analysis, Wirzba offers two meanings of nature – power, wilderness – and seeks to show how these contribute to an idolatry in which we treat the natural world as placed for human convenience.[109] Thereafter, the eclipse of creation is to be attended to by the recovery of a creation imagination that interprets the world as gift. In a conclusion that discusses various practices for the production of food, it is clear that Wirzba wishes to promote his argument as public but he does not explore the issue as to whether creation is a public concept in the way that his analysis requires. Additionally, his analysis of the term, nature, does not cover its range of meanings – including its importance for theological development precisely in the doctrine of creation – and so it is not clear how these critical issues are addressed by the doctrine of creation. The affirmation of creatureliness in and of itself does not set out how humans and nature negotiate the tensions in their interactions with each other and does not identify that these interactions are transformative and mediated by technological practices. Once again, it is interesting that there is a concern about a loss of order that presumably it is the task of the doctrine of creation to remedy. In a criticism of moral relativism, Wirzba laments: "There is no cosmic or transcendent order to which we are subject".[110] Yet the manner of the remedy is to invite "iconic perception" that enables "a deeper and more sympathetic engagement with the freshness, surprise, and mystery of creation".[111] In my view, this type of approach lacks an appreciation of the transformative aspects of human living. At this point, should we expect that some account of the *balance* of nature will be introduced? So we find: in a critique of modernity,

---

[109] Wirzba (2015), 54. This seems to reprise Lewis's criticism: "we reduce things to mere Nature *in order that* we may conquer them", cited in McGrath (2004), 36.

[110] Wirzba (2015), 55.

[111] Wirzba (2015), 94.

we are presented with "humanity 's inability to fit harmoniously within a world of others".[112]

The interpretation of nature as creation seeks to extend Christian meanings to present circumstance. At this point, we may appreciate with full clarity why nature cannot be converted into creation. For in such an act of conversion the problems associated with the concept of nature are simply transferred, unaddressed, into the doctrine of creation. In turn, this means that we cannot simply stipulate against the disgracing of nature by performing an act of substitution with the doctrine of creation. What Jonathan R. Wilson calls "the transformation of creation into nature" cannot be addressed by an act of mere reversal.[113]

2.7 CONCLUSION: WHICH NATURE, WHOSE SOCIETY?

The focus of this chapter has been the concept of nature and on making the turn to the postnatural. A brief account of the postnatural condition was presented in chapter 1 and in this chapter we have explored concepts of nature more fully. I have claimed that an order of life is social. Moreover, I have claimed that the best way to approach the social is by way of the concept of nature. Which nature? Taking the postnatural turn has involved engaging with the diversity of meanings of nature and exploring their social horizons. In joining nature and humanity by reference to the social, the notion of a greater society has been consolidated. A society comprises relationships and institutions; a greater society explicitly includes the non-human in its relationships. Furthermore, institutions are identified as where manifold reactions take place – I shall say more about institutions in chapter 5 where we shall resume this discussion by exploring a society of creatures in institutional relationships.

The concept of nature is comprehended and taken up by the concept of a "greater society", and supplemented thereby. An approach by way of "greater society" is one of complexification. Part explanatory and part exploratory, to call our society a greater society is not to require that domains of nature are called a society – that would be to deploy the concept of a "greater society" as replacement rather than supplementation – and I have already declared my agnosticism regarding this. It is rather to suggest as part of the postnatural turn that these domains are incorporated into a greater society: "manifold reactions" are comprehended by a plurality of orders of relationships. Moreover, we can reflexively locate the concept of "greater society" by reference to my discussion of nature: it provides a combination of all three senses of nature in which sense 2 is transferred into a version of sense 3, which in turn provides an essence, as in sense 1. That is, the social relations of a material world, including the human, are understood to be in interaction. A greater society extends relationships from intrahuman to extrahuman and

---

[112] Wirzba (2015), 120.
[113] Wilson (2015), 37.

thereby supplements the meaning of society in a postnatural turn. Eschewing organic metaphors such as web, metabolism and body, explanatory priority is given to active humanity in its relationships: an active and relational process at the scale of the transforming interactivity between humanity and nature.[114]

Moreover, by way of relationships and institutions the other sense of *greater* is honoured: a *societas maior* is not self-sustaining or independent. That is, a *societas maior* is a *societas* im*perfecta*; a greater society is not self-sufficient. An account of its relationships and institutions needs to take that lack of sufficiency and that dependence into account. The connotation of "social" in *social-institutional* is for a greater society whose interactive dependencies are considerable and constitutive.

A society may be understood as both general and abstract: it comprises relationships, institutions, and the condition in which both these are formed. The doctrine of creation, as we saw in chapter 1, also explores a tension between generality and condition: that creation relates to life and to normative states and processes. Of society, then, as part of creation, we may enquire: how is it as it is, and why is it so? In developing the concept of a greater society, I have been arguing that a greater society operates in a postnatural condition as an imperfect society: it is not self-sufficient or independent. Whose society is it? To consider this question more fully, we shall investigate the matter of order. To this issue, I now turn.

---

[114] As Dickens notes (1992), 56, interpreting society by reference to nature is not new: "Early forms of social theory were largely constructed using analogies between societies and nature". The point here, however, is to analogise *from* the social.

CHAPTER 3: ORDER – NATURAL

3.1 THE THEOLOGICAL PROBLEM OF ORDER FOR A POSTNATURAL CONDITION

As we have seen, Raymond Williams recommends that we consider a "right order of life". In this book, I am arguing that to advance a right order of life we pay attention to the postnatural quality of current circumstances in order to construct an account of right. How then shall we understand order for a greater society in a postnatural condition? This chapter offers a preliminary answer to this question with due reference to the trajectory of the historical-teleological.

We may begin by noting that one person's order is another's oppression, one person's disorder is another's freedom. Any way forward in theology is made more difficult by the use in 1930s Germany of the concept of "orders of creation" (*Schöpfungsordnungen*).[115] We encounter immediately some ambiguity in the meaning of the word, order. At one level, it is a descriptive term: "A body of people living by common consent under the same religious, moral, or social regulations and discipline" (OED), for example. In another sense, it identifies a correct operation or activity: that everything is in order and so working appropriately, of being in good order (see also "out of order" in two senses, not functioning properly, and inappropriate behaviour). These meanings are strengthened in any consideration of the historical-teleological in the doctrine of creation.

The doctrine of creation poses the question of order.[116] In what ways? First, we have the matter of how order is to be understood as discoverable in a postnatural perspective. Second, we have the issue of how an order is to be understood as alterable. What are the norms of judgement by which it can be assessed and changed? That is, we are confronted by the matter of right. In a discussion of nature, it would be simple enough to dismiss the natural as socially constructed and develop only a human-oriented account of order. Alternatively, it would be possible to affirm trans-historical structures as natural and insist that any comprehensive presentation of order must acknowledge such structures. As we shall see, neither option

---

[115] In earlier work, Scott (2010a), 25-30, I have explored the concept of mandate proposed by Dietrich Bonhoeffer, and sought to offer an ecological variation of these. Of mundane mandates, Bonhoeffer proposes work, marriage, and state – and argues that these have biblical warrant. The difficulty with such a proposal, I now consider, is that it is not clear why these structures have been selected and nor the extent to which the structures are to be regarded as invariant through time. As Pannenberg notes (1981), 29-30, the claim that mandates, etc. are different from natural law in its rational derivation from an abstract human nature is less persuasive the more an invariant basis is sought.

[116] See Scott (2004), 333-347.

is convincing in a postnatural condition. This, then, is the theological problem of human and natural order in the postnatural ordering of creatureliness.

We may also note the complexity of order by considering the difficult matter as to whether order should be understood as comprehensible by one set of regularities. According to Karl Rahner, there are three types of order: discovered natural order, imposed and appropriated ethical and logical order, and the constructed order of culture and technology.[117] When theologians press the matter of order, we shall need to ask from which type of order they are making their case. Postnatural right must, I think, be alert to all three types of order in its presentation – and hopes to secure this by reference to nature and technology, thereby referencing Rahner's first and third types. Additionally, there would be little enthusiasm today for declaring a particular order to be certain – clear, and not obscure – yet there remains a commitment, on creation grounds, to understand that order as universal and true. An important question then emerges: which conceptuality will be deployed as the basis of the universality? This is not a new issue: according to Lorraine Daston and Michael Stolleis, the concept of law – in the sense of "universal legality" – was selected in the early modern period as a way of understanding social and natural orders.[118] Such an option, as we shall see in section 3.5, remains influential.

So, in making an argument in the doctrine of creation, the issue of order cannot be avoided. We have already heard Cahill ask the following question out of the doctrine of creation: is it possible "to defend a foundation or minimum of human morality that survives the fact of sin and that can provide a natural basis for just social life"?[119] In starting to answer this question, I have extended the concept of social to encompass the non-human as well as the human; my argument aims at a greater society and a right order of life. Moreover, I have already queried the distinction between nature and society. Given my extension of the term "social", and my destabilising of the term "natural", how can we even speak of *natural* order?

To address these issues, in the next three sections (3.2, 3.3, 3.4) I explore how the notion of order functions in a discussion of two influential accounts of created order (O'Donovan, Demant). In the section thereafter (3.5) I explore the notion of order in natural (moral) law. In the penultimate section, I reconsider the matter of a natural order and suggest ways – which will be amplified in chapter 6 – to develop the notion in a postnatural direction by reference to the historical and the teleological.

---

[117] Rahner (1975b), 1110.
[118] Daston and Stolleis (2008), 5-7.
[119] Cahill (2005), 8.

3.2 CREATION AND ORDER

In this section, I wish to develop my argument by asking in what ways is the postnatural transhistorical? In other words, does creation identify a persisting order that is given by God through divine action? Such an order might be distorted through human action or ignored; such is the permissiveness of human freedom. However, on one view, such an order cannot be denied. Theological tradition has sometimes explored this issue by reference to enduring structures: marriage, family, procreative sex, work, sometimes the state, have all featured here. I have resisted simply abandoning reference to the natural and yet I have maintained that nature underlies rather than contrasts. In other words, central to my position is that there is an order proportioned to human nature and that such an order is to be found and discovered – indeed, it is available to be found and discovered even where it is not acknowledged and accepted.

To seek after a right order of life is to seek after a truer order of life. Yet such a truer order of life cannot be, as Donald MacKinnon notes of some strains of natural law, "curiously indifferent to historical change" and thereby in "neglect [of] the reality of novelty".[120] In what ways, then, is the postnatural transhistorical and yet not indifferent to historical change?

The doctrine of creation reminds us that we are dealing with an account of order as this relates to unity. As Regin Prenter writes, we are concerned here with "Human existence in its totality, because it [the doctrine of creation] always sees man [sic] as standing in a relationship to God".[121] Nonetheless, the question now emerges as to how to understand that totality. Given my affirmation of the postnatural, how shall that totality be thought? Does the relation somehow secure the totality of the human to God as advertised in the doctrine of creation? Is there a permanent order that, although not easy to discern, is discoverable by practical reason?

As a step towards answering this question, in *Love, Law and Language* Herbert McCabe makes a helpful distinction between two sorts of human unity. He calls these a *biological* unity and a *linguistic* unity.[122] He describes the two unities in this way:

In the first place [hu]mankind is a *biological* unity; human beings are interfertile. In order to be human you have to be born of other human beings, you have to be linked by physical genetic relationship with the rest of the human race; [hu]mankind is, in fact, an animal species. In the second place [hu]mankind is a *linguistic* unity; in order to be human you must, in principle at least, be able to communicate with other human beings. Just as sexual relations and offspring are in principle possible between any man and any woman, so it is in principle possible for any human being to talk any human language.[123]

---

[120] MacKinnon (2011), 115-29, here 119.
[121] Prenter (1967), 250.
[122] McCabe (2003), 36-37.
[123] McCabe (2003), 37.

Although I am not able straightforwardly to take over this distinction, preferring *communicative* unity to linguistic unity, I think that it is helpful to be reminded that the totality of the human is not simply a biological unity. In any theological discussion of a created order, a biological unity – for which the use of the term nature may serve as a proxy – cannot be allowed to stand on its own. As we shall see, to think of a created order in a postnatural condition is to think of the unity of the human as interactive with, and transformative of, the non-human.

I want to explore this issue further by discussing Oliver O'Donovan's *Resurrection and Moral Order*.[124] The volume has been influential in its own right, and in theology and the environment discussions because of its importance for Michael Northcott's *The Environment and Christian Ethics*.[125] O'Donovan presses this issue of unity by insisting that what is vindicated in the resurrection is a certain order: the "order and coherence" of the world.[126] This stress on the restoration of an order also encourages O'Donovan to argue for natural structures as teleological. That is, some permanent natural structures are never lost or surpassed in the movement of history. Procreative marriage seems to be his lead example. In presenting the matter in this way, O'Donovan's argument works against the main tenets of historicism: revelation and history are here opposed – as were reason and history in the eighteenth century and after – and a defence is offered of a common humanity and an order that has the same scope as natural law.[127] This, I think, associates his thinking with one aspect of the Enlightenment and early modernity: an emphasis on the universal but not the cosmopolitan.[128] I wish now to explore this position in more detail.

For O'Donovan, creation is identified as an order; it is received from God and is not God. The notion of order applies to humanity : "Man's life on earth is important to God; he has given it its order; it matters that it should conform to the order that he has given it."[129] The notion of order applies more widely: "Without "nature" around it in which it can take its place, "human nature" can be nothing but an insubstantial phantom . . . ".[130] We may note immediately that such an approach trades upon two of the meanings of nature: (1) [human] essence and (2) all that is. The world is an ordered totality; it is ordered by God and is ordered towards God. (As we saw in chapter 2, this is a thought that the concept of God enables.) If this is the vertical dimension, so to speak, there is also a horizontal dimension: the ways in which fellow creatures are ordered to one another. From these two directions – the vertical and the horizontal – O'Donovan argues we may derive

---

[124] O'Donovan (1994).
[125] Northcott (1996).
[126] O'Donovan (1994), 31.
[127] Davaney (2006), 16.
[128] A point reinforced in later work: see O'Donovan (1996), chapter 7.
[129] O'Donovan (1994), 14-15.
[130] O'Donovan (1994), 18.

two concepts of order: of end and of kind, of the teleological and the generic (or general). That is, kinds relate to one another because either one is for the other (teleological) or they are in a looser relationship of reciprocity (generic).

The next move is an obvious one: the ordering of the creature to the Creator is the only pure teleological relation; the creation is for the Creator. By contrast, within the created order there is greater complexity: teleological and generic relations, orderings-to and orderings-alongside are combined. One way of reading the creation narratives in Genesis is to see these as a sequence of increasingly sophisticated orderings-to and orderings-alongside. It is clear that as creatures, Adam and Eve are ordered alongside other creatures. Nonetheless, we should also note, O'Donovan contends, that fruit, the fish of the sea and the birds of the air are teleologically ordered to the human. In other areas, there is no natural teleology: that all human creatures bear the image of God recommends the conclusion that there can be no natural teleological ordering between humans; there is no natural superiority of one human group over another.

For O'Donovan, then, creation carries a specific meaning: a totality, a structured whole; "created order" is his preferred expression. This whole comprises two sorts of orderings: the teleological and the generic, of end and of kind, usually in some admixture.[131] There is some blurring, intentionally, as to whether nature refers to the human or to a wider nature in which the human is set. Given the discussion in chapter 2, the use of the term "kind" is interesting as it has resonances with what is given, what is born, and furthermore has association with rank or station.

This observation permits a first line of criticism: postnatural right identifies not an antecedent and prevenient totality and order but a dynamic, historical postnatural order. For the postnatural, it is difficult to disentangle orderings-alongside. A range of terms is available besides postnatural to explore this matter: for example, "hybrid" and "cyborg". Terms such as hybrid and cyborg are efforts to explore the increasing intensification of an order of kinds: of multiple and extended orderings-alongside. "Hybrid" and "cyborg" also call into question easy appeals to teleological and generic orders because it is harder to discern the kinds and their orders as these increasingly interact with each other. To use O'Donovan's term, reciprocity is deeper than his analysis seems to permit.

Moreover, it is not always easy to disentangle orderings-to and orderings-alongside. I am not denying these orderings but argue that their discernment is complex and practical. One of O'Donovan's examples is vegetables. In the perspective of O'Donovan's structured whole, there is an important difference in saying that "vegetables are food" and that "vegetables are considered to be food". The former accepts a teleological direction whereas as the latter is based on an arbi-

---

[131] Charles Curran also uses the terminology of "generic ends" in his discussion of natural law: see Curran (1996), 595.

trary decision by the human. However, in my view, in the light of, say, genetically modified crops, it is hard to maintain such a position. GMOs are still teleologically ordered to the human but also require the mixing of kinds. In other words, we begin from the mixing of kinds rather than a given order – or at least a claim to a given order. Is it credible to say that GM maize is teleologically ordered to the human as food? In the mixing of kinds, are there breaches in reciprocity in which the non-human is unwisely altered and unhappily dominated by human purposes?[132] Of course, GM maize can be eaten by humans but that, as O'Donovan would be the first to say, misses the point. The postnatural is thereby concerned with order but it is not confident about the settled order of a structured totality. The present order is already a strange mixture of orderings-to and orderings-alongside, many of these not well understood. There is no stepping out of history but that also means there is no stepping out of nature. It becomes harder to accept the blunt binary: "Either they [forms of order] are there, or they are not."[133]

One line of response that O'Donovan's position could make is to say, in partial agreement with mine, that it is not easy to say that GM maize is given as food. That is, it is not easy to say with confidence that GM maize is teleologically ordered as food to the human. Moreover, the reason why it is not easy to say that GM maize is for the human is because of this notion of a restored creation order: in effect, the "order" of GM maize in fact breaches a restored creation order. In the context of making the postnatural turn, such a response once more requires a conception of nature as in contrast with the present order. Once such a contrastive order is granted then the contrast is consistently reaffirmed by subsequent positions taken. The point remains: why grant the contrast? O'Donovan's position requires a contrast between the natural and the artificial, presented as a restored creation order.

A second line of criticism now emerges. Given that the postnatural turn invokes notions of hybrid and cyborg, from where does the confidence come to declare such a created order? One point of origin, in O'Donovan's analysis, lies in trying to think of "order" at all. To perform such a mental operation, he argues, we need the concepts of "end" and "kind". Moreover, for O'Donovan, these concepts "... belong to the world as it were stopped still in its tracks; they are given in the fact of creation itself".[134] How convincing is this approach? If we were trying to characterise such terms, we might call them "transcendental": concepts that are required if we are even to think of order. Nonetheless, such a transcendental status is a peculiar one for we should not conclude that such terms strip temporality out of our interpretation of present circumstances. Rather, we need transcendental terms that permit us to theorise order in terms that are more dynamic. Alternatively, at

---

[132] For as fuller discussion, see Scott (2010a), 161-185.
[133] O'Donovan (1994), 35.
[134] O'Donovan (1994), 32.

least, we need an explanation as to why such a temporality-free conceptual approach is justified.

A third issue presents itself for our attention. What is meant by "created order"? The reference to creation is clearly identified by O'Donovan as referring the human to its wider context: "... a divinely-given order of things in which human nature is itself located".[135] This, then, identifies an "... ontological ground for an 'ethic of nature'" and thereby an "objective order to which the moral life can respond".[136] In that the resurrection of Jesus Christ is the divine action that is the restoration of created order, we may now ask why the distinction between nature and history is a satisfactory way of interpreting the restorative outcome of the resurrection of Jesus Christ. Reference to the restoration of the created order neither requires the separation of the human from nature and nor does it require the drawing of a strong distinction between nature and history. The ontological ground renewed in and through the resurrection could, as I have suggested, be the sociality of humanity and nature: an order that is discovered through its construction and does not require an effort to separate nature and history.

The term "created order" should be interpreted more appropriately as referring to the realising of the freedom of human creatures and the flourishing of non-human creatures in the interactive concord of a greater society. Indeed, the resurrection of a human body and the return of that body to a greater society suggests that common distinctions between nature and society do not hold. As I have argued elsewhere, the resurrection of the divine and human body of Jesus of Nazareth is the transcendence of the natural limit of death and thereby the reconstitution of human society. At such, it is difficult to render intelligible the notion of resurrection except that the resurrection of a *body* is elucidated by reference to the concept of sociality. Moreover, if human society is always ecological society then this greater society also participates in bodily resurrection.[137]

This transcendence of the natural limit of death suggests that a return to Eden is not possible; there is no original ordering to which we should "return".[138] Moltmann reports a range of cognate terms for Eden: paradise, the primordial condition, innocence and the unscathed world.[139] Even if we accept the validity of these terms, the point remains, however: there is no right of return. Instead, the postnatural requires a dynamic and unfolding order that, I would argue, is not opposed by a doctrine of creation. At one point, O'Donovan argues that for the purposes of measuring movement we need something static. This is a way of justifying the use of a structured creation whole as a measure: we need something like a fixed

---

[135] O'Donovan (1994), 16.

[136] O'Donovan (1994), 19.

[137] See Scott (2010a), 161-185, here 177.

[138] To be fair to O'Donovan, he notes this but does not see that his position of the vindication of the created order suggests the vindication of Eden: see O'Donovan (1994), 55, 63.

[139] Moltmann (1985), 55.

point. This is true but not in quite the way O'Donovan claims. It is true that to measure movement we need a fixed point. However, it does not follow that we need always the same fixed point. Historical change may require the movement of "fixed" points; that is, what is required is new "fixed" points. We can judge the present order from the perspective of right that provides an historically situated "fixed" point.

To abandon the Eden-Fall-fulfilment schema is not thereby to abandon yard-sticks. Nature is not some independent and structured totality. Moreover, if we reject such a totality we are not obliged to conclude that nature is lost, irrecoverable or at an end. The affirmation by O'Donovan of an "ontological ground" is helpful but we need a different understanding of that ground.

3.3 THE NATURAL AND THE HISTORICAL

As already advertised, the second issue is this: in my presentation of the post-natural, is not nature dissolved into history? In the sense that nature then never enjoys its own telos (ordered to) and is thereby subsumed into history. Does the natural then become something transient and possibly momentary, produced by the human and therefore revisable by the human?

Once more, I follow the criticisms offered by Oliver O'Donovan. For O'Donovan, the enemy here is historicism because historicism ignores and undermines the theological commitment that creation enjoys a natural structure and a natural end. Christian ethics, O'Donovan argues, works with an account of the "natural structures of life in the world".[140] As such, these natural structures enjoy natural ends. The problem with historicism, according to O'Donovan, is that it undermines natural ends. In that the natural "serves only a supernatural end, the end of history" then "... natural order and natural meanings are understood only as moments in the historical process".[141] We might say that they lack their own natural integrity and await transformation towards an historical end. (As such, an historical end may not be a supernatural end, such historical ends may also be called natural!) From this position, O'Donovan insists that the doctrine of creation – or thinking with the doctrine of creation – identifies the whole and the given. As he writes, "Creation is the given totality of order which forms the presupposition of historical existence".[142] As such, creation is not reducible to historical flow. Instead, creation is to be understood as "... the order which was God's primary gift in creation".[143] Through all this, O'Donovan insists that "Natural ends are generic, historical ends are particular".

---

[140] O'Donovan (1994), 58.

[141] O'Donovan (1994), 58, 59.

[142] O'Donovan (1994), 60.

[143] O'Donovan (1994), 61.

As before, the theological root of O'Donovan's position is the resurrection of Jesus Christ which "vindicates the created order in this double sense: it redeems it and it transforms it". Moreover, O'Donovan argues that redemption and transformation refer us, respectively, "to the origin and to the end of the created order". Moreover, when we speak of the origin of life, we mean, according to O'Donovan, the "natural structures of life in the world". Natural structures cannot be repudiated but they can be transformed. This "integrity of the created order" – sometimes "nature's order" – is why O'Donovan resists the maxim: "[A]ll teleology is historical teleology"; the maxim that "there is no point in the regularities of nature as such" is to be rejected.[144]

We may agree with O'Donovan thus far: to grant a point to the regularities of nature is to accept that they have some ultimate significance; their generic ends are not fully subsumable by human action. Furthermore, to grant them a point is to grant them a rationale. The ecological feedback that we call climate change furnishes us with a helpful example of this. Climate change indicates that the goodness of creation rests upon a durable and stable non-human nature that is able to change but only within certain limits before the present set of regularities is replaced by a new, and less human-friendly, set of regularities.[145] Nonetheless, it is not clear to me, given its history and flexibility, that the earth's planetary ecosphere is best regarded as a structure. In his discussion of the generic ends of natural structures, O'Donovan offers only one example of such a structure: marriage. While it is just about plausible – although, as we shall see, not convincing – to regard marriage as a structure, it becomes harder to identify what these other structures might be. Other candidates are associated with human embodiment: requirements for food, warmth and shelter. In addition, there are forms of association other than marriage: for example, friendship and society.[146] None of these, however, are easily described as structures. The first group is better identified as a set of human needs and the second set arises from the nature of the human as social and so is better regarded as tendencies towards association. We might also add today the necessary dependencies by the human on a wider nature. While any transformation of these aspects might be regarded as the transformation of creation – these are all generic or general ends – yet none can, I think, be called structures, never mind invariant structures. Given these difficulties, it seems wiser to stick with the term, "institution", as already introduced in the previous chapter, rather than "structure".[147]

If we privilege "institution" over "structure", certain conceptual advantages emerge. For example, we can explore whether particular and generic ends may

---

[144] O'Donovan (1994), 57, 58.

[145] See Scott (2011b), 50-66 (here 60).

[146] See this chapter, section 3.5, for a further discussion of these aspects of natural law.

[147] In (1994), 69, O'Donovan does the term institution to describe marriage; this seems, however, to be a conventional usage.

combine in institutions. In other words, can generic ends host new/additional particular ends in institutions? Such a way forward seems to be blocked if we work with "structures". Let us consider, to develop this argument further, the well-known Marxist postulate that in the communist society – that is, post-socialist society – we can expect the withering away of the state. This position directly challenges the claim that human society requires political government. The governance of the polity is a given of human social living, we might say in response, and is its own end. Therefore, we should immediately be suspicious of a Marxist claim that the state will wither away if such a claim means the governance of a polity will not be required. Yet, in making such a riposte, there is no need to accept the "creation status" of the governance of a polity. At least, we do not need to do so if we refer to institutions rather than structures. For in an institution, as we shall see, generic and particular ends are not opposed; a new particular end does not cancel out a generic end. Indeed, the concept of "institution" can "process" the matter of the withering away of the state and acknowledge that such a claim to a withering away, however wrong-headed, does at least demand a defence of present governance. (We shall come to a fuller elaboration of "institution" in chapter 5.) It seems wiser then to avoid a term such as "structure".

O'Donovan's account contrasts a created or natural order with history and thereby insists that certain created or natural structures are ordered-to. To defend an account of creation that is ordered-to does not require the specification of structures, however, but instead the identification of needs or tendencies that are their own ends but can be realised in a number of ways – through a range of orderings-alongside. As I have said, we are dealing here with activities rather than structures. This is to acknowledge that the human acts in freedom to produce or reproduce; it is partly in agreement with McCabe's point that we should distinguish between the biological and the communicative; it is to acknowledge that the meeting of needs and acceptance of tendencies may be achieved by a diversity of orderings-alongside.

This postnatural approach contrasts with O'Donovan's stress that "Creation is the given totality of order which forms the presupposition of historical existence", a "completed design".[148] O'Donovan is surely correct to say that creation should not be understood as "the first phase in the process of history". (However, we should note that his preferred analogies for the extension of history – unfolding a scroll, a flowing stream – do tend in this direction. In other words, creation has its own ordering-to.) Do we then have to follow O'Donovan in drawing heavy black lines between what is given by creation and certain worldly structures?

Through a critique of Wolfhart Pannenberg, O'Donovan discusses one possible response to his position. Is it possible to identify certain historically particular ends and note their repetition? Through their repetition, would it be possible to

---

[148] O'Donovan (1994), 60, 63.

establish that these are in some way general, and thereby have the appearance of, or act in the same way as, natural ends? I suppose that procreative marriage might be one example; it is the only example offered by O'Donovan. Put differently, does the widespread "availability" of heterosexual, procreative marriage – repeated through many cultures albeit with some differences – indicate a natural end? For O'Donovan, such a position is not adequate: it denies the universality of the natural end of marriage and does not secure the natural end of marriage as based in the completed design of a created order. Instead, any such natural ends are sourced in a repetition of events: as Pannenberg notes, "... one can speak of a repetition of *the same* structures in an indefinite multiplicity of events".[149] For O'Donovan, such repetition provides an historicist resolution, and is thereby to be rejected: such repetition may support structures – including structures deemed to be universal – but these structures are neither universal nor given in creation.

The conceptuality of postnatural right requires both the affirmation of the reality of the otherness of nature and its interaction with the human ("the postnatural condition") and its ideal criticism from the vantage point of right. Postnatural right cannot therefore accept the historicism rejected by O'Donovan: natural ends are not merely reconstituted by humanity's historical projects; historical possibility is not the limitation of God's prudential activity; natural order is not dissolved into historical change. However, neither can postnatural right accept O'Donovan's characterisation of the weaknesses of historicism.

To develop an alternative position, we may note that Pannenberg, in an extended comment, draws out the differences between two rival versions of reality: one concerned with the reality of the appearance of what is and the other accounting for the arrival of futural reality:

Both ways have their religio-historical backgrounds: the one coming from myth's orientation to primal time and the archetypical, the other from being grasped by an eschatological future. The first is a well-beaten path and has been impressed on all our familiar habits of thought. The second way has until now been hardly considered. ... There is much to be said in favour of orienting philosophical thinking to that which always is. Above all, one may point to the possibility of forming general concepts and of making general structural statements that can be applied to the most diverse individuals and to changing situations. And yet, against this view is the truth that such a position, which sees what appears in the appearance only as a timeless universal, will inevitably underestimate or totally fail to recognise the importance for our experience of reality, of the contingently new, of the individual, and of time.[150]

It will be clear that postnatural right is attentive to the ecologically new, to the individual and the temporality of nature. As such, it cannot invest in the first of these ways, a version of which is preferred by O'Donovan. Nonetheless, Pannenberg's

---

[149] Pannenberg (1969), 142.
[150] Pannenberg (1969), 141.

presentation of the notion of repetition noted above, although attractive, requires some development. Thus, Pannenberg's account of repetition requires strengthening by reference to what I call *institutional repetition* and *universality*.

By *institutional repetition*, I mean that the concept of repetition has significance at the scale of the institutional. That is, repetition occurs as an activity through the stability of institutions. Of fundamental importance to my argument in favour of postnatural right is that generic and particular ends *combine* in institutional repetition. For example, in marriage the created order is continued through the procreative activity of human beings; these may be characterised as generic ends. Yet, such ends may be realised in different ways and thereby receive additional, historical and particular ends. This is the case theologically because in addition to being subject to eschatological transformation, creation also, as Daniel W. Hardy argues, delays the end: "Creation constitutes foundational structures and dynamics which lead to, and delay, the end". Although we may regret Hardy's use of the word "structure", it is clear that creation has capacity for both stability and transformation.[151] It is not simply that the created order receives its eschatological transformation. It is also the case that, as the infrastructure of life, creation delays the end. As such, creation is patient of the acquisition, so to speak, of further, particular ends towards the maintenance of the infrastructure of life, including social life. Thus, from the perspective of postnatural right, we may say that creaturely structures receive their future *by addition*; that is, by the acquiring of fresh ends. As such, institutional repetition secures the development by addition of the admixture of generic and particular ends. It is by addition that generic and particular ends combine in institutional repetition. (The earlier distinction between the biological unity and the communicative unity of humanity is also relevant at this point.)

Although we may note that my conclusion accepts Pannenberg's qualification regarding the significance of the future for postnatural right, nonetheless his position on *universality* cannot be accepted. In order to protect the contingently new, the individual and temporality, Pannenberg downgrades the notion of universality to that of a human construction, "useful by its ability to grasp a reality that is probably of quite another character, since it is conditioned by contingency and time".[152] Such a re-positioning is dubious in the light of creation's affirmation of the universal, given in the unity of all creatures as a whole, and as kinds, as they relate to God. In my postnatural perspective, the universal is given with creation: a whole, differentiated to be sure, but a whole nonetheless that offers the basis for *universality*. I shall return to this point in the next section.

For historicism, according to O'Donovan, what is natural is without differentiation and direction. The natural is subsumed under developmental tendencies

---

[151] Hardy (1996b), 157, 161.
[152] Pannenberg (1969), 141.

with the inevitable conclusion that "Action cannot be conformed to transhistorical values, for there are none, but must respond to the immanent dynamics of that
history to which it finds itself contributing".[153] One of the distinguishing, and dam-
aging, features of this historicism, he argues, is the one that maintains that history
is the process of human beings becoming self-conscious and taking charge of history. In theology, the best-known example of such a tendency would be the work
of Teilhard de Chardin. All this must be rejected, O'Donovan maintains. Where
it is not rejected, unfortunate consequences follow for the individual's relationship to nature and to society. With reference to nature, for example, everything is
intervention even when – as in wilderness parks – it is the intervention of non-
intervention.[154]

How does the postnatural respond to such a line of criticism? The postnatural must, I think, argue that the natural is not teleologically ordered only to the
historical. The natural is not superseded by the historical and nor is the natural
exhausted by the historical. A Platonic view of teleology in which matter is ordered to the rational (sc. historical) which is in turn ordered to the supernatural is
not persuasive. The postnatural claim that nature is ordered to God does at least
recommend the view that history does not act comprehensively as some kind of
corrosive acid to the natural.

What may be added to this recommendation? In denying transhistorical structures there is instead the affirmation of transhistorical *conditions* as the basis of a
transhistorical *order*. The necessary, revolutionary and social aspects of postnatural right are universal. These are the generic or general features of the ethics of
the postnatural and provide an account of orderings-alongside that needs also to
be related to the orderings-alongside of the human; indeed, strictly, these two sets
of orderings can be distinguished but not separated. By this argument, I contend
that in my account natural ends are generic and particular. The features of the postnatural apply generally but may produce different, concrete outcomes. However,
these features remain and are an ordering-to; they are teleologically significant
in their relation to God. Human practical activity as true and good is universally
ordered-to the necessary, revolutionary and social. In sum, there is no antecedent
and prevenient natural order. It does not follow, however, that there is no order.

O'Donovan's basic complaint is that natural structures do not have their natural ends properly identified; at the level of the natural, nature is understood as dissolved into the historical process. Natural structures are temporary stabilities that
are subject to historical reconstitution. The postnatural does not hold this view,
however. The postnatural does not operate with dualistic distinctions between historical process and natural structures. Instead, the natural is present through the
right-ful effort of making a habitable world. Such a basis, towards which all efforts

---

[153] O'Donovan (1994), 67.

[154] For an interesting discussion of humanisation and non-humanisation, see Antonaccio (2015),
31-46.

are ordered, is universal, identifies the human agent as of necessity to be ecologically located and in the name of unity calls into question the hierarchies created
between humans and their non-human counterparts. I think that Moltmann tends
towards such a view in his discussion of Cosmic Spirit and human consciousness; he also uses the concept of spirit to link human persons to their culture and
society, and to ecosystems, concluding that "human beings are participants and
sub-systems of the cosmic life system, and of the divine Spirit that lives in it".[155]

In summary, I agree with O'Donovan that "... we are not to conclude from
this that there is no *ontological* ground for an 'ethic of nature', no objective order
to which the moral life can respond".[156] I also agree with him that all creatures
are ordered to God and thereby it is not correct to say that nature is ordered to the
human (who is ordered to God). Such a position is too close to a Platonic teleological ordering that O'Donovan himself criticises. Nonetheless, through these
agreements, two issues – one substantive, the other procedural – separate my position from O'Donovan's.

First, I have suggested an alternative to a creation order with which we interact. There is instead an order that is given in, with and by common creatureliness,
and yet such an order is related to human activity – in chapter 8 I shall explore the
importance of human willing in this regard. As the analysis in chapter 2 shows,
converting nature into creation only translates difficulties into a different discourse
and idiom. The difficulty for O'Donovan's position is how to render intelligible
the appeal to a creation order. Put in terms of the concept of nature, what is has to
be secured with reference both to human and non-human worlds – to be universal – and thereafter to be granted normative force. Yet O'Donovan does not show
that how this is done and instead appeals to the recreation of an original order as
if the resurrection of Jesus Christ, human nature and cosmic order all align. If so,
how is this so? In other words, the effort to convert nature into creation, and then
declare an order, is not demonstrated; it lacks warrant. We may of course guess
at the warrant: an implicit appeal to a *creatio originalis* . Yet, as we shall see in
chapter 8, *creatio originalis* is also accompanied by *creatio continua* and *creatio
nova* .

Second, there is an important procedural difference between my position and
O'Donovan's. The account of right that I am developing has some similarities with
Fichte and Hegel and relates to a distinction between personal freedom and moral
freedom.[157] The argument of this book relates closely to personal freedom: the
order of right by which human freedom and non-human flourishing is structured,
secured and extended. O'Donovan's position relates, I think, closely to moral freedom: the capacity of the Christian to respond to the reality of redemption.[158] It is

---

[155] Moltmann (1985), 18.
[156] O'Donovan (1994), 19.
[157] See Fichte (2000); G. W. F. Hegel (1991).
[158] O'Donovan (1994), 102.

the burden of the complete argument of this book that the ethical issues that arise from our postnatural circumstance are better addressed by attention to personal freedom.

3.4 A NATURAL ORDER?

In *The Idea of a Natural Order*, V. A. Demant discusses the whole ordering of life for present society in an argument that bears some similarities to O'Donovan's.[159] Both are concerned with the doctrine of creation and the structured totality that, in their view, creation identifies. Writing under the heading of the doctrine of creation for the redemption of society, Demant argues:

> Either we can take our stand upon the permanent needs of human nature, or we can adopt some philosophy of human evolution in which human needs, apart from bare physical necessities, are in a state of flux. In the first case, the social order will be judged according to its power of meeting the essential needs of men in their total nature; in the second, man will be judged according to his ability to fit in with the processes of social change.[160]

We have once more the offer of a binary: "permanent" and "essential" are contrasted with "flux" and "process". Once more, we have the stripping out of temporality and the doctrine of creation deployed to ground fixity and stability. There are further similarities with O'Donovan's position: Demant discusses natural law but gives interpretative priority to the Gospel. Demant also speaks easily of a "natural order of life", a "norm of social ordering", a "common natural structure of human existence", and "man's fundamental nature". Like O'Donovan, Demant has concerns about historicism, and in addition vitalism, as these undermine natural order. Moreover, such order is partially secured by reference to God as creator. In that his argument is founded in a relation of microcosm to macrocosm, and trades upon two meanings of nature, the notion of balance is important to Demant's analysis. Although the term is mine, "balance" accurately captures Demant's commitment to human life as an ordered whole and the tendency of that ordered life to become disordered and so unbalanced.[161]

I begin my evaluation in the middle of Demant's argument, with the matter of microcosm. Demant proposes that the human person is a spirit-filled and spirit-centred creature. This is, to propose a description, a pneumatological "centrism": all human activities are grounded in "the spirit-centred structure of man"[162] and are thereby ordered into a balance or harmony (my terms). It is because the human is a spirit-centric being that, precisely as spirit, the human can move beyond

---

[159] Demant (1966 [1947]); reprinted in Demant (1948), 70-91.

[160] Demant (1936), 15.

[161] "Balance" may have Augustinian resonances: "*pondus* [weight] continually guarantees an overall balance, so that there is not, in the natural order, a chaos of conflictual agencies", Williams (2016), 65.

[162] Demant (1966 [1947]), 10.

such a centrism and focus too much on one sort of activity over others; to become, in Demant's term, "ex-centric". These activities include political, technical, cultural and trading activities as well as race and class. (These days we would add "gender".) Centredness – Demant prefers "centrality" – is easily lost and difficult to recover.

Moreover, such centredness has a personal aspect and a social aspect and in noting this distinction we move from the microcosm to the macrocosm. Just as in personal life the human person cannot through an act of will recover their true centredness so also in society the recovery of true centredness requires "a social order that provides a habitat for the soul".[163] Such a social order is based in the "natural order of human life", and operates as a "norm of social ordering", sometimes a "norm and operative force".[164] More often, "The natural order is violated".[165] Yet, even in the violations there are two indications that the natural order perdures: the persistence of morality and law on the one hand, and on the other that an overemphasis on, say, economic activities is eventually corrected in that such an immanent order does not enjoy equilibrium. We are reminded once more of the matter of balance.

By way of summary, Demant argues that the natural order of human life is transcendent, noumenal and eschatological. That is, natural order is dependent upon the transcendent God, with the result that human beings are not only natural and historical beings but also spiritual; noumenal in the sense that the order is not given but can only be discerned; and eschatological in the sense that said order is not yet fulfilled and will only be so in "God's final perfecting of creation".

In the context of making the postnatural turn, what is to be made of the claim that humanity is a "real kind", with " ... a norm of social ordering underlying ... "? Additionally, that there is an "essential nature of the human being" where nature means " ... what man is in the order of creatures" and that " ... man has a real structure ... "?[166]

First, it is helpful that Demant opens his enquiry by stressing that the aim of his essay is to assist in securing a change: that " ... problems of social good and evil were more in the sphere of the will than at present". This is crucial to my argument. The postnatural turn is an attempt to identify more accurately the practical conditions of social action. Discussions of *institution* in chapter 5 and *social freedom* in chapter 8 revisit the issue of human willing and social action.

Moreover, second, to give priority to the person is indeed only effective when the person is part of a "whole series of social relations that make up a natural order". Yet, we must recall the postnatural extension of "social" to encompass relations with other kinds and ecological relations more widely. This in turn means

---

[163] Demant (1966 [1947]), 12.
[164] Demant (1966 [1947]), 2, 15.
[165] Demant (1966 [1947]), 11.
[166] Demant (1966 [1947]), 2.

that the distinction that Demant makes between "nature" and "Nature" is called into question. For Demant, nature refers to human nature and Nature refers to the wider "natural world" in which humanity participates.[167] We have already seen reasons to call into question such a sharp distinction. Not least, the strong relation maintained in Demant's analysis between human nature, spirit and Spirit appears to use the doctrine of the Spirit in creation to secure a strong difference between the human and the non-human animal. With this, and related, comes a static account of eternity/transcendence. By reference to S/spirit, the human is somehow lifted out of history which somewhat undercuts the matter of the mutual reciprocity and orderings-alongside that we noted from O'Donovan's work. Moreover, the eschatological part lacks content. The emphasis on fulfilment does not identify which parts of creation are fulfilled and thereby raises the matter of the *telos* of the non-human and its relation to the human.

Third, although Demant is cautious about too great an emphasis on immanence and stresses that the individuality of the address of the Gospel is the basis of a Christian universality, and furthermore that the address of the Gospel is to history and not in history, nonetheless he offers a quite flexible account of "natural order". He stresses the family but in fact does not offer a lot of content about the family. He identifies other areas of human activity – production, government, culture – and argues, as part of his commitment to balance and equilibrium, that one should not be stressed more than another should. Demant promotes a decay narrative: the fullness of the past has been lost. Nonetheless, Demant offers a framework – which he calls natural order – in which to criticise historical developments. That is, his proposal is largely procedural. It differs from O'Donovan's in that for Demant the natural order is not restored; the order was never lost in the first place. This framework is thereby never fully present in any actual society yet it exists as a norm and a force. In contrast, a postnatural reading would offer an account of historical development, of breaking through to new institutions.

My account of postnatural right is related: it is universal, social but cannot be read off any social arrangements and has as its *telos* an eschatological fulfilment. What I am adding is that right must now be able to operate in a circumstance in which appeal to a given nature is problematic – Demant gets around this by arguing that nature refers to what is by nature human; that is, his natural order focuses on family, culture, economics, and politics. My account of nature and humanity as postnatural is equally noumenal and yet different. Right is not given but is instead a matter of achievement: we should not too quickly make the assumption "that mankind as a unity exists "by nature" ... [rather] that human unity is something towards which we move, a goal of history ... it is not simply given to us but also made by us".[168]

---

[167] Demant (1966 [1947]), 14.
[168] McCabe (2003), 67.

Moreover, for Demant, order can be justified theologically because it responds to the universality of the Gospel. The Gospel addresses the human in its particular setting from beyond the human. Whereas the setting is nature and history yet the Gospel itself is transcendent. Although human beings are in relationships to nature and history, the human is related to the One who transcends nature and history. For Demant, this transcendent relationship to God constitutes the human as "centric". When order oversteps its mark and becomes a general idea then it needs to be challenged by the Gospel in the name of particularity. Moreover, when particularity – for example, class struggle or evolutionary competition – assumes the role of general *explanans*, then this too requires to be challenged by the Gospel. Reason and vitality are common examples of false centres of the human (the true centre being spirit-ual). Demant argues for the metaphysical priority of family and culture – although economics and other spheres may have moral and/or physical precedence. This natural order is kept in balance only by the transcendent reference. The difficulty with this is that Demant's account does not refer to the ecological and presents a sort of personalism: what is grounded in the transcendent relation is the *human* spirit. Nonetheless, a universalism is maintained which is, after a fashion, open to the future: once the universal order becomes unbalanced it needs to be corrected. That a universal order is justified by reference to the universality of the Gospel is thereby to be preserved even if, for postnatural right, the universality relates more closely to the resurrection of Jesus Christ, who is the Gospel.

Through the last three sections, I have considered two different conceptions of order. Both stipulate that the doctrine of creation requires the articulation of a natural or created order. In turn, this raises the question of the relationship between said order and historical change. In chapter 2, I suggested that the relation between the natural and the historical should be reconfigured by reference to relationships and institutions. As we consider what the transhistorical is, we are concerned with the postnatural configuration of human beings: the freedom of the human to transform its circumstances in and towards a postnatural order. Such transformation is not well captured by the distinction between the natural and the historical. The human does not act independently in some historical realm to transform the natural but is instead always already placed in the social interaction of the natural and historical. To approach the activity of humankind is not to begin the task of separating out the historical and the natural.

Moreover, in my reading of Demant and O'Donovan, I find them much less successful in keeping to their avowed aim of affirming a creation order. Demant's position, it transpires, is largely procedural: the natural order provides a framework, and thereby a norm, for the equilibrium of human activities. Foregrounded is the "real" activity of human agents and the framework of natural order identifies when the activity becomes unbalanced. O'Donovan's position also requires certain concepts that will enable us to think "transcendentally" about order. With this, a different thought is introduced: that the ontological ground of a creation order is required if any sense is to be made of the notion of a restored creation order. Certainly, we should note that no logic connects the two thoughts.

Furthermore, to speak of an ontological ground brought back by the resurrection of Jesus Christ identifies a creation order of which Christ is somehow the summary and exemplification. Yet we can maintain this thought and maintain that Christ's body is that summary and exemplification but draw a different conclusion: a body in which humanity and nature are joined in the renewal of sociality through death identifies not a restored order but the indissoluble relation in sociality of humanity and nature. We may also note that O'Donovan is not able to maintain the strict separation he seeks between history and created order. O'Donovan leaves in place the hierarchical relations between humans and other creatures and matter in a fashion that exposes his position to the retort that there is history in his created order. Additionally, a focus on marriage and the family suggests a focus on a mediating activity – mediating, that is, between nature and history – in turn suggesting a calling into question of a strong distinction between created order and history.

3.5 LAW – NATURAL, MORAL

In the previous three sections, I have explored in a first step two versions of natural order, one proposed by O'Donovan and the other by Demant. In this second step in making the postnatural turn with regard to the theme of order, I continue this discussion by exploring natural law. We shall find that in natural (moral) law meanings of nature interact with each other in particular ways, and that this position is also unwisely correlated with the binary of natural/historical. In order to conduct this enquiry, we shall need to explore further the theme of the historical-teleological. This is important because postnatural right affirms the reality and otherness of nature but not in the usual ways. As such, and vested in the sociality of humanity-nature, postnatural right refuses the duality of natural vs historical. It is, as we shall see, in postnatural sociality that right is founded.

To begin, I must counter the objection that there is little point in postnatural right interacting with natural law on the grounds that postnatural right is sourced in the revelation datum of the resurrection of Jesus Christ and natural law is vested in an account of human nature known by reason. Although true, there are points of contact between the transcendence of the Gospel in the resurrection of Jesus Christ and the idea of natural law, as Demant points out. First, although the Gospel is addressed to individuals, Demant argues, nonetheless it is addressed to the person in their *setting*. Some account thereby needs to be given of the person in their setting. This presents the danger that two ways of understanding the setting – reason and vitality – may compete with the Gospel. Even so, Demant argues, reason and vitality are not equidistant from the Gospel in that law and gospel may join in the face of "the perpetual threat of vitalist, cosmic and historic interpretations".[169] Law and Gospel converge on universalism: Law engrosses all human groupings in reason; the Gospel in addressing each in their particularity generates a different sort of universalism of the uniqueness of each. Vitalism, cosmology and historicism do not, contends Demant, offer a universalism. Law may overstep its mark and seek to displace the Gospel and at that point it is to be rejected by the Gospel. Nevertheless, in its appropriate place, it is an ally of the Gospel. As such, a consideration of natural law seems appropriate, even if we note Demant's reservations.

In a period in which vitalist, cosmic and communitarian political options are available, we should note that the Gospel displaces these, sometimes with the assistance of natural law. As related to natural law, postnatural right also secures a practical justification in its resistance to an ethical "reduction" by vitalist, cosmic and communitarian perspectives. As such, postnatural right resists communitarian responses to ecological crisis and yet seeks to explore right-ful patterns of social living in specific settings. Postnatural right is thereby suspicious of attempts in natural law to argue that the content of natural law, or the procedure by which precepts are established, are given and settled. Demant's comment on the content of natural law – that what we have are "formulations and embodiments of custom" that address issues arising from the violations of custom[170] – is interesting. (As Stephen Pope points out, usury and marriage, slavery and the persecution of heretics have been both ruled in and ruled out on natural law grounds.[171])

To follow this lead, postnatural right understands itself as derived from violations of custom, which fits well with the method proposed by Raymond Williams that in the concept of nature we have concepts of society also. Moreover, from such a flexible position, custom in Demant's analysis begins from a "natural history of the family". The family is "common total life" and different from but related to "relations of association in which he must enter to pursue common tasks".[172] The priority of family and culture is not moral but metaphysical or sociological: the bonds of family are more inclusive and more personal, Demant argues, than relations in other areas (politics and economics, for example). He makes a closely related case for the metaphysical (and not moral or physical) priority of culture over economics and politics. Similarly, postnatural right is an ethical proposal that does not address ecological issues only but also a right order of life. In other words, postnatural right is not right-ful order only for the human but makes a much larger case for the right ordering of a greater society.

What is important in natural law for my argument, we may now appreciate, is the connection made between law and morality on the one hand and the refer-

---

[169] Demant (1966 [1947]), 7.
[170] Demant (1966 [1947]), 16.
[171] Pope (2005), 158.
[172] Demant (1966 [1947]), 17.

ence to universalist or species-founded moral aspiration on the other.[173] In other words, natural moral law seeks to ground morality in aspects of human nature. With some exceptions, the nature that natural law is based on is human nature. Such moral law functions as a contrast to the civil law or human law. Postnatural right affirms the basis of right in nature but argues, via the concept of a greater society, that the nature we have to do with here is an animal – rather than a human – nature. Moreover, postnatural right does not operate with a contrastive conception of nature: what is ideal about postnatural right does not refer to natural, that is, universal and unchanging, structures. Rather, what is ideal about postnatural right is the permanent reminder of the necessary ecological situatedness of the human and the teleological characterisation of that situatedness.[174]

How then shall we begin this brief enquiry into natural law? We may begin by noting that natural law is not a single thing. A. P. d'Entrèves argues strongly against understanding natural law as a uniform style of enquiry and recommends approaching it both *historically* and *conceptually*. Approaching natural law *historically*, d'Entrèves argues, allows its differences to be presented as well as its commonalities. Moreover, in taking this historical approach, d'Entrèves does not quite follow a common division of natural law into medieval/early modern/modern. Instead, he insists that proper attention be paid to Roman law also and the historical period for the consideration of natural law must be extended to before the medieval. Thus, he offers the following periodisation: *ius naturale*; *lex naturalis*; and *ius naturale*, corresponding respectively to the Roman period, the medieval and the modern.[175] Approaching natural law *conceptually* – D'Entrèves uses the term "philosophical" – attends to differences in the meanings of nature and the schemes of classification that try to capture its use.

I begin with neither history nor concept. Instead, I wish to begin with sources. For natural moral law, what is this "natural"? Given the range of meanings of natural law, and the presence of the theme of natural law without the name,[176] what are the sources of natural law? This approach is partly commended by a remark by d'Entrèves: "... the history of the law of nature is really nothing else than the history of the idea of nature in law and politics".[177] Such a comment raises the matter of sources: what are these natures? This is a crucial question for making the postnatural turn. And such an approach further permits my enquiry to be what d'Entrèves dubs psychological: we are concerned with "the function of natural law rather than the doctrine itself, the issues that lay behind it rather than

---

[173] See Oakley (2005), 19.
[174] Following Bloch (1986), chapter 20, we may also say that postnatural right is not concerned with narrative.
[175] D'Entrèves (1951), 7-14.
[176] For example, it would be interesting to compare O'Donovan's position with that of natural law.
[177] D'Entrèves (1951), 11.

controversies about its essence".[178] In making the postnatural turn, the underlying issue as regards nature is to construe the ontological ground of a right order of life as the basis of an order that advances a greater society; a postnatural order that affirms the otherness of nature but not in antecedent and prevenient ways.

What, then, are the sources of natural law? Dalston and Stolleis identify three: universal human nature, as presented in Roman law (this nature, as in Ulpian, may be extended to include non-human animals); dictates given by God and written on the human heart; and rational participation by humans in the divine law (often associated with the work of Thomas Aquinas).[179] I want to affirm this attributed emphasis in Roman law on humans placed with wider animals, an emphasis confirmed by d'Entrèves' analysis in which he argues that this aspect of natural law should not be dismissed. Moreover, in following d'Entrèves a little way, I also want to suggest tentatively that, although the bulk that is Aquinas' contribution to natural law looms large in this discussion, the Roman account of natural law – if we attend to *sources* as referenced by the concept of nature – is also helpful.

Ulpian, at least as attributed in Justinian's *Digest*, considers the following to be the core of *ius naturale*: "Natural law is that which nature has taught all animals; this law indeed is not peculiar to the human race, but belongs to all animals... ".[180] What sort of universal validity is this, we might ask? If law is a "common patrimony" – if it makes a claim to universality – what sort of universality is this? D'Entrèves argues that the rational basis or foundation of natural law, on this account, turns out to be Ulpian's "natural instinct", which d'Entrèves summarises thus: "... there are certain institutions which are inherent in all animal life. The universality of law is pegged to nature in its broadest sense".[181] Despite this reference to a broad institutionality, "basis" or "foundation" are the preferred terms at this point presumably because law is not to be understood in contrastive ways. (Such a contrast is present in the writings of Cicero: a contrast that has, according to d'Entrèves, both dominated the approach to and obscured the diversity of Roman natural law.[182]) Natural law does not precede and correct. Instead, d'Entrèves argues that the basis was not "speculative, transcendental" but instead was "a quest for the intrinsic character of a given situation".

In rather different terms, such an account of natural law offers us a "pedagogy of attention", and I shall in chapters 5 and 8 be associating my account of right with such a pedagogy. The aim here is then not to establish some rules, based in "nature", and deduce some principles for application. Instead, we are offered "a means of interpretation" that attends to the concretion of animal, institutional

---

[178] D'Entrèves (1951), 12.
[179] Daston and Stolleis (2008), 2.
[180] D'Entrèves (1951), 25.
[181] D'Entrèves (1951), 28.
[182] Cicero (1998), 68-69.

life.[183] We might then agree with Cahill that natural moral law may be interpreted more flexibly by noting that such a reading is already intrinsic to one interpretation of natural law.[184] To use Curran's terms, the "physicalism", "classicism" and "naturalism" that some have ascribed to natural law are not constitutive of it and a freer approach is possible.[185]

Recovering the account of non-human animals in Roman natural law is not to identify and privilege procreation, etc. but to indicate that humans are in continuity with other animals and said continuity is institutional. Therefore, any account of law is to be based upon an account of a common patrimony: shared relations, interests or goods. Hence, universality is to be understood *practically*. In this endeavour, is the position attributed to Aquinas a help or a hindrance? The standard reception of Aquinas on natural law argues that the focus of Thomist natural law is on human nature: that what identifies the human as human is reason, and it is by reason that humanity participates in eternal law. So far, this is a broadly Stoic conception.[186] Yet, Aquinas's presentation of natural law is more broadly based than this. Thus, as commentators generally note, Aquinas has a threefold basis of natural law:

The order in which commands of the law of nature are ranged corresponds to that of our natural tendencies. Here there are three stages.
There is in man, first, a tendency towards the good of nature he has in common with all substances; each has an appetite to preserve its own natural being. Natural law here plays a corresponding part, and is engaged at this stage to maintain and defend the elementary requirements of human life.
Secondly, there is in man a bent towards things which accord with his nature considered more specifically, that is in terms of what he has in common with other animals; correspondingly those matters are said to be of natural law which nature teaches all animals, for instance the coupling of male and female, the bringing up of the young, and so forth.
Thirdly, there is in man an appetite for the good of his nature as rational, and this is proper to him, for instance, that he should know the truths and about living in society. Correspondingly, whatever this involves is a matter of natural law, for instance that a man should shun ignorance, not offend others with whom he ought to live in civility, and other such related requirements.[187]

In the perspective of the postnatural, what is the significance of these three levels? David Ritchie opines that it would be helpful to maintain the distinction that Aquinas appears to make: "Here we have a very careful distinction between natural tendencies and the precepts of reason, which it would be well if all those

---

[183] D'Entrèves (1951), 29, 30.
[184] Cahill (2013), 247-89 (here 251).
[185] Curran (1951), 596.
[186] Aquinas (2006), 1a 2ae, 91, 2.
[187] Aquinas (2006), 1a 2ae, 94, 2.

who have talked about nature and the law of nature had always observed."[188]
Moreover, Ritchie will later link natural tendencies with "appeals to fact" and
argues that little is resolved thereby: which natural facts, he asks, should we respect? D'Entrèves, after listing the three points presented in full above, concludes:
"The natural law, the expression of reason, cannot fail to be an essentially human
concern."[189] The first, Ulpian-esque, point is noted but that is also superseded in
d'Entreves's reading by reference to society and God. Thomas Gilby also insists
that Aquinas presents us with a hierarchy: "The second [meaning of natural] refers
to a thing's status in the hierarchy of being: here man is regarded at the three levels
outlined in the article, namely as a substance, and especially a material substance,
as an animal, and as rational – "rational" here means intelligent, and need not be
confined to "intelligent through reasoning". Natural law enters at all three levels,
but specifically and properly at the third, where natural law is rational law, and
kata phusin is *kata logon*."[190] Despite the reference to rational as intelligent, a hierarchy is in place, avers Gilby: rational law and human society is the sphere in
which natural law is most strongly implicated. Does that suggest that Hooker's
distinction between two types of natural law – a law that governs natural objects
and another that governs voluntary creatures – makes him a good Thomist?[191] If
Ritchie and others are correct, it would seem so.

   I am not a Thomas scholar and so it is beyond my expertise to know whether
these standard interpretations are correct. In the light of the postnatural turn, however, I think we must query a strong adherence to an account of nature in which
human nature is privileged and in which natural law is most fully articulated with
the reference to human traits of friendship and worship. Moreover, there are some
scholars, such as Jean Porter, whose interest in natural law is in part resourced
by an account of the relation between human nature and its biological ground
in which she claims that the arguments in favour of the biological roots of human morality are now "impressive".[192] Put differently, and to draw a little from
d'Entrèves, the psychological problem faced by the medieval period was the co-
ordination of church and culture. The postnatural addresses a different psychological issue which, following Curran, we might call philosophical: in his own
account, Curran presents the three ends quoted from Aquinas above and yet notes
that there is disagreement within natural law on "the meaning of the criterion of
nature".[193] How should these ends relate to each other and which, if any, should
have priority? That is, the psychological issue addressed in the postnatural turn is
the relations between these ends: How is the human also an animal? What are the

---

[188] Ritchie (1894), 40.
[189] D'Entrèves (1951), 41.
[190] Thomas Gilby, in Aquinas (2006), 83.
[191] Hooker (1989), 59.
[192] Porter (1999), 26.
[193] Curran (1996), 594.

relations that govern a greater society? How is the human institutionalised with non-human animals? How does technological change affect the "intrinsic character of [our] given situation"?[194]

In the light of this analysis, the relevance of natural law to postnatural right is easily set out. Human action is not naked action but instead occurs in a determinate and determining context. As Porter puts it, "the distinction between the natural and the conventional [is used] as a warrant for interpreting human action in the light of the diverse forces that ground and limit it".[195] Moreover, I am not discounting the emphasis on reason, and discernment indicates a link between natural law and the image of God, "the capacity for moral judgment found in all men and women".[196] In a period in which all global voices need to heard – not least in face of the ways in which a changing climate will affect differently different locations – these are relevant positions. These two interpretations of natural law are resourced by two different sources of nature. The *first* interpretation notes that human nature shares in a wider nature and so human beings share in certain "traits" with other animals – food, shelter, and self-preservation are obvious examples. The *second* interpretation stresses the centrality of human reason in moral discernment. The use of reason is by nature human and natural law is the operation of this critical faculty.

I began this discussion of natural law by reference to sources. Eschewing theological and philosophical approaches, and privileging neither history nor concept, I have instead concentrated on the range of natures that source natural law thereby proving d'Entrèves point that "... natural law theories ... reflect or presuppose contingent concepts of nature".[197] In my view, and contingently, natural law requires some reworking along the lines of the postnatural.

For we should note that the transformation of natural law into natural right has reshaped natural law and this has implications for postnatural right. In other words, in the early modern period, natural law undergoes an important transformation: from a more objective to a more subjective emphasis. It is debated whether there are one or two breaks. Is the fundamental break between the mediaeval and the early modern period at which time law becomes right? Or, are there two breaks, the second one occurring more recently as natural right mutates a second time into human rights?[198] My argument does not have a dog in this fight

---

[194] Pope presents a distinction between general nature and specific nature as a way of de-privileging Ulpian, seemingly unaware that he uses two meanings of nature as if equivalent: see Pope (1994), 54.

[195] Porter (1999), 51.

[196] Porter (1999), 17.

[197] D'Entrèves (1951), 70.

[198] There is general agreement that there has been at least one break: whether the occasion of the break is Grotius, Pufendorf or Hobbes is debated (cf. Finnis (2011); D'Entrèves, 1951). Others, like David Boucher (2008) note the change between "law" and "right" but argue for a continuity nonetheless between these two; a more significant epistemological break occurs between "right"

because, in my view, all phases of law-right have been too concerned with the kind, human. However, the shift in balance towards the subjective is of concern and will be addressed most fully in the discussion of right in chapter 8.

Following this, it is easy to show how "nature" in natural law is contingent rather than given. In other words, it is easy to show that the nature on which such moral law depends is not universal or enduring. How is this so? It is to Hegel that we owe the insight that such a standard presentation of natural law needs to be reconsidered. Hegel argues that the emancipation of the human from nature – that is marked not least by its desacralisation – may be understood as the *realisation* of natural law. If the commonalities between human creatures and other animals present us with a task that creatures have in common to secure their existence, the unparalleled success of human moderns in securing their livelihood is to be understood as the realisation of natural law. Hegel's basic point is that the freedom partially secured by Roman Law – and generalised in thought by natural law – is secured by the division of labour: the realisation of the Idea of freedom.

This conclusion permits Hegel, in Joachim Ritter's interpretation, to interpret the transition from natural law to natural right in a new way.[199] Noting that natural right arguments relate to arguments regarding the "state of nature", Hegel argues that these arguments function as a break from the authority model of the medieval period. They function as a way of marking the break into modernity. For Hegel, the break is historical and practical: the emancipation of the human from nature marks the break rather than the positing of some "natural condition of humankind". As a result, the older natural law is doubly invalidated. It is invalidated once in that its content has vanished. It is invalidated a second time in that it has been reformulated into natural right theories (Hobbes, Locke, Rousseau). Yet it has been reformulated, and not lost. For natural law's emphasis on universality is retained in the modern period.

Thus Hegel argues that this nature-theory is better understood as the break of human dependence on nature and thereby the emancipation of human beings through the division of labour. This is a narrative of freedom. There is no permanent contrast, state of nature/social contract, because there is no "state of nature". Instead, there is the historical break into a new system of needs secured by the division of labour and the freedom of individuals in a (new) system of the meeting of needs.

Although this is his conclusion in *Philosophy of Right*, Hegel had considered the matter of natural law in an earlier essay of 1802-03. The trajectory of the essay is to resist pressures towards simplification that Hegel detects in natural law. In "On the scientific ways of treating Natural Law", Hegel distinguishes two ways of understanding natural law: the empirical and the formal.[200] Additionally, he subdi-

---

and "rights".
[199] Ritter (1982), 124-150.
[200] Hegel (1999), 106.

vides the empirical into pure empiricism and scientific empiricism. As empirical, there are important continuities with older forms of natural law that sought to identify the situatedness of the human through its efforts to secure its preservation and livelihood.[201] Nonetheless, Hegel finds both inadequate. The empirical does have the merit of not identifying and privileging some aspect or feature of the human: "For pure empiricism, everything has equal right with everything else, and it gives no precedence to any [one] determinacy, since each is as real as the other."[202] The difficulty here, as Hegel notes, is that there is too little discrimination: elements are juxtaposed and compete with each other. Nonetheless, this pure empiricism is preferable to scientific empiricism whose central fault is to single out only one aspect or feature. Stripping back alleged contingencies results in "the human being in the image of the bare state of nature, or of the abstraction of the human being with its essential capacities ... ".[203] Scientific empiricism, Hegel complains, provides no criteria for distinguishing between the contingent and the necessary. Moreover, it does appear as if that what is identified as necessary is established by a retrojection that justifies what is necessary. "According to the fiction of the state of nature, this state is abandoned because of the evils it entails – which simply means that the desired end is assumed in advance ... "[204] The variety of the retrojections – self-preservation (Hobbes), sociability (Locke), reform v. punishment (utilitarianism) – exposes the selection to the charge of being arbitrary.

Of the formal approach to natural law, Hegel identifies the *a priori* approaches of Kant and Fichte as operating a strong contrast between the abstract and the empirical, and as operating a strong disjunction between the legal and the moral, between what is required and human freedom. The strong emphasis on a moral will vested in an account of reason may seem an unlikely candidate to be discussed as natural law. However, what I think Hegel is challenging can in one way be assimilated to natural law: the modern emphasis on natural rights can be seen as a development of natural law thinking and the emphasis on reason and will does invoke the universal.[205]

At the heart of the argument being advanced by Hegel is his contention that positive law is not to be placed after natural law. As I have tried to trace, the depiction of natural law offered by Hegel notes the variety of ways in which society is present in natural law – despite the concerted efforts made by natural law to cover its tracks. So far, so good, we may agree. With Hegel, we may refuse some understandings of natural law. An inchoate presentation of "natural" powers and capacities is not acceptable. Nor is the refining of this pure empirical position towards a scientific empiricism in which a particular feature of the human active

---

[201] See, for example, D'Entrèves (1951), 25.
[202] Hegel (1999), 110.
[203] Hegel (1999), 111.
[204] Hegel (1999), 112.
[205] See, for example, D'Entrèves (1951), 48-62.

in some pre-social state is offered. For example, society is not formed out of an association of individuals pre-existing society who contract with one another to form a society. Consequently, the effort to disguise the contingency of nature as well as the hidden voluntarism of pre-modern and modern natural law is exposed.

Hegel's approach makes an important contribution and the objections that Hegel raises to natural law – especially in its empirical variant – will be met in chapters 5, 6 and 8. My account of postnatural right must offer a defence of a greater society without smuggling the conclusion in with the premise or by offering too narrow an interpretation of what is meant by social. Additionally, the contrast with which natural law operates between the natural and the conventional, to take the two terms used by Porter, will need to be developed along postnatural lines in chapter 6.

Moreover, there are two important aspects of Hegel's thought that can be built upon. The first is the creative suggestion that the human individual is a social whole. "For since real absolute ethical life comprehends and unites within itself infinity (or the absolute concept) and pure individuality in general and in its highest abstraction, it is immediately the ethical life of the individual; and conversely, the essence of the ethical life of the individual is quite simply the real (and hence universal) absolute ethical life – the ethical life of the individual is one pulse-beat of the whole system, and is itself the whole system."[206] I shall be seeking to amplify what is surely a version of the contrast between microcosm and macrocosm in chapter 6 in a discussion of concept of life and in chapter 8 in a discussion of the concept of institution. The second suggestion takes us to the tragic element of necessity in human living as this is provided by the reliance of the human on the inorganic. There is, we might say, economic necessity within the ethical totality provided by this tragic element. Hegel's presentation needs elaboration, however. The independence from nature of which Hegel writes presupposes the de-sacralisation of nature. Hegel considers this only abstractly, in a system of needs.

We should, however, be cautious about interpreting this abstractly: an abstracted division of labour facing an abstract nature. Instead, as I shall elaborate in chapters 5 and 8, we should see it in terms of institutions and agencies. Furthermore, we should note that fresh issues have arisen – here is our psychological interpretation again – as regards our domination of nature. That is, we are making the postnatural turn on account of feedback information that the task of the domination of nature – of our freeing ourselves from dependencies – is ill advised and likely impossible. In a helpful essay, entitled "Nature", Gordon Graham notes that Enlightenment and Romantic conceptions of nature have now been joined by an environmental meaning in which human actions are shown to be connected to wider natural ecosystems and in significant ways to be dependent on them. In the

---

[206] Hegel (1999), 159.

light of this emergence of a new meaning, how should the relationship between humans and nature be understood: as one of conflict, or harmony, or subservience?[207]
We are freed from nature in some ways but not in others. It is this new circumstance – a postnatural condition – that will also need to be theorised in an account
of order.

3.6 THE HISTORICAL AND THE TELEOLOGICAL

If we make the postnatural turn, what happens to natural order? To provide an
answer to this question the present chapter has been dedicated. In chapter 6 we
shall look more expansively at what sort of order may be called postnatural. For
the present, we may note that the form of life presupposed by postnatural right
is not one that requires a strong contrast between nature and history. Nor is an
appeal made to a notion of creation order nor is a hierarchical account of nature
proposed. Yet neither is the natural dissolved into the historical.

To explore this a little further, I want to employ a distinction reported by
d'Entrèves between objective right and subjective right: a distinction between
norma agendi and *facultas agendi*, between a rule of action and a right to act.[208]
In any consideration of order, both are to be investigated: if there is a right it is
because there is a law; there is freedom because there is order; freedom is always
a determinate freedom, enabled, shaped and framed by the postnatural condition.
Moreover, such a *norma agendi* is real on account of its postnatural condition;
there is no surpassing of the natural into the historical. Objective right relates to
an objective situation.

Yet, as will be clear by now, I have resisted attempts by O'Donovan, Demant and some natural law theorists to overspecify this objectivity. As Pannenberg notes, "As long as appeal is made to empirically enduring structural forms
of human life in community, there remains a vague remnant of the concept of
a natural order of society that is given with the essence of humanity."[209] Yet, as
we have seen in the discussion of "nature" in chapter 2, we should be cautious
as regards the convergence required of senses of nature to make such an account
credible. In addition, through this chapter, we have had cause to question the idea
of a "creation order", which seems to require not only the alignment of human
society with human nature but also the alignment of both with the cosmos.

It is more persuasive therefore to agree with Stephen Pope that we should be
considering "patterns of natural ordering rather than one natural order".[210] It is to
such patterning that the tension between the historical and the teleological needs
to be brought. For, as must now be clear, I wish to affirm the view that there are

---

[207] Graham (2013), 412, 415.
[208] See D'Entrèves, (1951), 60.
[209] Pannenberg (1981), 30.
[210] Pope (2007), 284.

"natural purposes or goals in nature". Yet if these purposes and goals are to be understood as teleological – as having their own end – they must also be understood as sharing in a pattern of a dynamic and so less hierarchical order: natural proclivities and tendencies are to be understood as saved into a greater flexibility or openness. That is, saved into a more extensive and intensive sociability – an active fellowship – of what I earlier called a greater society of relationships and institutions. It will be the remit of chapter 6 to explore these topics more fully.

CHAPTER 4: TECHNOLOGY

4.1 OPENING

Part 1 is called Making the Postnatural Turn. Having considered *nature* and *order* in making the postnatural turn, we now turn to the matter of *technology*, which we shall consider by reference to the trajectory of the *anthropological-eschatological*. By this, I mean the following: that technological activity needs to be understood by reference to human culture; it is not convincing, as we shall see, to restrict our understanding of technology to the use of neutral "tools". Furthermore, technological activity engages nature in transformation and projects an order. Additionally, technology is sometimes considered to be redemptive or to invoke in response the redemptive power of nature. These views are not credible and it will be the task of this chapter and chapter 7 to show why this is so. Herein lies the reference to the eschatological: the goodness of God is not distributed either by technology narrowly understood or by a resurgent nature but rather socially and institutionally. Another way of putting this matter would be to refer back to the discussion of order in the previous chapter and recall that order is discovered, appropriated and constructed. At this point, it would be tempting to argue that technology is best understood by reference to the constructed aspect of order. I am arguing that the matter is not simple, however. Through the social-institutional trajectory of human living, we may understand that a technological order is also discovered – by technology, *nature* is altered – and appropriated in and through the social life of institutions. This is the anthropological aspect of *anthropological-eschatological*. Interpreted as having a broad base, technology is not redemptive. Neither is nature, understood as reacting to technology, a site of redemption. This is the eschatological aspect of *anthropological-eschatological*. Through this opening section, I amplify these remarks.

I begin by noting that although it is easier to consider technology by reference to technical artefacts, in this chapter I assess technology more broadly. In other words, I shall be arguing that it is preferable to understand technology as devices within a technologised culture rather than a set of unrelated artefacts or tools. Understood as devices, as Albert Borgmann recommends, technology raises quite fundamental questions for culture and theology.[211] This, then, is a broadly based interpretation of technology. Following a suggestion from Peter Hodgson, we may understand technology as raising questions in three spheres of human life: self-relatedness, wholeness, and world-relatedness.[212] This is to press Hodgson's

---

[211] Borgmann (1984).
[212] Hodgson (1994), 200-201.

suggestion in a new direction in support of presenting the postnatural condition in which "north Atlantic" humanity finds itself. The phrase "postnatural condition" is my attempt to present together these three distinctive spheres of present life that affect how we should think theologically about technology.

First, technology in a postnatural condition has implications for how we think about the human in its self-relatedness: its self-understanding, powers, limits and responsibilities. How is our relationship with and to ourselves altered in a technological culture? In the theology of technology, this has been the main focus of enquiry – mainly with reference to powers, limits and responsibilities – and I shall comment only briefly on it in the next section. Second, the theme of wholeness in the postnatural condition invites consideration of the wider natural (cosmological, ecological and biological) relations of the human. What are these relations, and how might they be transformed? Third, the postnatural condition seeks to do justice to human technological *activity*. By way of its tools, human beings transform the world-related circumstances in which they find themselves: their self-understanding, their habitat and a wider "nature".

There is quite a lot at stake in this discussion. For example, religious people may be cautious about granting technological mediation any role in our self-understanding. Further, to stress wholeness may lead the enquirer to employ organic metaphors and thereby to downplay the ways in which technology does not simply interact with nature but transforms it. On the other hand, to stress the matter of world-relatedness may do little more than reverse this polarity: the stress is now on the urban, the machinic, the transformative, and the givenness of nature is occluded. (A further and consequent attempt at reversal – the "resurrection of nature" – will be discussed in chapter 7.) As Noreen Herzfeld argues, we have here a tension presented by modern technological practices. Modern technology does not "simply 'disclose' or shape nature but transform[s] and replace[s] nature".[213] In sum, technology requires attention to the self-interpretation of the human, materialism and praxis. In the following sections, I explore each of these aspects. In the fifth section, I offer a brief theological conclusion.

4.2 TECHNOLOGY AND SELF-RELATEDNESS

In *Christian Ethics in a Technological Age*, Brian Brock argues that a Christianity that considers that "... questions of technology are remote from questions of faith" has lost its way.[214] In agreeing with this assessment, we may also note that the effort by religious believers to keep technology at arm's length is at least understandable if not persuasive. As I have argued elsewhere, the understanding that Christianity is concerned with the personal rather than the technological may

---

[213] Herzfeld (2009), 9.
[214] Brock (2010), 7.

motivate such an effort.[215] On such a view, is not Christianity concerned with the "spiritual" rather than the "material"? Is not Christianity concerned with the naked human rather than the artefactual human?

A related way of way of proceeding is to suggest that technology be understood in some way as a tool. That is, technology is neutral until put to the service of some desire, some good. The meaning of technology in this line of enquiry is, broadly, benign or at least not malign. Herzfeld describes this position as "technology as morally neutral".[216] This approach often has its terminus in quandary ethics or ethical consequentialism. Nonetheless, I accept that the theological approach to technology cannot be by way of such ethical considerations. Such approaches may be understood as a further attempt to restrict the force and reach of technological practices by reference to powers, limits and responsibilities only.

Much discussion in the theology of technology now eschews this route. Instead, technology is regarded as more than a phenomenon concerned with technique.[217] As Romano Guardini says, "The development of technology is primarily an inner human process. ... Our age is not just an external path that we tread; it is ourselves."[218] The meaning of technology on this understanding is primarily *cultural*: "... technology is not just something that mediates between our mental intentions and the physical world about us, technology gets into our heads and affects the very way in which we conceive our reality."[219] To argue otherwise falsely restricts the reach and impact of technology. What is clear is that culture will be shaped and re-shaped by technology – and culture will in turn shape and re-shape technology. The distortions and limitations of any culture we shall then expect to find in the meanings and practices of technology. In addition, we may find that the powers of technology will intensify those limitations and increase those distortions.

In sum, science and technology may be understood as ideological. For Jürgen Habermas, science and technology function as an ideology, specifically as a dominating form of rationality: "... the rationality of science and technology is immanently one of control: the rationality of domination".[220] The rationality of technology is thereby not restricted to areas of technological production. Instrumental reason has occupied other spheres of society, and in so doing invites all political problems to be construed in terms of such rationality: above all, as problems requiring a technical solution. Note that the construal is a double one: political issues are not so much offered a technical solution but instead are raised as technical problems and, thus, as requiring "merely" technical solutions.

---

[215] Scott (2010a), 124.

[216] Herzfeld (2009), 6.

[217] Recent work by Brock and Pattison fits this description, as does my own work.

[218] Guardini (1994), 79, 81.

[219] Pattison (2007), 3.

[220] Habermas (1987), 85.

A difficult question now emerges: how to develop a theology of technology that is not itself technologised? That is, how to develop a theology of technology that does not try to address the matter of technology by construing it as a technical problem that needs to be "solved". As a possible way forward, Pattison quotes George Grant: "Thought is steadfast attention to the whole."[221] I turn to the matter of technology and wholeness in the next section.

4.3 TECHNOLOGY AND WHOLENESS

The theme of technology and wholeness presents us with the important matter of the cosmological, ecological and biological conditions of human life. That is, the impulse of life towards life. Broadly, in what follows I argue that such attempts to relate technology to nature are efforts to appeal to harmony and to marginalise the machinic. Such attempts turn upon an account of nature in which the human is to be interpreted from the perspective of the whole of nature – a version of sense 3. My analysis thereby takes a turn towards materialism and encounters specific difficulties, which I shall now discuss.

We might orientate ourselves by noting that this issue arises when nature in sense 2 – as shaping power or authority – gives way to a sense of nature as material world – as in sense 3. What then of the authority of the relationship between humanity and nature: what is authorised? As we saw in Hegel's argument, there is a certain liberation in the posing of this question. Naturalised authorities cease to be authoritative for it is possible to presume, as Stephen Pope accuses Gustavo Gutiérrez, "a complete abstraction of human relations from their wider natural setting" which can lead to understanding "... nature as matter subject to rational control and use in the satisfaction of human desires".[222] This is, I suppose, a downgrading of sense 2 and a deployment of sense 3 including a stress on the otherness of nature.

Such a discussion takes us back to the early modern period. Once the ordering authority of tradition had been marginalised, and the shaping power of human reason understood as pre-eminent, a number of questions were raised during that period. On what was the relation between humanity and nature, and between human beings themselves, to be founded? What sort of society would the mastery of reason produce? Who would be responsible for its production? In addition, what would be the "place" of nature in this society? "It is at this point", Paul Tillich has written, "that the problem of how nature can be grasped through human knowledge and how society can be constructed through human activity is of greatest urgency".[223] (Somewhat differently, Peter Dickens casts the issue in terms of the relationship of social theory and biological theory and the efforts by some theo-

---

[221] Pattison (2007), 100.
[222] Pope (1994), 34, 54.
[223] Tillich (1977), 49.

rists to "make analogies between the social and natural worlds" in the context of a neglect by social theory of "society's changing relationship with nature".[224]) What is the human relationship to nature? How could society be ordered and harmonious? (How should this relationship be thought?)

Tillich argues that the two answers given to these questions in the early modern period, "liberalism"[225] and democracy, are united by a notion of harmony.

Liberalism believes in a natural harmony that happens through the free play of productive forces. Democracy does not believe in *natural harmony*; it does believe, however, that nature can be subjected to reason. It believes in a metaphysical harmony that is certain to prevail in the historical process.[226]

We might then agree with John Milbank's view that "the early modern age already fled to the arms of nature as support for a new objectivity".[227] Indeed, this new objectivity is the heart of the Enlightenment project: the transformation of the natural conditions of human living through the process of objectification (especially in science and technology). Of this development, David Harvey has written:

The idea was to use the accumulation of knowledge generated by many individuals working freely and creatively for the pursuit of human emancipation and the enrichment of daily life. The scientific domination of nature promised freedom from scarcity, want and the arbitrariness of natural calamity. The development of rational forms of social organization and rational modes of thought promised liberation from the irrationalities of myth, religion, superstition, and release from the arbitrary use of power as well as from the dark side of our own human natures. Only through such a project could the universal, eternal, and the immutable qualities of all of humanity be revealed.[228]

We have here the running together of the two types of "objective harmony", natural and metaphysical, identified by Tillich. Yet this is not a form of objectivity in the abstract; it is rather to be connected, as Rosemary Radford Ruether has noted, to "the expanding world of European capitalism and colonialism".[229] This important reservation allows us to acknowledge that the project of the Enlightenment operates with specific understandings of objectivity.

Such claims to objectivity persist: In the 1933-34 seminar *Nature, History, State*, Martin Heidegger argues that "history and state are incorporated in nature, and the state in turn belongs within history".[230] In exploring the multiple ways in which nature is present to us in its relationship to *Dasein*, he shows the error in

---

[224] Dickens (1992), 20, 32.

[225] Although the word liberalism is of nineteenth century coinage, liberal thought emerges as early as the seventeenth century: see Macpherson (1962/2011).

[226] Tillich (1977), 51.

[227] Milbank (1993), 5.

[228] Harvey (1989), 12.

[229] Ruether (1981), 63.

[230] Heidegger (2013), 17.

simply treating it as the beginning of a sequence. Nonetheless, the presentation of nature as a whole that precedes history and politics is common, and enjoys a certain coherence and persuasiveness. The state of nature arguments of Hobbes and Locke provide one example from the seventeenth century.[231] A sense of a sequence may be found in contemporary appeals to natural law: we have already seen that Jean Porter argues that, "the distinction between the natural and the conventional [is used] as a warrant for interpreting human action in the light of the diverse forces that ground and limit it".[232] We may readily appreciate that such a view of natural forces tends to sidestep the issue of the deployment of technology in the construction of artefacts.

Additionally, we find that ethical naturalism appeals to nature as a whole. As Sebastian Gardner writes: "For naturalism, we are complex parts of a larger whole ... "[233] Moreover, according to Susana Nuccetelli and Gary Seay, ethical naturalism affirms that there are moral properties and facts that are mind- and language-independent – a position that natural law would also affirm.[234] Ethical naturalism may also affirm as part of its methodology that the only world we know is the world portrayed by the sciences but, as Fiona Ellis has argued, will wish to provide an account of objective value.[235]

We may notice immediately the restriction in the meaning of technology that follows from such a position. For the whole with which we are presented here does not easily draw our attention to the range of technologically mediated interactions between humanity and nature. Throughout, we are required to acknowledge a moral order based in a reading of stable properties and facts, and a set of ahistorical or pre-social needs to which a theory of technology must respond. However, as I argued earlier, the meaning of technology is better understood as cultural. In other words, technology refers us always to the self-relatedness of the human. One implication of this observation is that, in any discussion of nature as whole, the interaction between human actors and their machines in a wider technological culture must be foregrounded.

These criticisms notwithstanding, the reference to wholeness presents us with a vital issue: in technological perspective, how shall we consider the cosmological, ecological and biological bases of human life? In effect, we are searching for the material bases of human living. The question before us: is it credible to affirm either a natural or a rational harmony? (The first is originary; the second to be established as part of the progressive unfolding of the originary.) Are these material bases given and need only to be (re-)discovered? Alternatively, are they to be

---

[231] See Scott (2011a), 57-75.

[232] Porter (1999), 51.

[233] Gardner (2013), 22.

[234] Nuccetelli and Seay (2012), 1.

[235] Ellis (2014).

established through rational activity? (At first glance, this seems to be a version of nature sense 2.)

Alternatively, we may conclude that there is no harmonious, positive relation between nature and society and that nature is estranged from society. (This could be a variant of sense 3 of nature, with divergence between the human and non-human; to be added to it could be a sense 2 of nature-as-force from which humanity is alienated.) If that is the case, then we seem to be in the realm of a double alienation: nature is estranged from humanity and society in its turn is reified. Political hope, if a claim to hope is made at all, must then presumably be vested in the historical development or unfolding of both nature and society; any harmony can then only be *anticipated* in the historical process.

4.4 TECHNOLOGY AND WORLD-RELATEDNESS

If referring technology to nature does not seem convincing, then reference to world-relatedness seems an obvious option. We arrive at the consideration of technology in the context of humanity's active transformation of its circumstances. In other words, human beings live already situated in technological practices in and through which they both transform the world and are mediated to themselves. As Herzfeld puts the matter, "... technology is central to our understanding of ourselves and the environment around us".[236] Yet that understanding emerges from the active deployment, so to speak, of technology.

The temptation now is to derive a theology of technology from too static an account of world-relatedness. To accept some fixed human nature, some given order and thereafter to enquire how technology might or might not serve that order. However, such order is precisely denied by a cultural interpretation of technology. That is, from the technological interactions between humanity and nature: "tools, processes, and a social context", as Herzfeld puts it.[237]

At this point, I think that technology raises the difficult matter of historical contingencies. I have written about this matter of contingencies elsewhere, and will not pursue it further here.[238] Except to note that if theology accepts a cultural meaning of technology, how we are theologically to understand technology-related contingencies emerges as a difficult matter. What is required is the presence of eternity in technological reality that is not its stabilisation or demand for its miraculous overcoming. What needs articulation and development is a theology of technology that does not stabilise the contingent and thereby offer an underpinning of certain "natural" structures. On this view, nature is temporal and technology is effective because of that temporality. This in turn suggests that society is transient as well. The effort to develop a theological interpretation of tech-

---

[236] Herzfeld (2009), 9.
[237] Herzfeld (2009), 8.
[238] Scott (2010a), 134-37.

nology based on the givenness of the human in fact unravels at this point. If there is technological transformation of nature, then that nature is plastic and pliable. Human society as a technological work then seems to be a re-doubled transience: the transience of nature is redoubled through technology. Or, contingency upon contingency.

Such an affirmation of contingency may be related to theological insights. Take climate change as an example. That a warming climate may be related to contingency does not undermine the important theological theme of the goodness of creation. Such goodness may instead be understood to be manifested through the conditions that permit such warming. Planetary ecological systems are not taking their revenge upon the human but are instead in revolt. The contingency of these dynamic systems is that of a stable and durable nature that has some capacity for change – but beyond certain limits is tipped into a "new" nature. On this view, global warming is evidence of the goodness of creation: a climate suitable for certain sorts of life that operates within certain constraints.[239]

A temptation here might be to step back from such contingency by returning to a view of technology as artefacts. That is, understanding technology as essentially – nature sense 1 – neutral and thereby recovering some stable account of human nature or a theory of human needs as that which is served by technological artefacts. However, we have already explored the weaknesses of this position when considering the ideological functions of science and technology. An alternative approach would be to restrict the theological engagement with technology to ethical dilemmas. However, we have already seen that such an approach offers an arbitrary restriction to the effects of technology. We can hardly note the near omnipresence of technology and then restrict its scope in theological interpretation. Moreover, we may recall that one of the implications of the conclusion of the previous section reinforces the ubiquity of technology: in the consideration of technology, we are invited to pay attention to our material circumstances. As material beings, we are transforming our circumstances in the context of specific powers and forces that support and limit us. To propose a theological interpretation of technology is also to take with full theoretical force this materialist aspect.

4.5 POSTNATURAL TURNING: TECHNOLOGY

Our initial questioning seemed straightforward: what are the contours of a theology of technology in a postnatural condition? I was mindful that technology should not be construed narrowly as artefacts but should rather be understood as cultural: to be interpreted in the social-institutional life of humanity. However, we have encountered difficulties in developing a broad theology of technology. What is required of a theology of technology is to question technology in relation to three spheres of human life: self-relatedness, the material whole, and hu-

---

[239] Scott (2011b), 60-62.

man activity. Such technological activity is socially appropriated, encounters the non-human in discovery and constructs a postnatural world. With this comes the requirement to be alert to the three senses of nature.

We have established some protocols for thinking about technology in a post-natural condition. First, as regards self-relatedness, it has become clearer that technology is more than artefacts and tools but instead mediates between us and ourselves: technology is a mode of self-relating that invites the technicisation of issues and tends to the reversal of means and ends in which the resolution of problems is privileged. A changing climate is a good example here: although it requires sophisticated science to monitor a changing climate that should not lead to the conclusion that the resolution to climate change is technical. In developing this case, I have explored the ways in which technology exceeds the technological sphere. In turn, this demands the development of a critical theology of technology that persistently attends to the transgressive aspects of technology. In this regard, that technology is now cultural needs to be affirmed. (We are referred once more to the social-institutional aspect.)

Second, as regards wholeness, straightforward appeals to nature are unlikely to be convincing. Technology interrupts the meanings of nature required to sustain this position. Moreover, if such objectivity is not available a stress on nature as subject also did not appear to be convincing. The analysis that I have offered suggests that the way to consider technology in theological perspective is not best secured by reference to the objectification of nature.

Third, neither is it obvious that a theology of technology is best advanced by referring technology to world relatedness. For that way, the unity of humanity and nature seems to be obscured and the contingencies that technology presents to us appear to be contingencies only in a narrow sense. Nonetheless, that a theology of technology must encompass the transformative aspects of the human is evident.

In the consideration of technology, the postnatural condition advocated here thereby identifies the following aspects: ideology critique, non-difference, and practice. To develop these, all three will require an interruptive moment. Why is this? The task of ideology critique will be interruptive in the sense of call-ing into question technical solutions to non-technical issues and by resisting the refusal of materialism. Non-difference will also be interruptive in the sense of calling to account the transformative version of the relations between humanity and nature and enquiring whether the ways in which we interpret technology to ourselves are poorly aligned with the forces and powers of nature. Practice will be interruptive of claims to natural patterns and an epistemology of technologi-cal anthropocentrism. A theology of technology will therefore be reciprocally and constitutively interruptive of our three themes of self-relatedness, wholeness and world-relatedness. In this precise sense, such a theology of technology will be utopian.

What emerges is a requirement to understand the three aspects of technology –
self-relatedness, wholeness and world-relatedness – as reciprocal. Anthropologi-
cally, the conclusion is to affirm technological mediations via institutions, order
and historical activity. Theologically, the task is to explore how such interactive
reciprocity is already in some fashion available in theological tradition. In previous work, I have explored the concepts of activity, ground and force as a way of
characterising the differentiation in God that is required for a theology of technology.[240] Such differentiation is required, I argued, as a way of exploring how God
relates to the whole of creation and its parts. Nature is here not a universal but is
instead actual through the activity of God. The whole which theology proffers is
a diminished whole. Nonetheless, the divine activity resources the whole and that
means that creative activity is to be associated with the non-human as well as the
human. When we speak of creation, we identify the range of creatures. Yet there is
also differentiation: creation having its ground in God's activity suggests a pattern
or order. Moreover, such differentiation has its unity through the force of God.

At this point, it would be interesting to relate activity, ground and force to our
three themes, considered sequentially. That is, activity would relate to wholeness,
ground to world-relatedness and force to self-relatedness. However, perhaps activity, ground and force could be related to all three themes synchronously. That is,
the objectivity/subjectivity of nature (its wholeness) could be considered from the
perspective of God's activity in which the comprehensive aspect of nature could
be affirmed; by reference to ground the competition between nature as object and
nature as subject would be called into question; and the effort to think nature as
a whole would always be attempted. With reference to world-relatedness, the activity of God criticises efforts to separate the human from the non-human; the
ground of creation in God recommends a search for commonalities; and the reference to force suggests the effort by God to bring all of creation to its completion or
transformation. Such an eschatological impulse would be the resource for thinking about the renewal of nature. With regard to self-relatedness, the reference to
activity would stress that the self-awareness of the human is by way of all culture: that is, including those parts of culture that relate to embodiment (work and
reproduction especially); reference to ground would suggest that self-relatedness
directs us to the whole self; and reference to force that the divine effort is directed towards the integration of the human. Certainly, attempts to secure a core
self – by reference, say, to the concept of person – would not be immediately convincing. This, then, is the anthropological basis of my theology of technology. In
such fashion, the profile of a theology of technology in a postnatural condition
emerges. Yet, as already noted, technology should be understood by reference to
the *anthropological-eschatological* in the postnatural condition. Further attention
needs to be paid to the eschatological and will be the subject of chapter 7.

---

[240] Scott (2003), 38-42.

This chapter on the anthropological basis brings part 1, Making the Postnatural Turn, to a conclusion. To make this turn, I have been arguing, is to identify the condition in which theological ethics is to be developed. Three key themes were proposed: nature, order and technology. Why these three? Because the presentation of postnatural right affirms, firstly, the otherness of nature as discovered and yet insists that such otherness is articulated within a greater society. Secondly, a greater society projects an account of order. I have argued that we do not have to choose between nature and history and that it is possible to affirm the historicity of nature without falling into historicist traps. Thirdly, by reference to technological activity, I have suggested that any order must be a dynamic order. All three of these themes are concerns of a doctrine of creation. To make the postnatural turn is thereby to affirm the social as inclusive, the historical development of order, and the basis of technology in human activity. An account of action and freedom can be glimpsed. The way is open to the fuller consideration of postnatural right.

Part II

Acting Postnaturally

CHAPTER 5: POSTNATURAL GOOD

5.1 REPRISE

In part 1, we made the postnatural turn by exploring the themes of nature, order and technology. All three themes, I have been arguing, contribute to an understanding of our postnatural condition: that human beings participate through a wider creatureliness in a great*er* society. Furthermore, I have sought to amplify these three themes: *nature* has been amplified by reference to the *social-institutional, order* by reference to the *historical-teleological,* and *technology* by reference to the *anthropological-eschatological.* I have not denied the otherness of nature but instead have sought to understand human-nature relations by reference to the sociality of humanity and nature enacted in institutions of a greater society. I have not denied the matter of order in relation to nature but instead have sought to understand it historically and in terms of addition. I have not denied the centrality of technology in understanding nature and order but I have also argued for a cultural understanding of the transformative activity of technology.

In part 2, called Acting Postnaturally, we reconsider the three trajectories but now stress more fully the *institutional*, the *teleological*, and the *eschatological*. In this chapter, I pose the question: what joins humanity and nature? Social relations, I argue, in three modes: *in, beyond,* and *for*. These are three modes of *participation* in which humans and non-humans indwell each other, exceed one another, and are oriented on one another. These modes of participation are configured in and by institutions. In chapter 2, I noted that we are exploring a normative claim to do with the emergence of the good: we are pursuing a right order of life that is public. Nonetheless, this configuration is beset by misunderstandings and in the first part of this chapter I select a specific issue – the development of Ecosystem Services in the UK – to assess the ways in which institutions inhibit the emergence of this good and in which the modes of participation are misunderstood and poorly performed.

The vital point I am making here is that the discussion of humanity-nature relations in chapter 2 that sought to recover an adequate conception of nature and to reinterpret this conception as social requires now an account of its institutionality. It is in institutions that this eschatological good emerges and it is the task of postnatural right to judge the appropriateness of these institutional arrangements.

It would be worth pondering what institutional arrangements are presupposed by the approaches of stewardship and creation care as a way of introducing what may be an unfamiliar approach. If stewardship finally leads to management, what institutions would need to be in place for effective management? At the conclusion of *We have never been Modern*, Bruno Latour argues that we need a parliament of things – that is, a new institution – to take account properly of politics in what I am calling a postnatural condition. He argues furthermore that we need scientists in this new parliament to represent nature.[241] We might expand this insight further: if scientists are to be included, why not also farmers? Such a parliament would therefore be a new institution and an intersection of existing institutions. We might say that the practices of agriculture and the natural sciences are institutional contexts in which the human and non-human encounter each other. A parliament of things would offer a re-institutionalisation of such institutionalised encounters and thereby a new institution.

Ecosystem Services is also an institution in which humanity and nature meet: it is part of the infrastructure of the British state and directs investment, agriculture and rural tourism, among other things. It identifies the services provided by nature and seeks to protect, regulate and exploit them. We can ask the question: how does a postnatural good emerge out of such an institutional arrangement? If such a good is teleological, and so a public good, in what ways does Ecosystem Services permit and enable the public manifestation of postnatural good? The duality of public/private is crucial here, as we shall see.

5.2 ON INSTITUTION

First, however, I shall explore further what "institution" means, and how that amplifies the meaning of social-institutional. The social-institutional is important to my analysis as a way of explicating the meaning of a greater society. In chapter 2, I sought to explain how humanity and nature were open to the social by analogy. In this chapter, some specification on institution is required, not least because I have recommended that the encounter between an active humanity and an active nature is in institutions, and in chapter 3 I developed the concept of "institutional repetition".[242] What is a "social institution" in my argument?

First, the matter of scale: a postnatural institution does not operate at a predetermined scale. Hegel, for example, identifies three social institutions in *Philosophy of Right*: the family, civil society (including the economy), and the state. I do not think that we need to operate at such a level of generality. In my argument, although smaller in scale than civil society, Ecosystem Services counts as an institution: the human and the non-human meet in such services. That is, a postnatural institution features a meeting between the two parts of the third meaning of nature and where nature presents itself in a *pro nobis* way. As such, postnatural institutions are occasions of the organisation of nature and humanity. Nodding towards the ambiguity of nature discussed in chapter 2, responding to a sunset or a tsunami

---

[241] Latour (1993).

[242] Theology appears more comfortable with concepts such as "structure" and "system": see Gill (1977) and Ruether (2009).

does not therefore qualify for the status of "institutional" in this context as these are not matters of social *organisation*.

Second, "institution" refers to an entity that has been instituted. In other words, an institution has a beginning in time. Institution as a term thereby names a process and thereby notes that entities subject to process are also subject to change. This is significant for my argument in that it avoids the association with "structure" that may assert something invariant that perdures through time. In Christian theology, the orders of creation have functioned in this way, sometimes understood as pre-lapsarian and sometimes as post-lapsarian. As such, these orders are not considered to be the result of custom, and thereby are not *instituted*.[243]

If you adhere to an orders of creation approach, the matter of why these structures are to be acknowledged is voided. These structures are unavoidable; they are part of "creation order", to borrow O'Donovan's felicitous phrase. In my argument, institutions are, well, instituted. Thereby such entities are not given but are contingent. Such a conclusion raises the question: what is the ethical justification of these institutions? As we shall see, this question is tested by postnatural right. Such institutions are certainly *structured*, enjoying a settled and durable organisation over time. Thus, we encounter the issue of structural sin, when institutions become subject to distorting pressures. Cynthia D. Moe-Lobeda calls this "structural evil" and "social structural sin".[244] The way is open to consider, for example, institutional racism and other forms of structural sin.

In his account of Church as institution, third, Avery Dulles identifies some aspects of an institution: membership, a constitution, a set of rules, and leadership.[245] We can adapt these for present purposes. The trajectory of social-institutional invites us to expand what we mean by membership: the direction of travel here is towards the extrahuman. That is, the "membership" of postnatural institutions reaches across the divide between the human and the non-human. Modern agriculture would be a good example of this. It follows that a postnatural institution would not necessarily be one whose membership is restricted to species that are close companions of the human; the universality of the doctrine of creation invites a wider view. The constitutional aspect directs our attention to the matter of order: to what sort of order, liberatory or oppressive, are we directed as we pay attention to postnatural institutions? Such institutions operate to ways of working – often, as we have seen, these ways are anthropocentric – rather than sets of rules. As such, these institutions can be identified and thereby named as public. Moreover, as regards leadership, such institutions are founded in some way in human willing; they are custom made.

Fourth, in what ways do creatures participate in institutions? Following Frederick Neuhouser's analysis of Hegel's social theory in *Philosophy of Right*, I wish

---

[243] Scott (2004), 333-47 (here 339-42). See also Williams (2014 [1976, 1983]), 164-65.
[244] Moe-Lobeda (2013), 49-80.
[245] Dulles (2002), 26, citing B. C. Butler.

here to note two aspects that we might call "objective" and "subjective" as a way of understanding "the nature of good social institutions". The objective aspect of institutions refers to the social conditions for the realisation of freedom. Given the argument of part 1, we may appreciate that social in my argument encompasses nature and humanity. So the issue here is the way in which the five dimensions of postnatural right bear down on the objectivity of institutions. By the subjective aspect, I mean the ways in which individuals may "buy in", so to speak, to the activities of institutions. If Hegel is correct, social freedom can only be secured in institutions, functioning effectively along both aspects.

At this point, recall that I indicated some agnosticism in chapter 1 as to whether it was helpful to call nature a "society". Certainly, I thought that the openness to analogy between humanity and nature with reference to the social has its limits. Here, I express a stronger reservation about how the terminology of *institution* might be applied to nature. Although I wish to underscore that the non-human is present in institutions I am less persuaded that therein lies a justification for the use of the term "institutions" only with reference to nature. The concepts of society and institution are not identical, I consider. In relation to society, that both humanity and nature are constituted by relationships is an argument I made in chapters 1 and 2. If, however, institutions are products of human custom – that is, the human will – although nature may be encountered in institutions and *constitutes* them, it does not play a part in *instituting* them. As a result, I shall be cautious at this point and not use the term "institution of nature" or anything similar.

Fifth and finally, I introduce the notion of "institutional vision " as part of a larger discussion of the realisation of freedom in an institutional context. Institutional vision bears a resemblance to Moe-Lobeda's concept of "critical, mystical vision" that "reveals a future in the making and breeds hope for moving into it".[246] Institutional vision functions a little differently, however. By such institutional vision, I mean to refer to a future for postnatural institutions, tested by reference to the five dimensions of postnatural right. To test fully such vision we shall need some account of how institutions extend social freedom, in both objective and subjective aspects. I shall return briefly to this issue at the end of this chapter and pick it up once more in chapter 8.

Now, after this discussion of the concept of institution in and for a postnatural condition, we resume the discussion of the institution of Ecosystem Services.

5.3 "THE BADGERS HAVE MOVED THE GOALPOSTS"

In an interview with BBC television on 9 October 2013, then UK Environment Secretary Owen Paterson was asked whether he had moved the goalposts by extending by three weeks the badger cull against bovine TB in Somerset, England.

---

[246] Moe-Lobeda (2013), 112.

In his reply, Paterson argued that it was not he who had moved the goalposts but rather the badgers: "the badgers have moved the goalposts".[247] We are dealing here, Paterson opined, with a "wild animal", thereby proving the showbiz adage that one should never work with children or animals or, indeed, with metaphors on the loose. And with this profound insight, the interview proceeds: the badger is a wild animal, Paterson informed his audience, "subject to the vagaries of weather, and disease, and breeding patterns ... "[248] These remarks are revealing, I think, for what they imply about how we think about nature. That is, that nature is unruly: the animal is wild and the weather cannot be corralled in support of the cull.

I think that this stress on the activity of badgers is not a mistake or a slip of the tongue. Instead, it identifies a persistent difficulty that nature presents to us. Nature is other to the human, in ways we explored in chapter 2. What follows from this? Is the otherness one that requires managing or the otherness that identifies a strong difference between people and nature, to use the terms preferred by the UK Government's 2011 White Paper, *The Natural Choice*?[249] Or yet a third thing? One way of approaching this is to explore what it might mean to understand the publicness of nature. I shall be exploring a number of recent documents published by DEFRA [Department of Environment, Farming and Rural Affairs] and drawing these into conversation with the postnatural condition.

The interests that you might expect a theologian to have when thinking theologically about nature are present in the DEFRA documentation: *The Natural Choice* mentions the aesthetic and religious importance of nature to people, and the *National Ecosystems Assessment* discusses aesthetic and spiritual responses as part of "ecosystem services". I will explain what "ecosystem services" are in a moment. Moreover, given the complexity that surrounds nature, as concept and actuality, and its troubling status as both public and private, I shall not be suggesting some grand resolution. The DEFRA documentation points to genuine problems, practical and conceptual, in the humanity-nature relationship. I shall conclude that the DEFRA position, as far as I can discern it, is unconvincing. Indeed, the DEFRA position – perhaps an interlocking set of positions – is, I shall argue, a grand conceit: the separation of people and nature, and the deployment of abstractions (for example, society, economy). With these movements of separation and abstraction – surely these are linked – comes the laudable effort to treat nature as morally considerable. Yet the mechanism for doing this – an appeal to value – is also separative and abstractive. Services and goods; services and benefits; value; society – these are terms of my investigation. At the conclusion of my analysis, I shall reconsider the matter of the institutionality of postnatural good.

---

[247] That badgers are regarded with some affection is noted in the *UK National Ecosystem Assessment: Synthesis of Key Findings* (2011), 19. See also Barkham (2013).

[248] http://www.bbc.co.uk/news/uk-england-24459424 [accessed 30 12 13]

[249] *The Natural Choice* (2011), 3.

5.4 NATURE AS PUBLIC

Is nature public? Two contrasting answers can be given to this question, which, as we shall see, is a version of the issue adumbrated in 5.2 as to membership of an institution. (1) If by "public" we mean of concern to the wider community, the answer is an emphatic yes. Nature's goods – which the UK National Ecosystem Assessment works hard to identify – support individuals, communities and regions. These are "public goods".[250] (2) If by "public" we mean subject to public policy, then the answer seems also to be yes. For example, DEFRA is charged with the preservation of nature's capacity to deliver "ecosystem services". The 2011 White Paper, *The Natural Choice*, reports on a number of policy initiatives, and proposes more.

However, (3) nature seems to be private in the sense that it is the *object* of human management practices, marketised/monetised and so excluded from political community and extended democratic deliberation. Nature has ascribed to it an institutional place beyond community and deliberation. Behind this privatisation of nature, I shall argue, lies (4) the view that nature is private in the sense of being reserved or withdrawn. It then becomes the task of public policy to render a private nature accessible and productive: as the "deliverer of services". One of the cultural services that nature is required to deliver is (5) the view of nature as a source of (sentimental[251]) happiness.[252] It is hard not to draw the conclusion that DEFRA acts like a pimp – and that such pimping, as we shall see, presupposes institutions. I am arguing that we thereby find ourselves in a "grand dichotomy" of public policy and private nature.[253] Moving beyond this dichotomy requires thinking about nature differently not least in relation to institutions, and I shall be arguing that theology offers insights that support the view that badgers and other creatures are moving the goal posts.

5.5 ECOSYSTEM SERVICES

When trying to understand the relationships between humanity and nature, we are confronted by a complex and confusing picture. I shall be using the contrast between public and private as a way of analysing and gaining some perspective on this complexity. The arc of my enquiry recommends the view that the implicit understanding of nature presented by ecosystem services trades upon two appreciations: a reified nature as managed, and the sentimental viewpoint of nature as

---

[250] This phrase may be found in *The Natural Choice* (2011), 25.

[251] Originally, "refined or elevated feeling"; now, "addicted to indulgence in superficial emotion; apt to be swayed by sentiment" (OED, sentimental, *adj.*) [accessed 13 01 13]. At the back of this discussion are the contrasts country/city and urban/rural.

[252] *The Natural Choice* (2011), 45: "Our natural environment gives us a sense of place, pride and identity. Nature inspires and moves us." "… the natural environment can do much to benefit our health and education and make our daily lives happier and richer".

[253] I am adapting this presentation from Jeff Weintraub and Krishan Kumar (eds.) (1997).

"source of happiness". I am approaching these appreciations from the perspective of the distinction between public and private.

First, I present what DEFRA's reports mean by "ecosystem services" – sometimes "ecosystem goods and services". This is a specific construction of nature as public benefits and goods as managed by the state. I shall explore how two DEFRA documents account for the publicness of nature. Here I detect a difficulty that, to its credit, the ecosystem services approach identifies but then sets aside: how is the radical and total dependence of human beings on ecosystem services to be accounted for? It is this quality of dependence that, I shall argue, is captured in some religious, spiritual and aesthetic responses to environment, landscape, etc.[254] However, although it is captured by these "experiences", such quality of dependence is not fully articulated by these experiences. A fuller articulation requires a different, theological, thought. Moreover, this fuller articulation raises profound questions about the concept of "value" presented in the DEFRA documentation.

Second, I attend to the ways in which nature constructed as "ecosystem services" is regarded as private. Nature is present as services, and as mediated by expert knowledge, and as an environmental setting of various experiences. Although there is much discussion in the White Paper about establishing relationships, exchanging information, and the deepening of knowledge bases, the fundamental matter of how nature is infrastructurally present in democratic deliberation is nowhere discussed. Nature is not itself represented. How is the otherness of nature to be presented in a comprehensive way as part of society-wide deliberations: precisely as institutional(ised)?

This raises questions about what is meant by "society" in the DEFRA documentation (and issues to do with production and exchange), and whether "value" is presented as somehow external to nature. Here, the status of DEFRA itself is not discussed, but instead is assumed. In other words, the purpose of the state in this regard is not discussed. Additionally, we have the emphasis that nature has to be rendered more productive. This is evident in the sense of wishing to grant more people access to nature, not least for the purposes of health and education. These are grouped under the "cultural services" of nature.[255] While *prima facie* there is much to affirm in this position, the problem is that it appears to "zone" nature in an inappropriate way. The vital issue here is what is the significance of nature in these cultural services? For the experiences recorded in these cultural services are not epiphenomenal but are better understood as historically produced

---

[254] *The Natural Choice* (2011), 8, lists "spiritual or religious enrichment, cultural heritage, recreation or aesthetic experience". The *UK National Ecosystem Assessment* (2011), 13, proposes "cultural values based on ethical, spiritual and aesthetic principles".

[255] Other ecosystem services also have an impact on human health. For example, air quality has an impact on human health – see *The Natural Choice* (2011), 46. Air quality is located under "regulating services".

ways of representing the placedness of the human: as bodies, located in places; as institutionalised.[256]

5.6 DEFRA ON NATURE

In this section, I explore two ways in which we may understand DEFRA's nature to be public. First, it is public in the sense of being related to the collective: it supports the life of humans as a group. Second, it is public in the sense that it is subject to public administration; the managerial state is the gateway to nature's goods; as such, it is constructed as "services".

Current UK Government documentation uses the phrase, "ecosystem services". The *UK National Ecosystem Assessment* (2011) accepts that this phrase enjoys little recognition and understanding among the public. Instead, the *UK National Ecosystem Assessment* acknowledges that the terms that do resonate with the public are "Nature", "place" and "landscape".[257] What then does the phrase "ecosystem services" mean? The *Assessment* distinguishes between four types of service: supporting; regulating; provisioning; and cultural.[258]

1. Supporting services: These are the basic processes of life, and include processes as foundational as photosynthesis, soil formation and the water and nutrient cycles.
2. Regulating services: These include processes such as pollination and the regulation of pests and diseases, and the control of water and air quality.
3. Provisioning services: These include food, fibre, and fuel, and water also. Often, when we think of the countryside, we have in mind these activities. Such provisioning is dependent on supporting and regulating services and of course interacts with cultural services (for example, the morality of the treatment of farmed animals).
4. Cultural services: These include the goods and benefits that arise from people interacting with environments, including opportunities for learning about nature, recreation, and thereafter aesthetic pleasure, spiritual well-being and associated improvements in health.[259]

The Natural Choice makes identical distinctions but pays little attention to the supporting aspect of ecosystem services. Both reports speak occasionally of "ecosystem *goods* and services". Here goods refer to that which is provided by provisioning services: food, fuel and fibre.[260] And as for the goods of cultural services, we

---

[256] DEFRA reports do acknowledge that the people-nature relationship changes, and that our understanding of it changes.

[257] *UK National Ecosystem Assessment* (2011), 40.

[258] These distinctions are traceable back to the Millennium Ecosystem Assessment, at www.millenniumassessment.org [accessed 1 July 2013)

[259] *UK National Ecosystem Assessment* (2011), 18. Cf. *The Natural Choice* (2011), 7, 8.

[260] *UK National Ecosystem Assessment* (2011), 18. Cf. *UK National Ecosystem Assessment* (2011), 84.

have recreation, health benefits, etc. *The Natural Choice* sometimes substitutes
"benefits" for "goods".[261]

In the terms of my analysis, this presentation of ecosystem services is emphatically public: identified are the processes on which life depends and is constituted.
"Biodiversity is life. We are part of it . . . "[262] These are public goods, benefits and
services in the sense of being collective. These services are also subject to processes of public administration. Indeed, in a sense, these services are constructed
as part of a process of public administration.

It is tempting to see this listing of services – supporting; regulating; provisioning; cultural – as representing a hierarchy and there is some loose language
in the White Paper – for example, a healthy environment as a vital *foundation* for
economic growth – that might suggest as much.[263] However, I think that the principal difficulty with this position from a theological point of view lies elsewhere.
That is, what strikes me as being of most concern theologically is the link between
cultural services and supporting services. What appear most separated in the list –
the first and last items – are, in my view, closely related. There is a significant
relationship between these two. How is this so?

This is quite difficult to explain. To begin, I note that the *UK National Ecosystem Assessment* approaches this issue, if only obliquely, in a section dedicated
to exploring how processes of decision-making might take into account the economic values of ecosystem services. In a somewhat unclear sentence, the *UK National Ecosystem Assessment* proposes: "In line with standard economic analysis,
the methodology developed rejects attempts to estimate the total value of ecosystem services, as many of these services are essential to continued human existence
and claimed total values are therefore underestimates of infinity."[264] I am not certain what this sentence means but I think that it is groping after an important truth:
that the services identified as supporting services are basic to life and identify partially the basic conditions of life, including human life. Recall that supporting
services include the basic processes of life, and include processes as foundational
as photosynthesis, soil formation and the water and nutrient cycles. Other aspects
of ecosystem services – the regulating service of breathable air, for example, point
in this direction. In one sense, given how basic they are, these services cannot be
costed; hence the reference to "infinity". These services are constitutive of what
it means for there to be life at all – and not only human life. The relationship between human communities and these basic processes is one of strong dependence;
the relationship is institutional.

Elsewhere the *UK National Ecosystem Assessment* makes the same point
when it notes that efforts at economic valuation of ecosystem services do *not*

---

[261] *The Natural Choice* (2011), 7.
[262] *The Natural Choice* (2011), 17.
[263] *The Natural Choice* (2011), 3.
[264] *UK National Ecosystem Assessment* (2011), 42.

attempt "also to value the supporting services, crucial for the delivery of many provisioning, regulating and cultural services".[265] Presumably, this totality cannot be valued because there is a sense that without these processes-as-totality there would not be life at all.

5.7 MEASURING A WHOLE

We might begin by noting that there is a connection between the services that DE-FRA identifies as supporting and those identified as cultural. What is this connection? In cultural services, a sense that this world is given may be found. Moreover, an experience of the world as given does try to grasp this truth of dependence. It is in religious thinking that this thought emerges with clarity. Therefore, whereas the list suggests a hierarchy from supporting services to cultural services, in my view there is a close connection between religious appreciation of nature in cultural services and registering the dependence of the human on basic, supporting services.

Moreover, there is a sense that we can only think of this world as a totality because it is other to its Creator. We speak easily of the Creator/creation distinction. However, as we saw in chapter 2, it is not an obvious distinction and in circumscribing the present reality as creation, allows us to *think* the present reality *as a whole*. There are two parts to my analysis here.

The *first* part notes that one aspect of cultural experiences tries to give an account of human dependence on nature. The BESS Report *Aesthetic & Spiritual Responses to the Environment* is a remarkable attempt to present some of these experiences.[266] Aesthetic responses are described as "unexpected", turning the ordinary into the extraordinary; spiritual responses use terms such as "gift", "attending" rather than "looking", and nature as a counter to selfishness.[267] Moreover, a claim could be made that such religious or spiritual responses do not require a home in a specific tradition or belief and are instead to be sourced to an encounter with a generalised "other".[268]

The *second* part notes that this dependence can be extended in a theological thought to identify the totality of creation. That is, the idea that creation has an "external" source permits the thought that creation is a totality. Creation is not infinite, and nor is it eternal. For example, the claim that we find in *The Natural Choice* that nature benefits humans and humans in turn benefit nature is insufficiently bold.[269] For it suggests an image that nature and humanity are on the same level thereby obscuring dependencies that I have been discussing so far and that

---

[265] *UK National Ecosystem Assessment* (2011), 57.

[266] Rodwell (2013) www.nerc-bess.net/index.php/documents/2-uncategorised/129-workshop-rep ort-aesthetic-spiritual-responses-to-the-environment [accessed 12 12 13]

[267] Rodwell (2013), 4.2.

[268] Rodwell (2013), 9.2.3.

[269] *The Natural Choice* (2011), 9.

are captured in religious thinking. So far, so good – but how does this help us think about ecosystem services?

First, I note that immediately following the reference to "infinity", we have this sentence: "Real world decisions concern choices between options, with values being assessed in terms of relative costs and benefits of incremental changes in ecosystem services provision."[270] References to totality and infinity do not relate well to "real world decisions". So the claim goes. In one way, this is true: Christian religion is thereby trying to render visible a dependence and, in one sense, to measure it. Yet this religious scale is a very curious scale: the dependence of creatures on the basic conditions of their life. In an approach that seeks to establish economic values, what is the point of reference to infinity? More precisely, what is the measure here, and what is being measured? If we are counting, what is being counted?

Plainly, we are not counting economic values. In a strict sense, all that is is infinity and so cannot be measured. Instead, it can only be received. Without supporting services, there would be no possibility of the continuation of human life. What would counting tell you here? How does one count human life in its totality? It simply is. Indeed, one way of avoiding the receipt of this dependence is to measure it; one way of not acknowledging this dependence is to count it. The scale also suggests that although the human may be the measurer, the human is not the measure. Indeed, there is a sense in which nature-as-other is the measure: the de-centring of the human. Yet, this is as an ecological de-centering in which the human is relocated in a network of ecological dependencies. We are back to the social-institutional.

However, measurement is not ruled out. Once received, all that is can be measured – but in what way? What are the implications for scale, measure and counting? As regards scale, we are obliged to consider the whole range of services, even those that press us towards giving an assessment of the totality of our dependencies on a wider nature. We are forced beyond the man-in-his-environment image to something more profound, more radical. On this perspective, we are invited to measure not only a set of services but in a sense to measure the human also, in its fragility and dependencies.[271] Additionally, we are counting not services but the creatures and others that are parts of these processes. For example, bees and other creatures provide the vital ecosystem service of pollination. Processes are borne by actors – including non-human actors. The scale is all encompassing, the measure includes the human and what is being counted are not only processes but also the agents of those processes. Put in an explicitly theological idiom, we are exploring the difference of Creator and creation – where the latter includes all creatures.

---

[270] *UK National Ecosystem Assessment* (2011), 42.
[271] Rodwell (2013), 9.2.1: "… nature provides a context in which can learn what it is to be human, how to live and how to die". Cf. 9.6.1.

From this Creator/creation-creatures perspective, we can revisit the hierarchy of ecosystem services presented above, and make one further point as regards learning about creatureliness. Recall that the list of type of services begins with *supporting*, and thereafter moves to *regulating, provisioning* and *cultural* services. In this measure, cultural services appears last and as the least central: basic processes come first, and then food, etc., and thereafter cultural matters – in a hierarchy that smacks of a vulgar materialism. ("Eats first, morals after" – as Brecht satirised this position.) In the perspective that I have been developing here, we may appreciate by contrast that cultural services are not derivative but instead summative. (As Demant notes, in section 3.4 above, metaphysical priority and moral priority are not the same.) In other words, the religious appreciation of nature that I have been sketching here is rooted not in experiences of nature but instead the experiences of nature are found in a more basic *thought*: the dependence of creation on its Creator, and thereafter the dependencies of creatures on one another. The thought in which these experiences are based provide a scale, measure and indication of what to count. In this sense, then, the theological thought that I have been trying to sketch is primary.

My final point concerns *learning about creatureliness* – a pedagogy of attention. That public policy – its development and execution – requires an institutional infrastructure is, I take it, an unexceptionable point. We call that infrastructure, "government" and its agencies. Identically, the idea of Creator/creation-creatures is borne by religious communities that provide the infrastructure for its transmission, and this infrastructure provides the sites for learning about creatureliness. The role of religious communities in civil society is to keep reminding other sectors that this dependence cannot in the first place be measured. As we have seen, this is a vital insight. In this sense, the culmination of learning about our dependence on Ecosystem Services is provided by neither the state nor the economy, but instead by civil society. What this suggests is that the institutionality of nature cannot be left to the state or the market. As we have seen, nature is rendered other in specific ways – through a process of separation – and that inhibits the emergence of postnatural good in that the greater society is undermined. Instead, what is required is the development of an institutional infrastructure that identifies the sociality of human-nature relations in a greater society.

In this section, I have explored the publicness of nature. At the outset, I accepted that nature is to be understood as public, in two senses. First, it is public in the sense of being related to the collective: it supports the life of humans as a group. Second, it is public in the sense that it is subject to public administration; the managerial state is the gateway to nature's goods. However, although I have accepted that the designation of ecosystem services adheres to both senses of publicness, I have queried whether the notion of nature implicit in the DEFRA documentation is appropriate. The DEFRA position gives the state control over the status of affective responses to nature and thereby sidelines the importance of the witness of religious groups to a wider dependency. We are familiar with the ways in which the state tends to give priority to other matters of concern before the environment. On this view from the state, nature remains tap and sink. The position that I am sketching here gives to religious communities an important role in witnessing to an alternative scale, measure and way of counting.

5.8 NATURE AS PRIVATE

I turn now to the presentation of nature as private. In section 5.3, I claimed that nature is to be understood as private because nature is not present as part of demo-cratic deliberations, the nature-society relation and the value of nature are treated abstractly, and the "zoning" of nature leads to the consequence that cultural ser-vices are regarded as epiphenomenal when contrasted with making nature "pro-ductive". In this section, I explore these three issues.

In the previous section, I argued that the DEFRA documents approach the matter of supporting services as totality. That is helpful. The matter of supporting services provided by ecosystems does at least in part identify the ways in which nature operates beyond the human and the human needs to transform that other-ness in order to live. I also argued that this produces a peculiar scale, measure and way of counting. How is such a peculiar scale to be approached? A presentation either by reference to the economy or the state does not grasp the profundity of this matter. In other words, it is in neither management nor production that the depth of human dependencies on nature may be adequately grasped.

Instead, following on from 5.4, we should say that the publicness of nature may be recovered by ensuring that nature is the subject of democratic deliberation. It is nonetheless hard to see how this place in democratic deliberation is secured in practice. In the DEFRA documents, moreover, it is clear that the development of ecosystem services is the project of a democratically-elected government. How-ever, the treatment of nature in the documentation invokes an abstract concept of society and reference to the importance of nature to individuals. For example, in the *UK National Ecosystem Assessment* (2011), in a discussion of economic val-ues in decision-making, there is discussion of net benefits and losses to society.[272] Democratic deliberation is not central to this scale.

What abstract "society" is this? What is missing here is a careful and concrete account of the types of society-nature interactions. How precisely does human so-ciety transform nature, and in what ways are our processes of transformation sus-tainable (or not)? With concepts of nature come different concepts of society.[273] What sort of society is it that understands the nature with which it interacts as pro-viding services? What sort of society is it that deploys sophisticated technological

---

[272] *UK National Ecosystem Assessment* (2011), 43.
[273] Williams (1980), 71.

apparatus in the transformation of nature and yet seems unable to theorise this in
the development of policy? These questions are not central to the documentation.

With this abstract society also comes an emphasis on the replaceability of nature. In a discussion of "biodiversity offsetting", the White Paper argues in favour
of the offsetting of the loss of ecosystem benefits by expanding or restoring habitats elsewhere.[274] The procedure of biodiversity offsetting was re-affirmed by then
Environment Secretary Owen Paterson, according to a report by the BBC dated
4 January 2014.[275] Are landscapes and habitats interchangeable in the way that is
presumed by the policy?[276] I do not think we need to go as far as a deep ecological
position that says that a landscape restored to its former state is still a different
landscape. However, there is something troubling about this sense that nature can
be re-organised in this way. Such re-organisation presumes that nature is private:
nature is not required to be present in public discourse and the implicit account
of nature that offsetting presupposes is not discussed. Furthermore, we see that
the DEFRA publications do value cultural services. However, in the light of the
discussion of abstraction and offsetting, cultural services are different in that *specific people in particular places* have such experiences of and encounters with
nature. The replaceability of nature, and the substitution of such experiences that
is thereby implied, suggest once more that cultural services are of less importance
than the productivity of nature. Is this not another version of "eats first, morals
after" and thereby another way of construing nature as private?

5.9 VALUE

I now turn to the matter of the value of ecosystem services. The DEFRA documentation has a complex way of understanding the value of nature. In one direction,
value is understood as external to nature, and imposed upon it. Take *The Natural
Choice*'s use of the term "natural capital": "the stock of our physical natural as-
sets (such as soil, forests, water and biodiversity) which provide flows of services
that benefit people (such as pollinating crops, natural hazard protection, climate
regulation or the mental health benefit of a walk in the park). Natural capital is
valuable to our economy."[277] The White Paper notes that the financial value of
some of these benefits but the financial value of other services is not so easily
established. In a way, what the White Paper is trying to do is commendable: it offers a value to nature but also argues that the value may not be easily established
and/or that the value may not be measureable economically. Too often, natural
capital is taken for granted.[278] This is a highly significant development yet I won-

---

[274] *The Natural Choice* (2011), 22.

[275] http://www.bbc.co.uk/news/uk-25599249 [accessed 07 01 14]

[276] Cf. Rodwell (2013), 6.2.1: "… restored landscapes can also provide sites for nature conserva-
tion and aesthetic and religious experiences".

[277] *The Natural Choice* (2011), 11.

[278] *The Natural Choice* (2011), 35.

der if the word "value" was substituted by "use" whether the position would be altered at all? What else might an expression such as "The economy will capture the value of Nature"[279] mean? In other words, value is presented as separate from, and retrospectively injected into, nature. At one point, nature is said to have innate value[280] – but the analysis does not tarry here but moves swiftly on to the sorts of value that may be *ascribed* to nature.[281]

For the Ecosystem Services approach, it seems that there are values outside nature, imposed by sustainability, market and other concerns? The focus is on action by private firms, supported by the state. (The proposed extension of the "pay back" scheme is exemplary.[282]) Yet, is there a sense in which the process of the valuing of nature identifies value as that which needs to be wrested/produced/created from nature? This follows from the sense of nature as private and as requiring to be rendered public. Nature is private as withdrawn, reserved, and so as needing processes of management (public administration) to render it sustainable. These two commitments – value being applied to nature; nature as withdrawn – converge. For if nature must be rendered productive, it must have its value drawn out of it. On this view, value is not intrinsic to nature. Only as instrumentalised or operationalised does nature have value.

We come to a curious conclusion. On my analysis, nature is private in two senses. It is the object of economic valuation and thereby has a value applied to it. It is private in a further sense that it needs to have its productivity increased and may indeed be replaceable. There is also a minor report that stresses that the value of nature is innate and – although this argument is not made – this innate value is presumably the source of the religious and aesthetic valuation of nature. One implication of the position that I am sketching is the place of economy in relation to civil society must be re-thought. At present, the economy is placed outside civil society and is subject to more-or-less regulation by the state. That needs to change: in an institutional alteration, the economy must be brought back within civil society and clearly identified as a "sphere of necessity" (Hegel). That is, it must much more closely relate to family and neighbourhood. If we are to think about necessity more creatively, this must be related to family, care of children, etc., and place. There are constraints in the sphere of necessity and these need to be foregrounded more fully. In other words, nature is not to be subject to administration in the same way as the economy. On the other hand, how we think about the economy should change and thereafter nature should be thought about differently. This is a first step in the de-privatizing of nature.

---

[279] *The Natural Choice* (2011), 34.
[280] *The Natural Choice* (2011), p. 7. Sometimes, "intrinsic value" (*The Natural Choice* (2011), 2).
[281] Just because the human does the ascribing, it does not follow that it is through the act of ascribing that value enters into nature; ascribing is an epistemological act and value in nature is an ontological claim.
[282] *The Natural Choice* (2011), 52.

5.10 CONCLUSION: ON INSTITUTIONAL VISION

In this final section, I attend to larger matters raised by the foregoing analysis.

First, DEFRA is clearly trying to get people to *want* to change their lifestyles in order to reduce the demand on "ecosystem services". (We shall discuss this issue again in chapter 8, with Hegel's help and with reference to the subjective aspect of social freedom.) *The Natural Choice* claims that people will do that *only if* they feel that nature is somehow present to them. We shall only defend that which we feel attached to: "More people must have the opportunity for a lifelong connection with Nature."[283] Moreover, from such a connection to nature comes the desire "to enjoy it and protect it".[284] The White Paper assumes that connecting with nature generates obligations towards nature. And that connection with nature is generated by proximity to nature. Are either of these claims true?

One mode of connection is clearly provided by cultural services. A fundamental question remains: can that aspect of ecosystem services – aesthetic, spiritual and religious appreciation – carry the weight of this attachment or connection? These experiences are clearly very important and yet it is hard to measure them. The NEA notes that "… we are unable to assess the consequences of recent declines on changes in cultural services, because data on well-being values are lacking" and calls for the development of "a suite of appropriate indicators and measures".[285] Moreover, we lack criteria for determining whether these experiences are critical of dominant ways of transforming nature or are merely compensatory. How do such responses call into question "the dominant emotional and intellectual control"?[286]

Additionally, how do we trace the fundamental ideas that are the basis of these experiences? A quick example here: consider for a moment the implications of the title of the DEFRA Report, *Making Space for Nature*.[287] What idea is basic to the sort of experience that might validate the desire of 21st century inhabitants of England to make space for nature? Moreover, if we reversed the emphasis, how does the thought that nature makes space for us compel us to think and act differently? Finally, does God make space for both nature and humans? What sort of experiences – what sorts of cultural services and what types of institutions? – might correlate with these different ideas?

Second, we come to the matter of a sense of moral obligation – of the human obligation towards nature. What is the source of that moral obligation? What if a sense of moral obligation emerges only partially from proximity? An account of creatureliness is thereby required to ground this sense of moral obligation: that

---

[283] *The Natural Choice* (2011), 45.

[284] *The Natural Choice* (2011), 45.

[285] *UK National Ecosystem Assessment* (2011), 58.

[286] Rodwell (2013), 4.1.3.

[287] *Making Space for Nature* (2010) www.gov.uk/government/news/making-space-for-nature-a-r eview-of-englands-wildlife-sites-published-today [accessed 12 12 13]

humans and other animals, and other creatures, entities and processes are in this together. Much of the discussion refers to religious, spiritual and aesthetic valuations of nature. Yet, what is the moral reasoning behind the religious valuation of nature? What theology offers, however, is an account of a common creatureliness that might inform a religious appreciation of nature. Nature needs to be understood differently in having its own *telos*. It is almost impossible to turn the phrase "the *telos* of nature" into policy terms because policy is framed by a completely different account of the end of nature. The language of "eco-systems services" and the "natural capital" are overwhelming evidence of the mis-framing of nature.

Can we now count the publicness of nature? What, precisely, are we counting? A new metric is required by which we may measure differently: a greater willingness to measure nature's activity from a perspective other than our own.[288] The publicness of nature implicit in such a metric may lead to a different understanding of nature as mattering to us, as necessity. The crucial issue is the interaction between nature's activity and changes in human practice. We shall know that the badgers have truly moved the goal posts when we record nature's activity differently and that difference informs changes in human practices. That, however, will require new institutions.

This chapter has begun the task of considering what it is to Act Postnaturally. The case for a greater society – made in chapter 2 – has been extended by reference to the social-institutional, with a particular emphasis on the institutional. We have explored how one sort of institution – Ecosystem Services – renders nature public and private in unhelpful ways. Moreover, and by refreshing our memory of the concept of "institutional repetition" (see chapter 3), we may recall that any institutional organisation is open to revision and different ends.

How does postnatural good emerge from this discussion of institutions? My argument accepts that Hegel is correct in proposing *Sittlichkeit* – a strong moral ethos – that is learned through participation in institutions. Moreover, such institutions have both subjective and objective aspects – a distinction to be followed up in chapter 8. Postnatural right does not refer only to human action, however, but to the cooperation in action between the human and nature in postnatural institutions. Thinking of institutions is made more complicated by the western achievement of freedom that is now a nearly irreversible development and, although not eliminable, is deeply embedded in our institutions, as well as being their source. In all its ambiguities, freedom is one of the bases from which western societies understand themselves. Nonetheless, the emphasis on freedom comports poorly with the integration of non-human creatures for these non-human creatures are not free in the required sense. As we have seen, the notion of "institution" acknowledges this gap in its effort to coordinate human action and natural action. The difficult issue of freedom and institutions will be discussed in more detail in chapter 8.

---

[288] See Scott (2010a), 59-76.

If my argument is correct, institutions cannot be avoided. They can be reconsidered, however. We can ask about the membership of an institution, its order, way of working, and institutional vision. That is, we can ask about the ways in which it contributes to postnatural good in reference to what an institution provides by way of the fellowship or companionship of humanity and nature. The term, sociability, may also be used here to explore the universal, necessary, social, revolutionary and ideal dimensions of right. This matter of the institutionality of postnatural good requires further consideration from the perspective of order.

Chapter 6: Can there be a postnatural "order"?

6.1 Reprise

This study develops an account of postnatural right by reference to nature, order and technology. Between nature and order there is an unbreakable connection, as we have already seen by reference to social horizon and institutions. In this chapter, I build upon the discussion of order presented in chapter 3. We thereby return to the trajectory of the historical-teleological in a postnatural condition. We are exploring the difference made by the postnatural condition to a concept of order in which we act postnaturally. The burden of this chapter is to develop and defend an account of order that respects a natural teleology – that is, that defends the truth of purposes or goals in nature, including human nature – yet does so in an historically sensitive and non-contrastive fashion. I begin by reprising Rahner's concept of order before reporting on the findings of chapter 3.

As we recall, Rahner proposes three different types of order: that which is discovered, that which is appropriated, and that which is constructed. Orderings by which we are encountered, that we must somehow "subjectivise" and which, finally, we make. It will now be evident that these relate, broadly, to nature, order and technology. We must then appropriate an order that is discovered and constructed. A postnatural order will thereby be an order that is appropriated by participation and such participation encompasses a way of discovery and a path of construction. If the order was only discovered then nature as contrasted to history would be an appropriate conclusion, and such a conclusion thinking in the postnatural condition resists. If the order were only appropriated, then a constructive aspect would be ruled out. If the order were only constructed we would be working with the denial of natural teleology. Instead, a postnatural order must be constructed, discovered and appropriated: such an order is made and not given, is given but is not antecedent, is "internalised" but retains its otherness. How shall this position be elaborated?

To answer this question, I draw on chapter 3's conclusions regarding what is helpful and unhelpful as regards presentations of natural order. In the first place, we must note that the postnatural condition affirms the reality of the otherness of nature. It is true that in the postnatural condition that order is constructed and appropriated but it is nonetheless also discovered. (I am not attempting to override the complexity of the concept of nature; it is important to work with the complexity as a way of affirming the range of processes that nature identifies.) That discovery is rooted in teleology: there are purposes and ends in nature. These purposes and ends abide and are not subsumed into human history.

Yet, in a critique of the use of kinds and too narrow a focus on human nature, I suggested that we focus on a broader-based animal nature. In turn, this presentation means that although natural ends are to be affirmed yet the strong cutting of the world into kinds is to be resisted. Rather than kinds, I stressed activities based in proclivities and tendencies. The human, in a range of activities – some of which it shares with other animals – expresses its nature through institutional repetition by which it secures its own needs. The historical and the teleological are neither opposed nor contrasted. A range of institutions may promote human flourishing and these institutions may alter because of changing human – and non-human – circumstances.

Postnatural order is not invested in the human as a biological totality thereby grounding human order in a biological substrate (such as procreative sex). One of Demant's points about marriage and family is in fact very helpful here: what makes the family basic is its mediation *between* nature and humanity. That is, more often than not, what we call natural structures are *sites of mediation* between nature and humanity; the family is not prior to culture but is instead an activity where nature and culture meet.

A binary is to be avoided here. Either, nature raises the matter of pre- or trans-historical structures: are there aspects of the human that are not subject to the contingencies of historical change – aspects that we would then call natural? Or, is it preferable to say that the natural is subsumed by the historical and that the telos of the natural is history? The enquiry after a postnatural order avoids such a binary. At this point in the argument, we encounter a significant difficulty.

In order to avoid such a binary, is it better to start with the human or with a wider nature? In order not to be dazzled by this question – a question that does after all turn upon a binary – I begin by addressing a theological issue embedded in the concept of nature and I try to show the impact of this theological issue on the construal of a postnatural order. Next, I develop these postnatural issues by attention to Paul Tillich's concept of life through the consideration of "ecstatic life": that life is self-transcending. Finally, acknowledging that the theme of this chapter is order, I return to the matter of the historical-teleological: that is, in my account of postnatural order, what defence can be made of the purposes and ends of nature? I conclude by arguing that institutional repetition, understood ecstatically, encompasses natural orderings-to – that is, an affirmation of the universality of natural teleology – but nevertheless is more cautious about orderings-alongside and the division of the world into kinds. The relation between the historical and the teleological is secured by reference to institutional repetition – the natural proclivities and tendencies of animals are structured by ecstatic life – in which *addition* identifies the ways in which new elements may be encompassed in a postnatural order. Particular, historical and concrete ends may, through addition, become natural ends. This is not a matter that can be decided in advance by reference to some "creation order" but instead by reference to a norm or criterion of judgement here called right.

My approach cuts against our present habits of thought as resourced by a concept of nature: nearly always we think of a contrast between nature and history, the given and the made, and the natural and the artificial. In this cutting against, it does not follow that there is no natural teleology. The concept of ecstatic life requires it, as we shall see. So while we might say of postnatural order as Stephen Pope says of natural law: that "... our understanding of natural law must be dynamic, flexible, and open to new developments as a result of changing human circumstances", we must also affirm that changes of circumstances are not an abridgement, curtailment or suspension of natural teleology but its reconfiguration through institutional repetition "towards structures of living [we should say, institutions] that support human [we should say, animal] flourishing".[289]

6.2 ORDER AND METAPHYSICS

We are in the tracks of a postnatural order. Above I noted that we need to find a way of approaching this issue that does not begin from either humanity or nature. In a previous discussion, I suggested that the relations between humanity and nature could be placed beneath two broad headings: personalism and naturalism.[290] On this occasion, I want to follow Gordon Kaufman's analysis, first introduced in chapter 2, a little further. For Kaufman, the central issue is that the concept of nature is accompanied always by a metaphysics, in the sense of a commitment to interpreting the world from the perspective of a particular concept or schema. Furthermore, the metaphysics proffered, commonly traceable back to Spinoza, is usually indifferent to theology's investment in the God who creates. Surpassing Kaufman, however, we need not follow Kaufman's either/or and enquire whether the experiential basis of our interpretation of nature is either human placedness in nature or human separation from nature. Instead, a theology of postnatural right requires a theology of nature that renders active both sides of the ambivalence: to secure the universal right of the human as the ecological individual yet in the manner of a levelling movement that re-relates the human to the non-human. In that "social" captures both sides of this ambivalence, its use is validated one more time.

Still, Kaufman rightly places a considerable obstacle in the way of a concept of postnatural right. This obstacle is, we might agree, at root metaphysical. For Kaufman, the basic metaphysical schema offered by Christianity is "God, man and world".[291] Not only are the central themes of Christianity – sin, salvation, for-

---

[289] Pope (2005), 163.
[290] Scott (2003), chapter 2.
[291] Kaufman (1972), 349.

giveness – derived from the intrahuman, familial sphere but there is also a special relationship between God and humans that is presented by the term, *imago dei*. In this schema, the third metaphysical term, "world", is much less important, according to Kaufman. As Isaiah Berlin has noted, the Hebraic construal of God is formed out of the experience of community life and is quite different from, say, the Greek construal of the same period:

Let us look at another example – a parallel culture, that of the Bible, that of the Jews at a comparable period. You will find a totally different model dominating, a totally different set of ideas, which would have been unintelligible to the Greeks. The notion from which both Judaism and Christianity to a large degree sprang is the notion of family life, the relations of father and son, perhaps the relations of members of a tribe to one another. Such fundamental relationships – in terms of which nature and life are to be explained – as the love of children for their father, the brotherhood of man, forgiveness, commands issued by a superior to an inferior, the sense of duty, transgression, sin and therefore the need to atone for it – this whole complex of qualities, in terms of which the whole of the universe is to be explained by those who created the Bible, and by those who were to a large extent influenced by it, would have been totally unintelligible to the Greeks.[292]

Herewith lies the beginnings of the personalism that we have already encountered in Demant. Not only is this personalism a crucial historical development, Kaufman argues, but in this "backgrounding" of "world" the Christian metaphysical schema is being consistent: "An inner logic or consistency in Western religious traditions was being worked out here."[293] This consistency stressed divinity as personal and moral being, of which the human is the imaging partner. Thus, the metaphysical schema privileged the personal, the moral, the volitional and the free. This had important consequences for the description of "world" as it came to be understood as the context for human activity, and the material on which God and humans worked. Although the human creature was only ever a creature yet there were important *similarities* between divinity and humanity and important *dissimilarities* between humanity and divinity on one side and the world on the other. It is worth quoting Kaufman at some length at this point:

Thus, the conceptions of God and man, as they have developed in Western religious traditions, work hand in hand toward the distinguishing of man from (the rest of) nature. Nature is not conceived primarily as man's proper home and the very source and sustenance of his being, but rather as the context of and material for teleological activity by the (nonnatural) wills working upon and in it.[294]

It is important to underscore the significance of nonnatural wills for we see here, according to Kaufman's interpretation, the culmination of a view that privileges "moral and personal experience" over "a sense of dependence upon the unity with

---

[292] Berlin (2000), 3.
[293] Kaufman (1972), 351.
[294] Kaufman (1972), 353.

the orders and processes of nature".[295] It follows that there is a reciprocal relationship between the concept of God and the self-understanding of the human that
sees the latter as distinct from creation and interprets that distinction from the perspective of personal and moral experience. The Christian metaphysical schema
thereby exhibits an ecological deficit.

We can be yet more precise: the Christian metaphysical schema exhibits a
postnatural deficit. What is meant by this diagnosis? That, in the consideration
of nature, the focus in the Christian metaphysical schema is on the human: as
we have seen, "world" is backgrounded. From a postnatural perspective, the differentiation between humanity and world needs to be surpassed towards a more
interactive account of humanity and world: a greater society. Our first step towards a postnatural order is to overcome the differentiation between humanity
and world – to avoid personalism without falling into naturalism – and instead to
secure their greater interaction in a theological thought, that is, by reference to the
concept of God.

A contrast with the political is instructive at this point. Whereas the political
has often been downplayed or obscured within Christianity, it has never been lost
because of the experience of community from which Christianity draws its mate-
rials for consideration of the God-human relationship.[296] The same cannot be said
of the human-world relationship which is not present at Christianity's origins with
the same force and coherence as the God-human relationship. It is certainly true
that there have been serious and successful efforts to integrate afresh "political experience" into theology. Yet the same is less easily said for the human experience
of nature and the dependencies of the human on nature: the same foundational
effort has not been forthcoming. There seems to be little evidence to contradict
Dupré's judgement that Christianity no longer defines the fundamentals of the
worldview as presented by contemporary enquiries – philosophical or scientific –
into nature.[297]

Kaufman's conclusion raises some important questions for my argument. For,
as already advertised, the concept of right that I am developing is a levelling
concept, and thereby needs an account of the commonality of human and other
kinds. Yet, as Kaufman has also argued, such commonality presses down hard on
Christianity's metaphysical schema in which two differences are evident: between
God – and the human and the world; and between God-and-humanity – and (the
rest of) nature. A metaphysical account is required that bridges these differences
in order to secure the levelling force of right. Moreover, the levelling force cannot
be considered as that which merely places the human in nature. For that would
mean that the subjectivity of the human is overwritten by a naturalism. The force
would thereby be not so much levelling as subsuming. The metaphysical develop-

---

[295] Kaufman (1972), 354, 355.
[296] See Cavanaugh and Scott (2019), 1-11.
[297] Dupré (1993), 69.

ment required is thereby one that joins the human to other kinds and yet maintains the singularity-in-subjectivity of the human. Moreover, this development occurs within the doctrine of creation in such fashion as to secure metaphysically the participation of creatures in the creator God. The concept of a greater society, and the trajectory of the social-institutional, is one of the ways in which this work is undertaken in my argument.

6.3 LIFE: ECSTATIC ORDER

In *A Political Theology of Nature*, I have already proposed a theological metaphysics under the description of the common realm of God, nature and humanity. In an effort to avoid a subsuming naturalism and a transcendent notion of personhood, the key concept advanced was *sociality*. It is sociality, I argued, rather than human personhood or nature's immanent processes that should provide the lead organising concept in a theology of nature. Furthermore, I argued that all creatures participate in the transcendental of sociality and by that participation participate in the life of the social God.[298]

This position also allowed me to stress the agency of non-human nature and the encounter of the non-human with the human. In other words, when faced with the difficulty of the human subject facing the natural object, I stressed that nature is also a subject. Nature thereby offers a context of subject-ivity in which human subjectivity finds itself: the natural subject faces the human subject, and under the conditions of alienated living both subjects may be transformed into objectivities.

I propose to defend the appeal to sociality as ontological ground, through a discussion of life in relation to spirit: to encompass life in all its dimensions in morality, culture and religion, following Paul Tillich in volume 3 of his *Systematic Theology*.[299] Moreover, I shall take the force of the critique offered by Pannenberg in *Toward a Theology of Nature* that Tillich restricts the operation of the Spirit to faith, hope and love rather than the surpassing, energising field of the Spirit.

For my purposes, the most interesting feature in Tillich's pneumatological presentation is what he calls "the multi-dimensional unity of life".[300] Tillich insists that life should be considered from the perspective of a number of dimensions, all of which are present – even if only potentially – in life. Importantly, Tillich argues, just as there is no competition between depth and breadth, just so there is no competition between the dimensions of life. I shall return to report in some detail on these dimensions in a moment. For the present, I note that along with "dimension" Tillich also proposes the use of the word "realm". This is interesting in that I have in earlier work independently come to use the same term. Similarly, I have deployed the term because its provenance is social. As Tillich writes, the

---

[298] Scott (2003), 43-52.
[299] Tillich (1963).
[300] Tillich (1963), 12.

metaphor of "realm" " . . . is not basically spatial (although it is that); it is basically social".[301] And he continues: " . . . in the metaphorical sense a realm is a section of reality in which a special dimension determines the character of every individual belonging to it, whether it is an atom or a man".[302] All dimensions are potentially present in a realm and, Tillich notes, some are actual – yet we must argue, realm by realm, for that which is the characterizing "special dimension". Now, Tillich identifies "man" as such a realm. However, in the light of the postnatural condition, "man" cannot be identified simply as a realm. An account of postnatural order is vested in a wider realm, precisely a common realm of God, nature and humanity, a greater society. Moreover, we must stress that with reference to nature, order and technology, humanity is "active"; we are addressing the personal freedom of humanity in a common realm. Thereby, the characterising dimension cannot be a dimension that pertains to humanity alone for the realm in which we are invited to act postnaturally is not an human-only realm. That is, "the section of encountered reality"[303] that the postnatural invites us to engage with is not populated only by the human. Moreover, in this realm many agents are active. To advance my analysis, we need to discuss the dimensions proposed by Tillich.

Tillich offers five dimensions of life. Beginning with the inorganic, Tillich notes that generally a "'theology of the inorganic' is lacking" in theology.[304] Indeed, Michael F. Drummy has identified Tillich's work on a theology of the inorganic as a major but little noticed contribution by the German-US theologian.[305] In sum, and as an indication of its comprehensive importance, " . . . the inorganic has a preferred position among the dimensions in so far as it is the first condition of the actualization of every dimension".[306] Next is the organic dimension, which has two aspects, so to speak: the vegetable and animal. (The term "organism" is here germane.) The animal also refers to self-awareness: that is, the higher animals, including humanity, enjoy inner awareness and hence relate to the psychological dimension. The next dimension is the personal-communal or the spiritual; this dimension is restricted to the human. Beyond this is the historical dimension, "the dynamics of life", " . . . a last and all-embracing dimension of life comes to its full actualization only in man, in whom as the bearer of the spirit the conditions for it are present".[307] As such, the historical dimension is manifest in all dimensions of life: "actual – if subdued – in every realm of life, for history is the dimension under which the new is being created".[308]

---

[301] Tillich (1963), 16.
[302] Tillich (1963), 16.
[303] Tillich (1963), 17.
[304] Tillich (1963), 18.
[305] Drummy (2000), 75-82.
[306] Tillich (1963), 19.
[307] Tillich (1963), 25.
[308] Tillich (1963), 26.

In this presentation, I want to pause to return to some of the difficulties that we encountered in the discussion of moral order in chapter 3. Before doing that, I note a very interesting comment by Tillich: "In historical time or causality, all preceding forms of time or causality are present, but *they are not the same as they were before*".[309] This judgement offers a further perspective on why a creation order cannot truly be separated out from an historical order. Contra O'Donovan, we can privilege the personal-communal but we cannot deny the impact of historical temporality. Any appeal to a "creation order" must also accommodate all five dimensions that comprehend the unity of life. Of course, Tillich's presentation is permissive: on phenomenological grounds one of the five dimensions may dominate in the consideration of encountered reality. Nonetheless, the historical can never be set aside.

Moreover, we should be cautious about a judgement made by natural law that law applies only to the upper levels. That is, that natural law is best expressed not in the activities that humans share with non-human animals but rather in those that separate humans from other animals. For this denies the inorganic and organic dimensions of human life. Moreover, these last enjoy institutional repetition, and are thereby unsurpassable. Indeed – and this makes resurrection ethics and the natural law ever more peculiar – family and the sphere of the interpersonal are rooted in animal self-awareness and so in the organic realm. It may be correct, as Demant does, to privilege the realm of the personal and thereby to grant metaphysical and sociological primacy to culture and moral priority to economics. Nonetheless, the other dimensions are always also present. To employ Tillich's terms of potency and actuality – a contrast traceable back to Aristotle – even the dimension of the inorganic enjoys the potential for historical development. Indeed, the inorganic has its own history.

Is the postnatural a dimension? The answer to this question is in the negative. No, and yet the postnatural presses the theme of actualisation more strongly in relation to all of the levels. That is, potential/actual is not a zero/sum game. Thinking theologically in the postnatural condition invites taking more fully the importance of the inorganic and organic as dimensions of the unity of life, including human life. Dimensions do not compete, as we have seen. Therefore, it is the task of a theological ethics in a postnatural condition to stress dimensions usually not privileged. Yet, the way to do this is not to say that there is a creation order/human nature that is actualised without the dimension of history. Human activities like marriage and family actualise through the activity of birthing all the levels, including the personal. These cannot be overcome and are thereby teleologically significant.

It follows that it does not make sense to de-historicise the personal-communal and call it a "creation order" when all dimensions relate to the dimension of his-

---

[309] Tillich (1963) 18, emphasis added.

tory. Yet, there is a unity – and that is the teleological point. For O'Donovan and accounts of natural law discussed in chapter 3, the personal-communal is privileged. Yet, the point of postnatural right is not to privilege the personal-communal in this way but rather to explore how a greater society identifies a part of reality as a unity under a characterising dimension. Or, rather, must there be *one* characterising dimension? Instead, the postnatural suggests that we must work with a range of dimensions in the context of the social realm. Moreover, at this point we may now notice that Tillich misses the social-institutional – that is not a dimension but rather the realm identified. It is in the interaction between the realm of the social-institutional and the five levels, in a unity, but characterised by the historical, that relates best to the postnatural condition. The unity points towards the revolutionary aspect of right and also toward the ideal; the realm grasps the social; unity identifies the universal aspect; all five levels speak to necessity.

With a little more help from Tillich, we can explore the historical dimension further. The historical emerges out of a "constellation of factors", Tillich argues. If we are to refer to time and space, we should say that the organic is closest to space; the historical is closest to time.[310] Nonetheless, once more we may note that the dimensions are not in competition and the distinction between potential and actual is important: "... the actualized historical realm includes the actualized inorganic realm, but not vice versa".[311] We should immediately note an important implication of this position for creation order and natural law type arguments: these types of argument based in the personal-communal are closer, so to speak, to time rather than space and so cannot have time stripped out of them. To do otherwise is to misunderstand the dimension along which these arguments are made. We are reminded of the wisdom of Demant's comment that activities such as marriage and family are, to coin a phrase, sites of mediation between nature and humanity (and not nature only).

That the dimensions are not competitive allows Tillich to stress that historical existence and natural existence – Tillich calls it universal existence – must be thought together: "But historical existence is embedded in universal existence and cannot be separated from it. 'Nature participates in history' and in the fulfilment of the universe".[312] Moreover, picking up from the discussion in chapter 3, Tillich also uses the language of repetition: "Time, so to speak, runs ahead toward the new, the unique, the novel, even in repetitions."[313] Therefore, repetition includes the possibility of the new and the possibility of breaking through to new structures. "In a historical group a double causation can be observed; the causation from a given sociological structure to the creation of cultural content and the causation

---

[310] Tillich (1963), 315.
[311] Tillich (1963), 319.
[312] Tillich (1963), 320.
[313] Tillich (1963), 319.

from this content toward a transformed sociological structure."[314] Institutional vision, a concept advanced in chapter 5, is an example of such movement.

At this point, we may pause and explore how helpful Tillich's position is for
thinking theologically in a postnatural condition about a greater society. I begin
by noting that for Tillich space and substance are associated with the inorganic,
time and causality with the communal and the spiritual. Drawing on his notions of
space and substance, Tillich argues that "Substance under the historical dimension
can be called the 'historical situation'".[315] Tillich argues also that a given culture is
such an "historical situation". Nonetheless, the emphasis appears not to be on the
ecological aspects of such a situation, although the dimensions of the inorganic
and the organic would permit such a theoretical development. More interestingly,
Tillich makes a case for the teleology of substance: "Historical situation or substance, if drawn into the dynamics of historical causality, contains the quest for
a universal historical substance (including all forms of dimensionally qualified
substance) or a situation which transcends every situation." The name for such
transcending, Tillich claims, is the symbol, the Kingdom of God, which identifies
a universal unity. The affirmation of the teleology of the category of substance is
welcome but seems to be directed to understanding substance and space as always
potential in the movement of history. This is true but underplays the ecological aspects of space and substance. Ecological substance, I am arguing, is always also
identity conferring. As such, said identity conferment is a permanent feature of
any historical situation.[316]

Indeed, Tillich comments on this in a discussion of the movement of history,
in which he notes the interplay of "necessity and contingency in the dynamics
of history".[317] For Tillich, necessity emerges from the substance and space of the
historical situation, already discussed. Despite this emphasis on necessity, Tillich
insists that all reference to "historical laws" is to be avoided and in turn prefers
to use the term "trend" to identify "certain regularities in the sequences of events,
rooted in sociological and psychological laws, which, in spite of their lack of
strictness, participate in determining a historical situation".[318] Yet there is no men-
tion of ecological "laws" which certainly participate of necessity in determining
an historical situation. Above all, "trend" seems too mild a word to denote ecologically determining pressures, although Tillich does add that there are "situations
in which trends are almost irresistible".[319] It is clear what Tillich is keen to avoid:
totalising explanations of historical development or movement that undermine hu-

---

[314] Tillich (1963), 325. Cf. 326: Time provides irreversibility, causality the new; space and substance are the static elements.
[315] Tillich (1963), 325.
[316] For comments on place and identity, see Scott (2015b), 155-168.
[317] Tillich (1963), 326.
[318] Tillich (1963), 327.
[319] Tillich (1963), 327.

man agency. Nonetheless, it is less than clear that the order that we are presented with is postnatural: an order of *life* that transcends nature and yet follows nature. As Peter Hodgson has opined, there are certain necessary and natural features of human existence apart from death: birth, genetics, the unconscious, growth and maturation.[320] Moreover, this is before we have considered the wider inorganic and organic dimensions – to use Tillich's terms – that provide the enabling conditions for such teleological change.

Finally, a comment on the teleology promoted in Tillich's analysis. True to his analysis of the interaction between life and history, Tillich argues that the processes of life remain operative in any historical movement. Life aims for self-integration, creates, and transcends itself. Life may also, within such directionality, disintegrate, destroy itself, and fall into profanity. Additionally, self-integration, self-creativity and self-transcendence are in the historical dimension one process, toward an aim. Thus, history aims for universal and total integration, the universally and totally new, and the universally and totally transcendent.[321] Yet, in exploring the relation between life processes and history, the focus is the "personal-communal realm", which Tillich also calls the spiritual realm. Why should this restriction be in force at this point? In a final comment on teleology, Tillich argues that the aim of history can be understood by reference to the aims of the processes of life: self-integration, self-creativity and self-transcendence. Yet, in line with our postnatural commitments, we must still ask after the aim of the dimensions: not only of history but also of the inorganic and the organic. Perhaps Tillich would reply that these dimensions also have time in their specific ways. Nonetheless, what is the teleological end of such life processes, on which the effectiveness of ecological and biological factors in structures relies and is the actualisation of? If, as Tillich commends, these dimensions are not in competition, what is their teleological end?

Praising their efforts to overcome "spiritual subjectivism" by identifying the spirit with life rather than with the mind, Wolfhart Pannenberg has argued for the development of Tillich's (and Teilhard de Chardin's) pneumatology. He argues that Tillich restricts ecstatic movement associated with the spirit to experience of God in faith, hope and love. It would be truer to Tillich's pneumatology, Pannenberg argues, to maintain that all spiritual experience – and not only the virtues of faith, hope and love – exemplifies "the self-transcendence of life".[322] I am not sure that this is accurate or fair as a presentation of Tillich's doctrine of the Spirit. For example, Tillich maintains that "The Spirit of God is the presence of the Divine Life within creaturely life".[323] Yet, in his fuller discussion of the Spiritual Presence, Tillich does appear to restrict the meaning of spirit to the human. In

---

[320] Hodgson (1994), 201.
[321] Tillich (1963), 332.
[322] Pannenberg (1993), 129.
[323] Tillich (1963), 107.

a discussion of the concept of Spiritual Presence, Frederick J. Parella seems to confirm this: although Spiritual Presence presupposes creation and redemption nonetheless "... the Spirit makes the transcendent union *of the human* with the divine in unambiguous life possible".[324] Is it possible to understand the ecstatic activity of the Spirit more broadly?

Pannenberg thinks so and argues that it is possible, through a reconstruction of Teilhard's concept of energy, to argue that "[entities] participate in the universal field of energy only by transcending themselves, or by way of ecstasy, and the degree of their capability for that ecstatic experience would mark the degree of their spirituality".[325] Moreover, such an account of ecstatic life relates well to modern biology's insistence that especially organisms have an environment on which they depend. As Pannenberg puts the matter: "[E]very organism depends on specific conditions for its life, and these conditions do not remain extrinsic to its own reality but contribute to the character of its life. ... In this sense, every organism lives beyond itself."[326] Thus, we arrive at a sense of ecstatic life: all life, especially evident in the life of organisms, transcends itself, and seeks unambiguous life in the life of the Spirit. Further, Pannenberg argues that in the ecstatic movement of life the organism relates to its own future and to the future of its species (knowingly or not). In relating itself to its own future an organism relates itself to the future of its own self-transformation: participation in a dynamic, ecstatic movement. This is the further specification of how humanity and nature interact, as promised in chapter 1.

In a way that Pannenberg does not, we may immediately note the significance of this position for teleology. As we have seen, Tillich restricts ecstatic self-transcendence to the response in the human spirit of faith, hope and love thereby restricting such self-transcendence to religious belief and experience. Pannenberg seeks to refurbish Tillich's doctrine of the Spirit by extending it to explore the themes of self-integration, self-creativity and self-transcendence by reference to spirit/community/personhood. Thus, spirit is associated with life, and life transcends ecstatically from and into the Spirit of life. To what purpose? The answer to this question we have already seen: to participate unambiguously – as far as is possible – in the aims of self-integration, self-creativity, and self-transcendence. That is, in the realm of the spiritual/personal/communal, to be a moral, cultural and religious being. Moreover, all organisms, as far as they have self-inwardness, are spiritual beings and thereby exhibit rudimentary moral characteristics, the cultural habits of making a home, and seeking a future. In this way, I extend these teleological considerations to life, and so to the interaction between the human and the animal and beyond.

---

[324] Parella (2009), 74-90 (here 79, italics added).
[325] Pannenberg (1993), 132.
[326] Pannenberg (1993), 133.

My focus here is morality in the sense that right identifies an ordering, an historical achievement that identifies the postnatural dignity of the human, a dignity that is only comprehensible and capable of being practised postnaturally, that is, by reference to other animals and other agencies. Such a position is possible, as Pannenberg notes, by the de-restriction of Tillich's position on ecstatic life:

[S]elf-transcendence is to be regarded at the same time as an activity of the organism and as an effect of the power that continuously raises the organism beyond its limitations and thereby grants it its life. The functions of the self-creation and self-integration of life depend on the ongoing process of its self-transcendence.[327]

Realm by realm, we must therefore pay attention to those entities that I call institutions in which organisms – including human organisms – transform their conditions of life in an acknowledgement of their dependence on these same conditions in ways that seek ecstatically their future through integrating and creative processes (and, unhappily, their opposite). These processes are teleological: the purpose of the human, as with other organisms, is integrative, creative and ecstatic. All this takes place in processes of ecstatic order or repetition: when successful, participative; when unsuccessful, exclusionary. Sometimes these processes are competitive and on other occasions collaborative.

These processes or activities are universal. Life is ecstatic; life is teleological. Yet there is a further sense in which humanity is universal: it can imagine the world in which it finds itself. Similarly to the higher animals, humanity is not oriented in the world only by drives and desires but can relate to that world also by thinking. Yet the human does not do this solely as an individual. (We have seen a version of this argument in chapter 3 in Demant's stout defence of "the person".) What is universal then relates also to the community: the individual emerges in its concrete form in community. Pannenberg concludes in this way:

[T]he human is a social being, not simply as a member of the flock, but by recognizing the community as manifesting a unity of human nature superior to one's individuality. Since, however, the society is composed of individuals, the final basis of its unity is to be asked for beyond the concrete institutions of social life: as social being, the human being is at the same time the religious being.[328]

Pannenberg argues from organic life to the individual, and then to social/community life and finally to the religious being. What does the human as a religious being mean here? It seems to identify the ecstatic aspect of human living: that self-transcendence – the ecstatic – is the fulfilment of the human as integrative and creative. Yet, from a postnatural perspective, this is to focus on the human in isolation from the conditions on which it depends and which it transforms. To think theologically in a postnatural condition is to be committed to the

---

[327] Pannenberg (1993), 135.
[328] Pannenberg (1993), 136.

view that in the doctrine of creation we have the interaction of humans and other organisms and inorganic processes. That is, by its ecstatic movement, the human spirit embedded in and transformative of life processes interacts with other spirit-bearing creatures. It does this in repetitive ways in institutions by its participation in an ecstatic order. All creatures, to the extent that they are spirit-bearing, self-transcend as spirit and in the power of the Spirit.

6.4 HISTORICAL AND TELEOLOGICAL ORDER

So far in this chapter, I have argued in support of an account of postnatural order. I have sought to develop an account that is related to but also significantly different from the accounts of natural order criticised in chapter 3. In this chapter, I have been developing a presentation of order that is discovered, appropriated and constructed in the context of a postnatural condition. This has meant resisting any appeal to a creation order and "natural structures" and yet insisting on the teleological significance of social-institutional activities. Moreover, I have argued that such social activity encompasses creatures other than the human and is directed, in analogical ways, to integration, creation, and transcendence. Ecstatic order identifies activities that are both historical and teleological; order changes and yet has purpose secured through institutional repetition. An important relation here is that between participation and exclusion. How then shall we understand these teleological activities – tendencies and proclivities – that are not surpassable in history?

We may in retrospect appreciate that the discussions of Kaufman, Tillich and Pannenberg have opened up a postnatural way. My line of enquiry is an attempt to de-fund a theological habit of mind that sees nature as in contrast to history and the natural as a structure. The point, then, is to deny soteriological significance to claimed natural structures. The issue here is not to propose structures in which humans find a validation for their restricted personal and moral experience but instead to propose theological ways of thinking in which a sense of dependence upon, and requirement to transform, our natural conditions is central. A certain emphasis from natural law that associates the human with other animals, reviewed in chapter 3, is important here. The focus of attention is a social realm: the interaction of many creatures in a greater society founded in the resurrection of Jesus Christ rather than an attempt to shore up an account of order by reference to, for example, Christologically-framed divine command. Moreover, I have stressed a postnatural emphasis on the dimensions of the inorganic and the organic rather than attention to structures – some of which ironically function as sites of mediation between humanity and nature. This provides a levelling pressure to them.

In a discussion of natural order in chapter 3, I invited the reader to make a postnatural turn. "The natural" is not to be understood as in contrast to "history" and is to be extended towards a common creatureliness. This informs the notion of order that I am exploring. Such an order is discovered, appropriated and constructed and is a right order of *life* present in a greater society. We noted that the unity of humanity is not to be found solely in a biological unity. Moreover, biology was too narrow a basis for unity as it identifies an order to be discovered only – rather than one also to be appropriated morally and constructed through technology. Through an emphasis on appropriation and construction, as well as discovery, postnatural order is less concerned with specifying the *content* of a creation order. That is, of identifying specific structures that are assigned the status of being given in a creation order and thereby having a teleological significance. Such a process of identification is not my concern. Instead, I suggested that the term "institution" is to be preferred to "structure". At this point, in order to take account of the emergence of the new and as a way of affirming the direction, permanence and stability of postnatural activities, I introduced the concept of "institutional repetition".

Moreover, I argued that this notion of institutional repetition is a way of addressing the issue of teleology: general ends and particular ends are maintained in and by institutional repetition. To consider this, we need only go back to the discussion of Ecosystem Services in chapter 5. The postnatural activity that Ecosystem Services serves is, among other things, the security of UK food production. Such activity meets basic human needs. Nonetheless, this meeting of a need is conducted in an institutionally specific way: the potential of the "natural need" is made actual through Ecosystem Services as an institution. That the institution repeats itself, so to speak, leaves open the matter of change in ways of meeting that need. A different institution is possible and thereby a different way of meeting the need is possible. Moreover, through institutional repetition we may affirm that the need itself may change: for example, the significance of food is open to cultural variation and thereby how that need is understood, practised and satisfied may vary. Through this notion of repetition, terms such as "balance" and "centredness" do not find favour.

My presentation of institutional repetition does not deny that institutions enjoy stability. In chapter 5 I suggested that membership, order, way of working and authority are features of institutional life. That does not mean that membership never changes or that order might not be reshaped, that the ways of working that operate in an institution never change, or that institutions might never be redirected. An institution such as the meat production industry has clearly changed in terms of scale, procedures for killing, and processing. In and through those changes a question can certainly be posed: has its purpose or end changed? In other words, has the shift to industrial scale and administered production involved a reconsideration of its ends, *from* meeting a need *to* generating a need that the industry then meets?

Yet an ethical question remains: how is such an account of postnatural order an ordination to the good? If order demonstrates direction, permanence, and stability, how does postnatural order do this? In short, how is postnatural order also a teleological order? I have already started the answer to this question. In institutional repetition, general ends and particular ends combine. What is it that stops general ends being subsumed by particular ends? To respond to this question, we can revisit the amendment proposed, following Pannenberg, to Tillich's position. This amendment I called "ecstatic order" in which life processes – we do not need to specify at this point which processes are under discussion – aim towards self-integration, self-creation, and self-transcendence. Moreover, we must note immediately that I am discussing life processes in all five dimensions (inorganic, organic, self-awareness, spiritual/personal/communal, and historical). If the basic teleological question is "What purpose does x serve?", then such a question must be asked of all five dimensions, always bearing in mind that these dimensions can be distinguished but not separated. To ask what is purposive or functional about postnatural order is thereby to ask what ends these activities serve in institutional repetition.

From this position, we may note that order relates to nature, that the historical-teleological relates to the social-institutional. Given such an emphasis on the social-institutional, it is not easy to separate ends from relations: it is difficult to disentangle the orderings-to and orderings-alongside. However, that does not mean that there is no "order": right requires an ontological ground. This order is rooted in the universal, necessary, social, revolutionary, and ideal.

1. As universal, postnatural right is informed by the emphasis of the doctrine of creation on unity – the unity of creatures, given by God in creation *ex nihilo*: a gift, and not the product of an emanation or a divine principle.
2. As necessary, postnatural right requires us to affirm at every point that humanity interacts with other creatures and the inorganic.
3. As social, postnatural right works in the context of an entangled creatureliness.
4. As revolutionary, right is placed otherly; it is levelling and antagonistic.
5. As ideal, postnatural right critically assesses institutions.

From a teleological vantage point – the freedom and flourishing of creatures – right identifies an order that is and may be; the postnatural declines a natural order/historical freedom dualism and insists on the encounter and interactivity of creatures. We live in a postnatural world of interactivity. Nature does not serve humanity *simpliciter* but instead all creatures are ordered to God and ordered to each other variously. This ordering is sourced in the universal, necessary, revolutionary, social and teleological: the order of right in which creaturely freedom and agency is structured, secured and extended.

At this point, we enter some interpretive thickets. It will now be evident that in theology teleology is used in two quite different ways. The first sense denotes the purpose of creation. I think that this is presently an unproblematic sense: both history and nature serve God's purpose and have an end in God. We might call this "transcendent teleology" or the destiny of the natural in the supernatural. The second sense refers to the ends or purposes served by dimensions of life. What are these purposes and, most especially, how do these ends relate to the end of history? We might call this "immanent teleology".

Clearly, the two meanings of teleology are related, and the link is eschatology. If there is to be a resurrection of *bodies* – meaning that bodies are eschatologically significant – something of the this-worldliness of bodies must persist in the Kingdom of God. Nonetheless, the two meanings identify two different clusters of issues. The first meaning raises the matter of the relation between personal, historical and cosmic realms of eschatology. Although related to this, the second presses the matter of whether or not teleological descriptions are defensible and whether teleological descriptions are only preliminary and are finally taken up into human historical action. Put differently, yet still within the terminology being advanced in this book, if human action occurs in institutions, *understood teleologically –* does such action have unrevisable significance?

To explore this matter further, I propose that we attend more directly to specific issues in the consideration of teleology. According to Andrew Woodfield, certain words should alert us to the fact that we are within the circle of teleology: for example, "purpose", "end", and "function". (Stephen Pope adds "goal".[329]) In other words, that x is for y: marriage is for procreation, vegetables are for human food, the natural world is for humanity, and creation is for God. Using a different set of verbs this time, we may rephrase: marriage aims for procreation, creation seeks fulfilment in God. And differently, one more time, using "in order to": people marry in order to have children, God gives nature to human beings in order to sustain them, and God creates in order to fulfil creation.[330]

Although the issue of theology and teleology is not Woodfield's concern, we may immediately notice that teleology is important for accounts of natural order, including postnatural order. It is deep in theological habits to say that God creates for a purpose, that purpose is restored in Christ, and that purpose awaits final fulfilment in the Spirit. We may also note that the emphasis on distinct kinds also supports a particular teleological reading as it answers the prior question: if God creates for a purpose, what is it that God has created? Pope's comment – "Natural law ethics evaporates if nature is purposeless"[331] – applies also to the positions of O'Donovan and Demant; it applies to postnatural right as well. An account of purpose must apply at the cosmic as well as the human level, and the Tillichian terminology of self-integration, self-creativity and self-transcendence – suitably extended – helps at this point. We must note too that the Tillichian dimensions are a way of relating human purposes or goals or ends into wider processes of life. As such, Pope's requirement that teleology must be considered at both the cosmic level and the human level is met. Postnatural order is an ecstatic order in which the

---

[329] Pope (2005), 159.
[330] Woodfield (1976), 17.
[331] Pope (2005), 159.

human, in its self-transcendence, achieves an awareness of its dependence on other processes of life – the postnatural condition – towards integration and creativity. Put in a different theological idiom, the human experiences that dependence as gift, and responds accordingly.

Making the postnatural turn, the human acknowledges dependencies as gift and, learning to act postnaturally, explores its creative responses through postnatural interactivity. There is a profound ordination to the good here: to integration, creativity and transcendence, to be judged by right, which is universal, necessary, social, and revolutionary. Postnatural right operates with an ordination to the good, comprehensively understood along the five dimensions, as discovered, appropriated and constructed by an ecstatic postnatural order. Such an order is teleological: it is for the flourishing of creatures, human and non-human, through the ecstatic movements of institutional repetition. That is, this good is directed more widely than human flourishing alone. Moreover, as my account of right requires, judgements must be made about appropriate institutions in which such ordination to the good is embedded, articulated and developed.[332]

Following Woodfield once more, we can also affirm that there is not only one sort of teleological description. There is some variety in what is to be explained (the *explananda*) and the sort of explanation offered (growth, movement). Further, the teleological explanation (the *explanans*) may offer more than one sort of end or purpose; an *explanandum* may be patient of more than one end. Let us in this regard consider the example of the family. First, what is it precisely that is the subject of teleological explanation? Must a certain understanding of familial arrangement be presupposed? If the family is for the raising of the offspring of their biological parents, then the answer is yes. However, that "the family is for the raising of children" – that is its purpose – can still be understood as a teleological statement without reference to biological procreation. Although it would be possible to make more specific the relation between parents and child, nonetheless "The family is for the raising of children" remains a teleological statement. I offer this example only to indicate that there is more than one form of teleological description. How does this help in the discussion of postnatural order?

Consider the statement, "Nature is for . . . ". The following three statements all qualify as teleological statements: 1. Nature is for God. 2. Nature is for humanity. 3. Nature is for itself. In the area of transcendent teleology, the end of nature is God; in the area of immanent teleology, the end of nature is humanity and also its own flourishing. Elsewhere, I have argued that the second and third teleologies are dependent on the first but that is not our concern at this point.

Instead, my concern is what is the impact on the second and third teleological descriptions in the light of the first teleological description? The answer is formal: an end in God buttresses nature's end of its own flourishing and, in that the human

---

[332] This matter is the topic of volume 3 of this work, entitled *Postnature: A Theology of Culture*.

has its end in God also, supports the view that nature is for humanity. These are teleologically significant conclusions but these are conclusions derived from the postnatural consideration of ecstatic order.

By way of contrast, I wish at this point to return to Woodfield in order to note that much teleological language is associated with an artefactual approach. In other words, objects understood as teleological are said to have a function because of the intention of their maker. Sometimes this is a direct ascription (a computer is an artefact made by a designer for a purpose) and sometimes an analogical one (a beaver making a dam, for example, may not have an intention that it can actually set out but nonetheless its "intentional" activity is goal directed). As Woodfield points out, some objects are not made by human intention (one meaning of nature, as we have seen, is that which is not sourced to human willing). At this point, Woodfield suggests that it is possible to re-establish the artefact model by reference to God or Mother Nature (or, we might add, evolution). With reference to a creator God, we may appreciate that, say, a notion of creation order could be traced to an artefact model: the creation order has a purpose given to it by its creator. It is in the intention of the creator to create and thereby bestow purpose on creation. We can, following Woodfield's discussion of Kant's "projectionist" teleology – with which he disagrees – take a second step in our analysis. Central to Kant's case is the positing of an "End of Nature" as his significant teleological term and he argues, according to Woodfield, that organisms – as designed and in interaction in a wider whole – are the best example of such natural ends. Kant argues that such an end of nature exhibits "intrinsic finality" or "internal teleology". Any causal process that culminates in such a natural end is described in terms of "extrinsic finality" or "external teleology".

There is, we may appreciate, a certain attractiveness in this position for theology. First, the natural end as artefact, and God as the artificer, seems to resonate nicely with the concept of a creator God. Second, the notion of intrinsic finality as it secures natural ends could be used as the basis of an argument in support of a creation order: certain designed wholes are ends that cannot be overcome. If such an account is the dominant way of conceiving of a natural order, then this would raise questions against attempts at teleological description that do not require the artefact model and has a more expansive, historical and flexible account of natural end resourced by a social interpretation of human beings entangled with other kinds. In the next section, I seek to show that this more expansive account is credible.

6.5 Ending

My position is of a postnatural teleology. However, that does not mean that natural order is subsumed into historical human action. Instead, I propose an account of teleology that does suggest that activities at least in part have their purposes given to them, through a creatureliness understood in the line of five dimensions. So the question is: how is this creatureliness to be understood? As the next two paragraphs try to argue, the direction, permanence and stability of teleological activities are discovered, appropriated and constructed.

Teleology – the description and validation of purpose – in the postnatural condition proves to be complex. In rejecting a distinction between natural structure and historical action, I am also defending the teleological standing of the dimensions of the inorganic, the organic, self-awareness, and the personal-communal. Because these dimensions are present – are actual – in social-institutional activities, these activities cannot be given an immanent teleological standing. Instead, these activities must be interpreted from the perspective of the dimensions. This means that natural structure and historical action must give way to an account of humanity and nature based in their similarities. What needs to be identified is what is common to creatures, and then the ways that the human is different. Yet, it is by what the human shares with other creatures – its right – that enables and supports the theological ethic being argued for here. The theological ethic proposes an account of human dignity by right: the postnatural ordering of society commends a necessary, revolutionary "individuality" that relocates the individual in a teleological way into a greater society. The social nature of animals cannot be overcome and so we are directed to the right of pre-citizenship. All that is required to enact such a right is to be "alive". Moreover, it is not easy to restrict such right to the human. This I have called "ecstatic order".

The distinction that Hegel makes between *Ding* and *Sache* is helpful at this point. In Hegel's usage, *Ding* refers to a thing that has a certain independence, and can become "thingified"; *Sache* refers to a thing or entity that can embody the self-determination of the (human) will.[333] Encounters of social creatures requires that the human rely upon the otherness of nature and its capacity to be thingified. Additionally, the human relies upon the availability of the non-human in institutions to be the instantiation of human will. In encounter, both otherness, and participation in the social life of others, is affirmed. Human action renders the world (sense 3, that which is other than humanity) objectified and humanised; the world resists and embodies human action. It is important to note that the dynamic works also in the other direction: for non-human creatures, the human is an object and is "naturalised", and in this process nature enters into encounters towards its own fullness – although institutions are founded through the custom and practice of human willing alone. Nature enjoys both an independence of human action and the capacity to be the recipient of human action. These encounters may only be understood comprehensively by reference to the historical-teleological, the social-institutional, and the anthropological-eschatological. In this comprehensive treatment, the realisation of the truth of God as creator of the world is identified. In

---

[333] Ritter (1982), x.

short, this comprehensiveness can only be understood in a theological thought of a greater society. Greater specificity is here given to the matter of "multiple reactions" that was first broached in chapter 2. Ecstatic life is social life – and life is a theme of *creatio continua*, which we shall explore further in chapter 8.

The "ecstatic order" is thereby teleological in the transcendent sense in seeking, and being given, an eschatological fulfilment. A postnatural order is thereby ecstatic towards its supernatural fulfilment. The "ecstatic order" is teleological also in the immanent sense in that processes of integration and creativity which presuppose interactions in encounter in a creaturely society are the penultimate *teloi* – the aim is an increased sociability. These ends are secured in and through dimensions of inorganic, organic, self-awareness, and personal-communal through which creatures seek their flourishing through the transformation of their circumstances. For human creatures, such teleological activity is universal, necessary, social, and revolutionary. As ideal, right is the judge of this postnatural order of a greater society as discovered, appropriated and constructed.

In the next chapter, the final chapter of part 2, we turn once more to technology and its transformative aspect as the final step in our enquiry as to what it is to act postnaturally.

CHAPTER 7: REDEEMING TECHNOLOGY

7.1 REPRISE

Throughout this part, we have been exploring the three themes of nature, order and, in this chapter, technology. What is it to live in a postnatural condition with reference to the social-institutional, the historical-teleological, and the
anthropological-eschatological? In this chapter, we explore this question by reference to technology as anthropological-eschatological.

In chapter 4, the counterpart of the present chapter, the anthropological basis of technology was presented by reference to self-relatedness, wholeness and
world-relatedness. Such an account takes us far beyond understanding technology
as technical means towards the making of artefacts. In this connection, Deane-
Drummond, Bergmann and Szerszynski write of "technology's deep impact on
human lifeworlds, as well as on different kinds of natural environments … ".[334]
They also note that the linking of technology to salvation is standard.[335] In other
words, that technology is related to efforts to fix body and world although, given
the range of meanings of salvation, it is not always evident how the links between salvation and technology are being made. In approaching salvation, Ernst
Conradie identifies three clusters of images: liberation, healing and deliverance;
reconciliation; and reconstruction, moral regeneration, and education and development.[336] Given the anthropological breadth of the three aspects of technology
presented in chapter 4, we should expect many of these soteriological terms to
occur in theological discussion of technology.

It is easy to see how the three aspects of the anthropological basis of technology present us with accounts of nature and order. First, self-relatedness identifies
a way of life as the location of technology. Technology is not only artefacts and
nor can what is "truly human" be sealed off from a technological culture. The
nature that technology transforms – including human nature – is secured through
social-institutional arrangements and thereby the consideration of technology can
never be restricted to tools nor separated off from other areas of life. Moreover,
technological activity projects, and attempts to secure, an order. That is, such
activity is directed towards some end. Second, wholeness or unity reinforces a
sense of the relations between humanity and nature and that technological activity is the transformation of the human as well as of the non- or extra-human.
This raises in turn the matter of what has been called the humanisation of nature:

---

[334] Deane-Drummond, Bergmann and Szerszynski (2015), 1.
[335] I, too, have noted this: see Scott (2010a), 109ff.
[336] Conradie (2015), 261.

how, and the extent to which, human technological activity impinges upon nature, from preservation to restoration and transformation.[337] Finally, world-relatedness stresses once more the transformative aspects of technological activity and thereby raises the historical-teleological dynamic of such activity and the construction of a postnatural order. In summary, by reference to self-relatedness, wholeness, and world-relatedness, technological activity produces a postnatural order that is social-institutional (nature in the postnatural condition is always relational and relates to human beings via institutions) and historical-teleological (order is re-shaped by technological activity and is oriented on the good).

In explaining technology by reference to the anthropological-eschatological, the issue of the aim or direction of technology is raised and what the relation-ship of technological activity is to redemption. In a postnatural condition, what is meant by "redeeming technology"? The phrase has been deliberately selected for its ambivalence: does technology redeem or is it in need of redemption? In the following sections, I set out various ways of understanding technological activ-ity that are, I think, ruled out by the postnatural condition, and other approaches that might be understood as better related to the anthropological-eschatological activity of human beings. The aim is to explore in more detail what it is to act postnaturally in the anthropological-eschatological aspect of technological activ-ity.

7.2 ESCHATOLOGY, THE FUTURE AND CREATION

Before that discussion, however, I want to be clear about my use of the term, eschatological. For present purposes, both technology and eschatology refer us to a future, and eschatology and creation should be understood as closely related.

The relation between eschatologies and futures has been strongly presented by Michael Burdett who deploys the contrast between *futurum* and *adventus* as a way of framing different futures.[338] Burdett's main target is transhumanism, which presents in its strongest form what is wrong with a *futurum* eschatology. "It has become evident that there has been... an inverting of the future as *adventus* to *futurum*".[339] In transhumanism, we have the victory, so to speak, of *futurum*: the culmination of utopian thinking in technological futures; transhumanism is the strongest form of this technological future in its utopian aspect. The critical issue here is that in such utopianism the future is built rather than received.[340] What is required, Burdett argues, is to amplify the meaning of *adventus* as a more con-vincing way of grasping the eschatological future.

---

[337] See Antonaccio (2015), 31-46. The meaning of "humanisation" does not emerge clearly in this essay.

[338] Burdett (2015). These terms are to be found in Moltmann (1996), 25-26.

[339] Burdett (2015), 80.

[340] Burdett (2015), 100, 224.

To engage in technological activity is, we might say, always to project a future. Given the discussion so far, this future will be the future of a greater society and thereby will project an order. That is, the future will be social and ordered. Creation and eschatology are, in my view, intimately linked therefore. So the question becomes: how does technological activity contribute to the future of creation as social and ordered? To answer this question, the concept and task of eschatology require ecological extension and development.[341]

The grounds for extension of the *concept* have been presented already in chapters 2 and 5. In the consideration of nature, I have argued that humanity is to be understood as interacting with non-human agents in a social-institutional infrastructure. The future of creation is therefore also the future of the social-institutional. We might call this an ecological-eschatological extension yet, as we have seen, it is more complicated than that: the future of creation relates to the future of the institutions of a greater society.

Moreover, the *task* of eschatology needs development. To consider this, we may note a doubled statement that Karl Rahner offers in his account of the "hermeneutics of eschatological assertions". First, the eschatological future remains mystery and yet, second, is always related to humanity. Put differently, God's eschatological action transforms and fulfils after a pattern: the transformation and fulfilment is presently in its fullness unknown and yet does truly relate to humanity. Such transformation is not the cancellation of humanity but its fulfilment.[342] We may immediately see that, in the light of the historical-teleological direction of the construction of postnatural order, the task of eschatology must be considered with the transformation of the historical-teleological, in which *all* dimensions from the inorganic to the spiritual, are treated.

What is the import of this for technological activity? First, we may appreciate that the anthropological roots of technological activity must be related to the organic and inorganic basis of *human* living. Attempts to construe technology as a human act in which only that which is other than the human is transformed are not convincing. Elsewhere, I have noted, in a discussion of Fordist technological practices, that even the worker is changed in and through such labour.[343] Second, appeals to a non-technologised nature – beyond or before technology – as the basis of redemption will, given both the extension of the concept and task of eschatology, also be unconvincing. Third, given its broader-than-anthropology basis, eschatological transformation and fulfilment will encompass the technological and its projection of a future. Therefore, interpretations of redemption that strip the human of its technological attachments are also unconvincing. We may explore these theological judgements in connection with our technological spheres of self-relatedness, wholeness and world-relatedness.

---

[341] See Scott (2000), 89-114.
[342] Scott (2000), 92-94.
[343] Scott (2010a), 100-103.

7.3 GREATER SOCIETY AND TECHNOLOGICAL CHANGE

At this point, as we develop the discussion of technology with reference to self-relatedness, we may note the depth of the transformation of the human through technological activity. Machines occupy this social body and thereby humanity and nature are involved in technological practices. It does not seem helpful, therefore, to understand this society of humanity-nature by reference to an interpretation of society as an organic body. If there is to be no retreat to some technology-free contemplative space and no worship of large-scale techno-fixes,[344] how are we to think theologically about the redemption of technology in the context of a greater society being transformed by and through technological activity?

What needs to be stressed at this point is the technological transformation of the human and the acceptance of this development by a theology of the post-natural condition. Of course, the transformation of the non-human is central to technological activity but nonetheless the transformation of the human must not be overlooked. It is the task of theology for a postnatural condition to refuse the abstraction of the human from its technological practices. Technological change happens in a greater society in which the human and the non-human are changed. The infrastructure of the greater society – social-institutional operations – is the location of this change.

We cannot therefore think theologically of the redemption of technology except by reference to the social nature of humanity. This social nature is based in a sociality of humanity-nature and manifested in a greater society. In this argument for postnatural right, technology may be regarded as redemptive as it contributes to the universal, necessary, social, revolutionary, and ideal vocation of the human in a postnatural condition. In other words, as universal and social, technology is to be located within the social life of humanity. As such, technology cannot be understood as a salvific power operating from beyond humanity that may intervene in human affairs with "solutions" and "fixes". As universal, its activities cannot be restricted; as social, its activities cannot be externalised. As interpreted from the perspective of the necessary and the revolutionary, a postnatural interpretation of technology requires that the natural and anti-hierarchical bases of such activity also be theorised. The vocation of the human as a technological agent is to be found in the midst of nature, as identified by thinking theologically in a postnatural condition. Efforts always to assume the priority of human interests in technological activity are also here confounded. As human activity, technological activity is also teleological activity: it operates within the social life of humanity, is regarded as universally and necessarily operative, and embodies anti-hierarchical practices that are also oriented to the good.

Technological activity is thereby to be interpreted as social and institutional and of eschatological significance. That is, when we speak of the fulfilment of

---

[344] For excellent discussions on climate engineering, see Clingerman and O'Brien (2016).

humanity in a postnatural condition we are speaking of the fulfilment of *technological* humanity.

7.4 TECHNOLOGY, WHOLENESS AND A RESURRECTED NATURE

In the previous section, I discussed the anthropological basis of technology. A different perspective is available: from the perspective of the wholeness of humanity and nature, that is, an appeal to a redemption of technology from the perspective of a resurrected nature looks like a possible way forward. Such a basis means that one way of thinking theologically about technology is from the perspective of a non-technologised nature. What does this sort of argument from the resurrection of nature look like?

We have here a difficult matter of interpretation concerning the status of nature as subject in relation to the modern objectification of nature. An appeal to nature as subject needs to be understood as part of a development premised upon nature as object. As we have seen, this tension between nature as object and nature as subject is common in ecological literatures, although not necessarily using precisely those terms. Maria Antonaccio, who explores a distinction between universal nonhumanisation of nature and the universal humanisation of nature, provides a recent example. Although the stress here is on human activity – that is, humanisation – towards nature, two different accounts emerge: an emphasis on the integrity of nature (which does not include human beings) and a stress on the totalising activity of techno-humanity.[345]

In chapter 4 I argued that there is no innocent objectivity, and hence there is no innocent harmony, as regards nature.[346] The character of the objectivity and harmony posited there is, as Rosemary Radford Ruether reminds us, to be interpreted under the specific headings of capitalism and colonialism.[347] Moreover, it is precisely the drive for accumulation that characterises capitalism and colonialism that lies close to the heart of our current ecological crisis. Furthermore, it may, as John Milbank observes, be best to explain the enthusiasm for this "turn to nature" by relating it to the sorts of divisions that a capitalist social order secures and reproduces: "'Nature', like private life, is turned into the repository of what capitalism denies or relegates: community, mutuality, objective aesthetic value".[348] Marx notes this tension in *Grundrisse*, when he insists that Romanticism is part of the reaction to the bourgeois development of productive forces:

---

[345] Antonaccio (2015), especially 41-46.

[346] Throughout this chapter, I use the terms "objectivity" and "objectification". The first refers to the otherness and wholeness of nature as a basis of human life. The second refers to those processes of manipulation, control, transformation, etc. by which nature is transformed by human beings. Confusingly, the objectivity of nature is founded in nature-as-subject.

[347] Ruether (1981), 63.

[348] Milbank (1993), 7.

It is as ridiculous to yearn for a return to that original fullness [Marx is referring to the writings of certain Romantics] as it is to believe that with this complete emptiness history has come to a standstill. The bourgeois point of view has never advanced beyond this antithesis between itself and this romantic viewpoint and therefore the latter will accompany it as legitimate antithesis up to its blessed end.[349]

Such a tension between nature as objectified and nature as balm is of benefit to the current dominant social order. (For instance, it plainly has immediate connections with the patriarchal emphasis that associates men with rationality and women with embodiment, men with culture and women with nature.) A theology of technology for a postnatural condition that reproduced this dualism would then be precisely producing the intellectual conditions for the reproduction of the current hegemony. The turn to nature may appear as a way of grounding the interdependence of humans and non-human nature. Yet this turn to nature is precisely modern, and it is to this modern turn (particularly scientific investigation and the application of technology) that the contradictions of modernity may partly at least be traced.

Although the turn to nature as subject seems to be concerned with the conditions of nature-human relations, the difficulties of such an approach may be noted. First, the objectivity of nature was affirmed in the early modern period. Second, the notion of nature as objectified called forth a Romantic reaction. Nevertheless, both the domination of nature and its Romantic appropriation assume a basic humanity/nature dualism. A theology of technology that operates within this dualism is, arguably, caught in a difficulty. If the theological approach to nature is an appeal to nature as grounds for a new harmony, then some account needs to be given as to how this appeal to nature is not simply incorporated into the objectification of nature in science and technology. How is such an appeal to nature *not only* the Romantic repetition of the positing of nature as subject over against nature as object – *but also* its criticism? The issue that needs to be resolved at this point is the relation between nature as subject and the objectification of nature. If an appeal to the "resurrection of nature" is to be the basis of a theology of technology, this needs to be specified in order to avoid the incorporation of nature as subject by powerful forces governing the objectification of nature.

The turn to nature seems to be caught within the movement of the positing of objectivity in nature, and a subsequent Romantic reaction. Theology may then be tempted to invest its emancipatory interests in a fresh account of nature that is neither objectified nor a repository of that which capitalism devalues. One way of doing this is to suggest the "resurrection of nature". In other words, nature may escape its determination as object; it is not possible to "fix" nature in a subject-object schema. Here we have the suggestion of the revivification of nature as subject that insists upon a new form of living. Nature, the unconscious, and wilderness have

---
[349] Marx (1973), 162.

been offered as starting points in this kind of argument. Such a move attributes to nature a profound transformative power. It is, we might say, a de-colonising strategy: technology objectifies all things, leaving nothing unchanged. Are there any sites of resistance that have escaped such colonisation? If our response is no – not even nature, the unconscious, and wilderness serve as sites of resistance – is the claim of a resurrected nature of any merit?

Jürgen Habermas has suggested that the emphasis on the resurrection of nature is available in the work of Herbert Marcuse. According to Habermas,

> [For Marcuse] social emancipation could not be conceived without a complementary revolutionary transformation of science and technology themselves. In several passages Marcuse is tempted to pursue this idea of a new Science in connection with the promise, familiar in Jewish and protestant mysticism, of the "resurrection of fallen nature"." This theme, well-known for having penetrated into Schelling's and Baader's philosophy via Swabian pietism, returns in Marx's Paris Manuscripts, today constitutes the central thought of Bloch's philosophy ... .[350]

If followed through, this argument would suggest the possibility of a new science and technology. There would then be two types of science: the dark science of the rapacious forces of capitalism, and the redeemed science of critical theory. What is the result? According to Habermas, "the viewpoint of possible technical control would be replaced by one of preserving, fostering, and releasing the potentialities of nature: "there are two kinds of mastery: a repressive and a liberating one"".[351] Now Habermas insists that there is no alternative technology in this sense. The remainder of his argument is taken up by trying to show how Marcuse is correct in seeing that science and technology function as an ideology and have effectively depoliticised the public sphere, but also that there is no requirement for – indeed, no possibility of – a resurrected nature, a New Science and a New Technology.

We may use Habermas' critical discussion of Marcuse to highlight the difficulties in thinking in theological terms about a "resurrection of nature". If Habermas's reservations are correct, the notion of the resurrection of nature is questionable. Habermas and Marcuse, we might accept, are correct in their insistence that science and technology do not simply propose the benchmark of rationality in a scientific "world"; science and technology are also ideological. Political problems are transposed into scientific or technical problems, with the result that decisions about the shape and direction of human society – the work of the *polis* – cannot be made because they are not raised in political form.

If this is so, then the notion of the resurrection of nature suggests that what is required is a "new" nature; a nature that is outside culture and resources praxis against the dark forces of capitalism. Yet, for Habermas, this suggests that the only response to science and technology must come from outside the realm of human

---

[350] Habermas (1987), 85-6.
[351] Habermas (1987), 86-7.

practice, i.e. a utopianism. Tillich voices a similar concern in a comment on what he terms the utopian element in Marxism: "it looks forward to a miracle of nature that transforms human nature as well as non-human nature".[352] The resurrection of nature suggests the reconstitution of nature (including human nature) from "beyond" human practice: in short, a miracle. Put differently, the praxiological aspect of technology – that humans by technology transform their circumstances – and themselves – is here bypassed.

The difficulty with such a miracle is, as Gordon Kaufman and Sallie McFague have pointed out, that it can be construed as the invitation to human beings to wait upon a god with a particular form of miraculous power, rather than to assume responsibility for their own actions.[353] Habermas's concern with the Marcusean version of the resurrection of nature is that it distracts us from appreciating and engaging with our natural constitution, both as "given" and as extended by the (re)organisation of our powers in specific relations (including the practices of science and technology). The resurrection of nature is utopian, but in a bad sense. This option struggles to give an account of the reified and alienated technological practices of our present society and how nature is constructed through such practices. In a sense, this position naturalises society – and to overcome this naturalisation, calls for the resurrection of nature.

For my account of technology in a postnatural condition, the notion of wholeness presented in this section cannot, if the analysis of this section is correct, be accepted. Although there is a sense in which the resurrection of nature as a theological trope has an eschatological aspect yet the eschatological aspect does not emerge out of the social being of humanity-nature. It is rather the resurrection of nature from "outside" the greater society and not the fulfilment of nature in all its dimensions.

7.5 TECHNOLOGY AS TELEOLOGICAL

Now we arrive at the matter of world-relatedness in the perspective of technological activity. I have already noted that eschatological transformation will include the technological: that is, we should expect that technological activity might contribute to redemptive activity. (I shall return to this matter in the final section of this chapter.) Such an insistence that redemption does not strip the human of its technological attachments brings forward my insistence that in the discussion of postnatural right we are not dealing with the "naked human" and entanglement of many varieties is instead to be affirmed.

In a discussion of the theology of technology, there are nonetheless a number of ways of refusing such technological entanglement. One way is to understand technological activity as separate from spiritual activity. That is, we might under-

---

[352] Tillich (1977), 73.
[353] See Kaufman (1985); McFague (1987).

stand the human in and through the contrast between the spiritual and the material, the personal and the entangled. As I have put it elsewhere, on this view piety is opposed to technology.[354] Yet the discussions so far in my argument in connection with natural and postnatural orders render problematic such a duality. We need at this point only to recall the five dimensions presented by Tillich ranging from the inorganic to the historical to learn that it is not possible to separate out the material and the spiritual. As Tillich notes, the spiritual-community is dependent on the other dimensions and the human creature engages these other dimensions partly through technological activity. We are concerned with a postnatural order that is discovered, assimilated and constructed – and the constructive aspect relates closely to technological activity. We are brought thereby to the matter of contingency.

We are not able to address the issue of contingency without first undertaking a ground-clearing exercise with regard to technological determinism. In other words, it is easy to develop an argument based in technological determinism that obscures contingency and undercuts teleology (while appearing to secure it). Technological determinism is not a single thing but for present purposes it is sufficient to note two different understandings of such determinism. The first understands technological developments as emerging in an arbitrary fashion. Such developments have no anthropological basis or foundation. On this account, technology certainly creates worlds but without reference to any anthropological necessity. We might call this a strong determinism. The second understands technological development as related to anthropological interests. Technological change is contingent and yet its emergence is not properly understood as arbitrary. In other words, technological developments relate to stable human interests. We might call this a weak determinism.

From the perspective of acting postnaturally, neither of these approaches are satisfactory. Strong determinism seems to place technological activity outside of teleology. There seems to be no "direction" to technology and it cannot be thereby understood as being related to orderings-to. Weak determinism partially addresses this issue by firmly placing technological activity within a teleological account of human activity. Nonetheless, what additionally seems to be required to make this position operative is some settled account of the human and its needs. Yet, as chapters 3 and 6 have sought to argue through a steady critique of notions of a settled order, we should be cautious about such claims to stability. If these claims to a stable order are overstated, then they cannot be used to secure the teleological orientation of technological activity.

Nonetheless, if there is a link between technological activity and an ordination to the good, there must be some relation between a contingent technological order and teleology. The end of the present-and-future order must enjoy a relation to its

---

[354] Scott (2010a), 125-128.

technological frame. That is, although such an orientation to the good is eschatological, yet such a good cannot be only mystery but must relate, as we have seen, to this greater society. What sort of contingent order is this?

It has been my argument that the primary habit of thought that we must discard is to secure the (false and falsifying) stability of an order by reference to God. That is, God is not a stabilizing factor. The activity of the social God in the social life of creation is not opposed to contingency but instead works through such contingency. Such a contingent order is received from God and yet is reshaped through practical activity of the *anthropos*, including technological activity. How then does such contingent technological activity relate to the teleological? How does the world-relatedness of technological activity contribute to an ordination to the good? What, in sum, is technological activity *for*? I shall answer this question in three points.

First, as we have already noted in the discussion of GM foods in chapter 3, technological activity is unkind to kinds. In other words, in a postnatural condition we are not able to rely on the cutting of the world into kinds as a route for giving technological activity an orientation to the good. That is, the direction of technological activity is not given by a teleology of kinds as if we are able to say that the direction of technological activity is suggested by the ordering of kinds. There are kinds and they form an order but it is not true to say that such an order provides direction to technological activity. We may explore this issue by reference to the "big technology" of geoengineering. This technology is understood as "the deliberate large-scale manipulation of the planetary environment to counteract anthropogenic climate change".[355] Writing about geoengineering projects, Forrest Clingerman asks: "Is the concept of "geoengineering" a promise of redemption or a life out of balance?"[356] For Clingerman, the matter is ambiguous and no response one way or the other can be stipulated. This judgement suggests in turn that the actuality of climate change by itself is not a guide to technological action. In a situation where even the weather is hybrid, we cannot appeal to an order of kinds as guidance. To the extent that geoengineering appeals to a return or recovery of balance, thinking theologically in a postnatural condition will be very cautious. Despite the ecological extension of eschatology, the ordering of kinds offers no secure redemptive guidance, a conclusion reinforced by Sigurd Bergmann's judgement that attempts " … to achieve salvation through technological innovations" either achieve little or open ways to "violence and destruction".[357]

Second, does this conclusion suggest that there is no relation between technological activity and human ends? Put differently, the question, Who is technology for?, receives no clear answer. Certainly, it cannot be stated with confidence that

---

[355] Report of the Royal Society, *Geoengineering the Climate: Science, Governance and Uncertainty* (2009), quoted in Clingerman (2015), 180.
[356] Clingerman (2015), 190.
[357] Bergmann (2015), 115-37 (here 119).

technological activity is for humanity. We have seen this already in our discussion of order: is the task of technological activity the confirmation of existing orderings or also their alteration? Because of their constructive making of hybrids, teleological relations cannot be easily settled. How technology redeems cannot therefore be asserted as a set of given teleological relations.

Does this mean that the relation between technological activity and natural ends is arbitrary? In one sense, yes: as we have seen in the previous chapter, there is no natural order to act as a guide for technology and as we have seen in the discussion of nature there is no settled account of humanity that we may appeal to as a guide for our technology. What is required instead is the placing of technological activity in the postnatural context of social activity. We may note once more Demant's point of the different areas of activity in the human realm: the technical and the economic as well as family and culture. Whereas the economic and the technical may often have a moral priority – people must be fed and housed – yet culture and family have metaphysical priority. That is, in culture and family humans are their most spiritual. Neither culture nor family are removed from technology of course. Nonetheless, it is in these spiritual areas that the teleological dynamic of human living as integrative, creative and ecstatic is most fully displayed and considered.

Is this the denial of purposes or ends in nature? By no means. At this point, I would agree that two extremes discussed by Maria Antonaccio in understanding the aim of technological activity are ruled out. Antonaccio calls the extremes "universal nonhumanisation" and "universal humanisation". The first extreme – although Antonaccio does not put the matter this way – is the same as the death of the human for if the human cannot change its habitat using its tools, it does not survive. The second extreme identifies the domination of nature by the human. Antonaccio prefers a third option of "incomplete humanisation" and refers such incompleteness to maintaining the value of nature and noting double binds in our attempts at humanisation.

For my purposes, the crucial terms are once more integrative, creative and ecstatic. Such a direction is related to the purposes and ends in nature in a postnatural order. Yet, the integrative, creative and ecstatic direction is based in the five dimensions of the unity of life in which the five dimensions serve each other towards integration, creativity and ecstasy. The inorganic and the organic are potential in all activity. They are not surpassed through technological activity. To the extent that technological activity serves such integration, creativity and ecstasy in a concrete future such activity has eschatological significance. We recall again a point made at the beginning of this chapter: that the eschatological transformation and redemptive fulfilment identified here are always an ecological transformation and fulfilment. The concept of eschatology has already been extended ecologically in this postnatural argument: the human is always *anthropos in oikos*.

Third, consideration of the anthropological-eschatological dynamic of technology should also be referred to the matter of "institutional repetition". To comprehend this point, we may recall that relations between creatures are secured in and by institutions in the manner of repetition. The "institutional" aspect denotes stability and direction whereas "repetition" identifies openness. Such openness is, I proposed, nicely understood by reference to *addition*: new elements may be added to a postnatural, institutional order. A useful example of such a development is the addition of robots to what remain formally Fordist production lines.

It is in and through such institutional repetition that self-integration, self-creativity, and self-transcendence are secured. Through institutional processes of integration, novelty, and transcendence, institutions are saved into a more extensive and intensive sociability. Thus, while not quite arbitrary, these developments are contingent as they emerge in an order that is discovered, appropriated, and constructed. It is in this fashion that technology may be understood as redeeming as it contributes to a reflexive self-relatedness, an interactive unity, and a world-related greater society. This is an account of the future proffered by a redeeming technology in a postnatural condition.

7.6 CONCLUSION

This chapter brings to a close our discussion of technology. In my larger argument for postnatural right the consideration of technology is important for two reasons. Both reasons address the matter of technological change. First, as Brock argues, ethical enquiry should not be insulated from technological change and thereby overlook the ways in which technology is a cultural phenomenon with implications for forms of thought, including theology. Second, technology poses a difficulty for postnatural right: I have maintained throughout that right has an objective basis but how is that basis to be understood in the light of changes wrought to any social order by technology?

In chapter 4, attentive to the concepts of self-relatedness, unity, and world-relatedness, various meanings of technology were explored. In this chapter, our focus has been on redemption: in what ways does technology redeem? The concepts of self-relatedness, unity, and world-relatedness have remained central to this chapter's enquiry. Yet, instead of paying attention to the implications of technological activity for the postnatural condition we have paid attention to the eschatological rather than the anthropological significance of technological change. Behind this enquiry, traces of earlier sorties into concepts of nature and order are evident. If technology redeems, it cannot do so at the expense of a concept of complex nature nor by reference to a fixed order. If technology redeems, it cannot do so through its reversal by a concept of nature nor by the baptising of technological change. If technology redeems, it must do so by reference to a particular future.

My argument about redeeming technology is as follows. First, that the fulfilment of humanity is always the fulfilment of social creatures. Technology is to be judged by its contribution to the institutionality of creatures. The teleological direction of technology is given not by reference to some order but by efforts within institutions that are integrative, creative and ecstatic. Second, that there can be no sidestepping this affirmation by reference to a resurrection of a pristine nature. Only, third, in this fashion is technology to be understood as projecting an ecstatic order oriented towards God.

Such a conclusion suggests that technology cannot be discarded at the point of eschatological transition. As technological activity is central to human life, the final destiny of such activity is a mystery but also must be related to the technological life of humanity. Rahner's axiom that eschatological destiny is mystery and yet is related to the human and more-than-human is operative here. That suggests an openness to eschatological fulfilment: the destiny of animals – in all dimensions – is an active destiny of redistributive goodness. Traditional images of a post-mortem destiny may therefore require revision: images of a gloomy underworld, a rich garden, and a praising community will need to be supplemented by something more social. Nonetheless, the purpose of my argument is to show that what is required is new institutions if nature and freedom are to interact in a different way. This, to anticipate the argument of chapter 8, will be a deepening of liberty and not a restriction of it.[358]

This chapter ends the second part of this book. Through this part, we have been exploring how to act postnaturally by reference to nature, order and technology. In the next and final chapter, we explore more fully the concept that has been present through the enquiry so far: postnatural right. In other words, following on from the discussions of nature, order and technology, how is a right order of life to be more fully understood and achieved? That is a matter of postnatural right, and to this discussion we now turn.

---

[358] The majority report understands our present ecological difficulties to be leading to restrictions in human freedom. A minority report within the majority report, as in those who deny anthropogenic climate change, claims that there is not even a problem.

Part III

Re-founding Right

CHAPTER 8: POSTNATURAL RIGHT

8.1 REPRISE OF THE ARGUMENT

Through parts 1 and 2, I have been arguing that we need an account of "What is going on?" before we can answer the question as to "What is to be done?" I have developed a postnatural analysis to show what I consider is going on. In other words, an ethical proposal relates to an account of its context. This is hardly new: philosophies of nature such as deep ecology, social ecology, and socialist ecology attempt to characterise the present situation, often structured by reference to anthropocentrism vs ecocentrism perspectives, as well as provide proposals for ways forward. There are other examples I might cite: the land ethic and ecofeminism, for example, are no different in this respect. "What is going on?" is a foundational question for an ecological ethics.[359] The same applies to enquiries based in environmental ethics more narrowly conceived: in the second edition of his *Environmental Ethics*, after seeking to delimit his enquiry, Robin Attfield offers an account of possible sources – population, pollution, technology – of ecological problems that we may appreciate as a response to the question, "What is going on?"[360] In the foregoing, I have provided my own account of what is going on; right relates to what is going on, a postnatural order.

This chapter – the sole chapter of part 3 – brings my argument for postnatural right to a conclusion. At the beginning of this book, I argued that a theological ethics is required for a postnatural condition. I have sought to explicate this condition by reference to nature, order and technology. Each of these themes has been considered twice, by reference respectively to the trajectories of the social-institutional, the historical-teleological, and the anthropological-eschatological. The aim throughout has been to explore the transformative and institutional order in which we find ourselves that will serve for an account of postnatural right towards a right order of life. That is my answer to the question: "What is going on?" I will sketch a fuller account of postnatural right in the next two sections. For the remainder of this section, however, I shall reprise the argument so far.

My argument began in the doctrine of creation. A consideration of the doctrine of creation – *creatura* rather than *creatio* – permits a theological consideration of a right order of life. With its *extensive* reference, the doctrine of creation recommends that right be more widely grounded than only in the human (person). Hence, the trajectory of my argument has always been to consider life extensively by reference to a greater society of creatures, human and non-human. In

---

[359] I have taken these approaches from Scott (2003), and Jamieson (2001).
[360] Attfield (2014), 17-21.

other words, to consider the concept of right in a postnatural condition. Such right refers to a patterned or ordered basis: a *logos* or *ratio*, we might say. What is that pattern or order when traditional distinctions between humans and other animals and others are no longer convincing?

To respond to this question, the analysis in the preceding chapters moved in two steps. First, there was an exploration of the three themes of nature, order and technology as reinterpreted for a postnatural condition as social, historical and anthropological. Second, the themes of nature, order and technology were explored in a more constructive manner to discern nature as institutional, order as teleological and technology as eschatological. A brief recap of this analysis now follows.

In the first part of the consideration of *nature* I reprised an earlier argument of mine that human-nature relations are best understood by reference to sociality and the concept of a greater society. In a postnatural condition, I argued, it no longer makes sense – if it ever did – to operate with a contrast between nature and humanity. This is not strictly to refuse a notion of natural givenness; as was noted later, an order is *discovered* as well as appropriated and constructed. It does mean, however, that a more sophisticated appreciation of nature is required. In the second part of the consideration of *nature*, I attempted such an appreciation: how might the re-institutionalisation of nature contribute to the emergence of the good and identify the modes of participation between the human and the non-human? Through the example of Ecosystem Services in the UK, we considered the institutionality of postnatural good as it emerged in public and private and considered a need for a new institution – based in institutional vision – informed by the postnatural condition.

In the first part of the consideration of *order*, I queried the term "natural order" without refusing a sense in which nature is other. That is, what can be made of the phrase "natural order" if nature underlies, and does not contrast with, the human? Developing the notion of institutional repetition, I argued that particular and generic ends converge in such repetition that may lead to the proliferation of ends. In such fashion, a postnatural order is not invested in a natural structure but nonetheless enjoys a certain stability. Order is historical but it is not *only* historical; such was my argument in chapter 3. In the second part of the consideration of *order*, I argued that we might on postnatural grounds, following Tillich, interpret the order of life by reference to its multi-dimensionality. Moreover, I argued that such a unity is teleological in two senses: as directed towards a supernatural end and as directed towards securing the unity of life in its multi-dimensionality.

In the first part of the consideration of *technology*, by reference to the term "anthropological" I set out the significance of technology. Technology is not to be restricted to artefacts but also has impacts on how we understand ourselves, the non-human and practical activity. We cannot think accurately and persuasively about order and nature without also considering the change secured in and by technological activity. In the second part of the consideration of *technology*, certain claims regarding salvation often associated with technology were treated cautiously as was the claim to a resurrection of nature in response to technological pressures. Instead, drawing on a recommendation by Rahner regarding eschatological thinking, eschatological fulfilment and transformation encompasses the technological also. We are concerned then with integration, creativity and ecstasy in relation to technological activity.

We have thereby consistently been taking two steps. First, with reference to nature, order and technology, to characterise the postnatural situation that western humanity now finds itself in. Second, to explore how this dynamic, postnatural order might be lived in, so to speak. In these two steps, we have been addressing how we shall, in a theological thought, understand a right order of life as discovered, appropriated and constructed. That is, we have throughout been interacting with postnatural right: from a universal, necessary, social, revolutionary and ideal perspective, we have been exploring the realisation of a right order of life by reference to relations of right.

In this final chapter, I set out more fully the contours of postnatural right. As human beings struggle to create a right order of life, postnatural right offers a theological-ethical approach: an orientation that invests in an account of order that is neither natural nor static but is always postnatural and technologically dynamic. Thereby, postnatural right offers ethical guidance in a situation where order cannot only be discovered. The blurring of the boundary between nature and humanity, and technological change, ensures that an order of life is not only discovered but constructed and appropriated also. To secure a right order of life means therefore to be orientated by postnatural right: a universal, necessary, social, revolutionary, and ideal ethic. Postnatural right is rooted in an order of life and offers normative judgements towards a right order of life. Right relates to life; life is de-restricted and encompasses the shared order of the human animal-other animal-and-inorganic life in three modes: *in*, *beyond*, and *for*. In these three modes of *participation*, humans and non-humans indwell each other, exceed one another, and are oriented on one another. Institutions configure these modes of participation. For such a perspective, it is clear that the moral aims for society cannot stand alone: ethical theory and social form accompany one another.[361]

The pale outline of postnatural right, as actuality and concept, hoves out of the mist. Postnatural right stresses the interaction between humanity and nature as social and privileges the ways in which these encounters occur in institutions. Additionally, postnatural right is historical and teleological in specific ways. Right does not comprise a set of invariant principles but may through historical development acquire additional ends. As teleological, postnatural right understands the good as emerging historically but may not be definitively achieved. Furthermore,

---

[361] For copious evidence, see MacIntyre (2007).

right relates to the anthropological aspect of a transforming technology and tests a commitment to eschatological fulfilment. Postnatural right is concerned with the realisation of freedom – a social freedom that incorporates and affects nonhuman others and takes place in an ecological context.

8.2 RIGHT

For a term as complex as "right", a settled meaning should not be expected. Difficulties in interpretation are to be expected therefore. An interesting example of difficulty in interpretation may be seen in Leo Strauss's *Natural Right and History*. Consider the following remark by Strauss: "It is granted on all sides that there cannot be natural right if the principles of right are not unchangeable".[362] We may immediately appreciate that such a judgement is doubtful. It fits well with the claims made by some natural law theorists who maintain that the aim of such law is pre-conventional and a-temporal comprehensiveness. Yet we also noted the claim by d'Entrèves, discussed in chapter 3, that such an approach is – at the very least – open to question. Let us take another text: Ernst Bloch's *Natural Law and Human Dignity*.[363] Translated from the German, we may note that the title in German begins "Naturrecht". "Natural law" is an accurate translation of the German – I am not disputing that. Nonetheless, in the choice by the translator of "law" over "right" certain associations are invoked. Indeed, given Bloch's sustained effort to offer a very different account of law, reinterpreted in relation to certain Hebraic commitments, avoiding the term "law" might have been wiser. Given such hermeneutical difficulties, how shall we proceed?

At this point, I need to distinguish my concept of postnatural right from the notion of right as it has emerged powerfully in post-Hobbesian political theory, with its deep impact on Anglophone political philosophy. Previously, I have argued that Hobbes' position on right is not best understood as the continuation of the medieval natural law traditions.[364] Instead, the contrast that Hobbes draws between right and law (*Leviathan* XIV, 1, 3)[365] is one in which right is understood as the liberty – as Hobbes puts it – to do or not do. *Ius* loses its reference to a just situation and is transposed into a sort of power – for Hobbes, the power of individual liberty. Clearly, such an account of right – with its failure to identify and operate from an external situation – is heading in a different direction than the one proposed here with its stress on an external reference to society. Against Hobbes' voluntarist construction of the rule of a "sovereign" in which the human gives up natural right, I maintain a sense in which the human – as a creature with other creatures in a greater society – never gives up postnatural right.

---

[362] Strauss (1953), 97.
[363] Bloch (1986).
[364] Scott (2011a), 57-75 (here 62-67).
[365] Hobbes (1994).

The German tradition is quite different from the English. How then should we translate Kant's never plural *recht* (an equivalent to the Latin *ius*)? It is not a moral or legal claim of a particular person or group of persons to a particular benefit or cluster of benefits. Instead, "rather like a mass term, it connotes a total situation of external lawfulness (as contrasted with inner morality)".[366] According to Guyer, it should not be translated as justice as this term has a "compensatory or punitive connotation" in English. Moreover, Guyer concludes that "Kant's concept of right does not straightforwardly correspond to any single concept in traditional British political philosophy".[367] We have seen this before: in my argument postnatural right is not founded on a concept of lawfulness but instead in the actuality of a greater society (and its transcendental underpinning).

What, then, is right? Translating the German *Recht*, Latin *ius*, and French *droit*, right identifies a circumstance of external order or lawfulness, as we have just noted. As such, right keeps company with law (but not laws, *Gesetz*, *lex*, *loi*,) and justice (although not in a judicial sense). Right is not here concerned with entitlement claims, moral or legal, made by a person or persons; right is to be distinguished from rights.[368] As we shall see shortly, my use of the term right depends more on German than Anglophone traditions. In what follows, therefore, I shall draw on Hegel's *Philosophy of Right*.

Hegel's own technical presentation of right – which in its voluntarism owes something to Rousseau and which he distinguishes from Kant's definition – is somewhat forbidding: "*Right* is any existence in general which is the *existence* of the *free will*. Right is therefore in general freedom, as Idea" (PR §29).[369] Right refers us, as Allen Wood notes, to the objectivity of freedom, the will as "*external existence*" (PR §26): "A right is a thing in which the free will has successfully ac-tualised itself or accomplished its ends."[370] Yet we should note immediately, with Richard Dien Winfield, the structural implications of this notion of freedom for an account of justice: "What immediately sets Hegel's philosophy of right apart is that it is devoted to establishing and determining justice as freedom, not by postulating freedom as the prior principle of justice, but by developing the struc-tures of justice themselves as the constitutive reality of freedom."[371] In my terms, the constitutive reality of freedom is social-institutional. We are speaking, to bor-

---

[366] See Kersting (1992), 364, footnote 1 (by Paul Guyer).

[367] Kersting (1992), 365, footnote 1, citing Guyer.

[368] I shall not explore the relation between right and rights, which is a complicated matter. In a com-prehensive treatment, the difference between natural right(s), moral right(s) and legal right(s) would need discussion; as would an account of "representation" operative in this discourse, es-pecially the matter of self-representation and other-representation (are rights about securing my interests or the security of a shared domain?).

[369] Hegel (1991).

[370] Wood (2010), 72.

[371] Ritter (1982), translator's introduction by Richard Dien Winfield, 2.

row Frederick Neuhouser's term, of "social freedom".[372] Such social freedom can be realised only within institutions and these must be organisations that can be judged as ethical – that is contributing to postnatural sociability – and in which both humanity and nature may flourish towards a right order of life.

Moreover, as Idea, freedom depends upon a larger context for its full reality – that is what the identification of freedom as *Idea* means. I have been arguing that human freedom will require an interaction with nature as part of that larger context. In other words, the context in which freedom is actualised exceeds the human. On this last point, Hegel would not have agreed. In *Lectures on Natural Right and Political Science [The First Philosophy of Right]*, he argued:

The sphere of right is not the soil of nature – certainly not of external nature, but also not of subjective human nature, insofar as human will, determined by human nature, is in the sphere of natural needs and instincts. On the contrary, the sphere of right is the spiritual sphere, the *sphere of freedom*. It is true that nature also has a place in the realm of freedom, to the extent that the idea of freedom expresses itself and gives itself existence, but freedom remains the foundation, and nature only enters in as something dependent. (NRPS §2)

The contrast that Hegel makes between the human and nature is not uncommon. In secular and religious ethics in general, there persists a difficulty in granting moral considerability to the non-human – in granting moral status to nature. In this book, with no little irony then, I follow an Hegelian clue: humans act ethically – and learn to act ethically – through participation in institutions under the guidance of an institutional vision. This participation in institutions has subjective and objective dimensions, in which individuals find fulfilment and are constructed in and through their participation – see 8.4 for a discussion of this point. Is it possible, then, to develop institutions for humans *and other creatures* in which creatures might encounter each other and act in mutual support? In other words, the search for human freedom reaches a new issue: encounters with the non-human. Freedom can no longer mean human development without paying attention to the ways in which human beings transform their contexts, especially in their use of non-renewable resources, which are also contexts *for other creatures*. Hence my neologism, postnatural. Although the reduction of authority and the increase of liberty remain the aim these must be thought and practised differently. Moreover, as already argued, such institutional or discovered participation will involve the appropriation and construction of a social order, a shared greater society. Additionally, I have argued that construction is partly achieved through technological activity and its interpretation as redemptive.

Therefore, although I affirm the centrality of human freedom for an account of right, I disagree with Hegel that such freedom is to be understood as a strong contrast with non-human nature. This freedom must be a social freedom that en-

---

[372] Neuhouser (2003).

compasses more than the human. We may therefore agree with Hegel's critique of Kant: freedom cannot be abstract self-determination. Yet we cannot fully agree with Hegel, because freedom will have to be reconfigured in a postnatural direction. That is, how we think about freedom will need to be governed by the universal sociality of right: that freedom in a greater society encompasses more than the human. Right is universal and as such the order it relates to is not restricted to the human. Moreover, we have hardly begun to develop postnatural institutions that acknowledge that humans are in coalition with animals and other creatures. The reference by postnatural right to technology ensures that institutions cannot be considered conservatively as if found in an order beyond change. Institutional action is teleological and eschatological: it incorporates natural action and is concerned with redemptive practices.

Clearly, mine is an uncommon meaning of right, and it is not the way we employ the term in ordinary use. We would not normally speak of, say, an institution in terms of right. We would more usually speak of a "right *to . . .* " or of "an action being right in the sense of just".[373] Nonetheless, in what follows my usage is closer to Hegel's: right refers to the realisation of freedom, of a greater – that is, societal – freedom, to – as Hegel says – freedom as Idea.

By "right", then, I mean the attempt to identify the external moral situation of creatures: to indicate the moral situatedness of the human with other creatures – the inorganic as well as the organic – as the location of the realisation of freedom. *Pace* Hobbes, right insists that there are moral considerations that exceed positive law, especially the sourcing of the law in the sovereign will. Right – this is my argument – is founded in sociality; as a concept of both being and act, sociality encompasses both rule and right, both *norma agendi* and *facultas agendi*, both objective and subjective right.[374] As we have seen, Hobbes sunders such a correlation between a rule of action and a right to act. Postnatural right assumes the correlation and develops it "socially", by reference to a greater society.

Right is thereby a normative proposal that seeks to offer some repair work regarding ethical theory and yet preserves the will-based mediations of the human. To work with the Idea of freedom in a postnatural condition means to consider wider and wider contexts in which human freedom is operative. One of these contexts is nature. With its technological attachments, the human is already interacting in freeing and oppressive ways with other creatures. Humanity-nature is an event of intersubjective encounters, of mutual discovery by reference to the otherness of nature. Yet this otherness is only encountered in the publicness of institutional mediation. This otherness is therefore constructed and overcome in practices. If we are to speak of the common good with reference to humanity-nature, here is the source of such speech.[375]

---

[373] Wood (2010), 72.

[374] D'Entrèves (1951), 59-60.

[375] Additionally, contemporary western societies are not marked by the thick moral experience that

The overall aim of my argument has been the recovery of the full dimensions of right: as social, historical, and anthropological – and thereby as postnatural. In order to develop my analysis, I have proposed that What-is-going-on? may be understood in three ways: as social-institutional; as historical-teleological; and as anthropological-eschatological. That is, the institutional order of freedom may be understood as extending freedom in ambiguous ways that may be corrected to-wards a postnatural order that is oriented on an eschatological good. Freedom is thereby never freedom in the abstract: it is infrastructure as justice that emerges in and through "historical" activity. Right is the criticism of social arrangements that are not regarded as universal, necessary, social, revolutionary and ideal. In other words, postnatural right tests the present towards the realisation of justice by stressing its universal remit, that it invokes the necessary or ecological aspects of creaturely life, insists that life is social, offers a revolutionary criticism of hier-archy and operates from an ideal. Right is antagonistic ethics.

8.3 THE CONCEPT OF ABSTRACT RIGHT IN HEGEL'S *Philosophy of Right*

Philosophy of Right makes an important contribution to this enquiry because Hegel's argument marks a significant break in the tradition of thinking about right presented by Kant and Fichte. For both Kant and Fichte, although differently, the beginning of thinking about right is rational: for Kant, the rational apprehension of the individual's duty; and for Fichte, the self-conscious awareness of the freedom of the acting individual.

What is the basis of the link between right and ethics? In *Fichte's Ethical Thought*, Allen W. Wood argues that for Fichte and Kant right and morality are separate.[376] This is strongly the case for Fichte, Wood argues, in that right and morality are based in two different systems. For Kant, the concept of obligation is borrowed by right from ethics, which means there are not two systems but one; nonetheless right and morality are separate. With Hegel, the picture changes and right is historicised: beginning from the abstract will leads immediately to the consideration of how freedom is instantiated in society – and so to private prop-erty. The epicentre of Hegel's understanding of right is freedom thereby. Hegel locates his argument within a European philosophical tradition that understands freedom as the freedom of the human will (*PR* §33).[377] Yet this human willing has a number of stages, objective and subjective, through which it develops. Ba-

---

Hegel assumes. This new development must also be faced by a theology of postnatural right. Part of my argument in volume 3 of this work is that the fragmentation in moral ethos can in fact be supplemented by attention to the intersubjective encounters of humanity-nature towards a renewed moral culture.

[376] Wood (2016), 256-259.

[377] Neuhouser (2003) instructively compares Hegel's position to that of Rousseau.

sic to Hegel's argument is that, although the will freely wills itself, yet it requires instantiation. The first instantiation is objective yet abstractly so: private property.

As Alan Patten points out, Hegel is here adopting a traditional argument: that private ownership is intrinsic to the exercise of human freedom. At an intuitive level, this has some plausibility: I need some means to exercise my freedom and these means secure non-interference from others. Private property secures such means. Additionally, Patten points out that private property, it may be argued, contributes to the stability of a society by requiring that the liberties of private property owners be protected. However, Patten argues that neither of these accounts is central to Hegel's argument in favour of private property. What *is* central, so Patten argues, is a "developmental thesis": that through private property I secure the objectification of my personality; through such Abstract Right, my free personality is secured.[378] The bare will, understood as subjective and arbitrary, and so as formal, is "infinite, universal and free" (PR §35) and attains objectivity by posting a reality or existence to Personality as other (PR §39) in the immediacy of possession or, as Hegel concludes, as property. It follows from this, Hegel argues, that included with this Abstract Right is contract – that is, how property owners relate to each other – and then the difficulties in such relating (wrong and crime) (PR §40).

Whether or not Hegel provides good reasons for considering the individual person as a willing I over against external nature we might debate.[379] Certainly, his arguments function to reconcile the reader to private property, arguably a vital institution of capitalist society. Famously, Karl Marx will later complain about the artificiality of this approach.[380] For now, however, I want to concentrate on the ways in which Hegel's argument permits the drawing of a strong contrast between the human and the non-human. For example, Hegel deploys the concept of the will to note the way in which the human transcends its body. Although he concedes that the person is "*alive* in this *organic body*", nonetheless we each possess our life and body only in so far as it is willed by each of us (PR §47). Alternatively, as Hegel also puts it: "I have these limbs and my life only in so far as I so will it; the animal cannot mutilate or destroy itself, but the human being can" (PR §47). Which in turn permits the drawing of the human/non-human contrast: "Animals are indeed in possession of themselves: their soul is in possession of their body. But they have no right to their life, because they do not will it" (PR §47A).

If the human has a right to her life, may she also alienate it? No, argues Hegel – conveniently enough, we might think – because life is not external to personality but is rather this personality (PR §70). Yet we might conclude that this is a rather strained argument turning upon a distinction between possession and ownership. It would presumably be possible to begin with what joins the human animal with

---

[378] Patten (1999), 140.

[379] See Hardimon (1994).

[380] Marx (1975), 243-257 (here 250).

other animals: that we find ourselves alive, in possession of ourselves, so to speak. It might be relevant to adduce empirical data at this point: a bear caught in a trap will gnaw off its leg and so mutilate itself. It has an ability to distance itself from itself. However, perhaps it is better simply to note at this stage that there will be difficulties in approaching non-human nature if we begin from the will, and Hegel helpfully if accidentally draws our attention to these. This means in turn that it will be difficult to think about institutions of human-animal co-habitation. Whether Hegel's argument in favour of private property is successful is doubtful therefore. However, that is not what most concerns my analysis at this point. For the present, I wish to note two matters.

First, that Hegel sets aside, as Joachim Ritter notes, the "social problem of property".[381] By grounding the issue of property in the development of free personality, Hegel sets aside the issue of the distribution of property in this present stage of the development of the Idea of freedom. Hegel claims that Abstract Right does not include a right of equality of ownership. Such claims to equality fail to take into account the "external contingency of nature" and the "infinite particularity" of spirit – by which we should understand human nature. Moreover, we should not appeal to nature at this point, Hegel argues, to ground an argument for equal distribution (fair shares for all!) as nature is not free and so is neither just nor unjust (PR §49). That is, the social-institutional context of this account of Abstract Right is set aside. This has consequences for our understanding of right. To develop Allen Wood's argument, Hegel's argument regarding private property not only has to show that "*in its actual consequences* this institution is compatible with a social order in which the status of a free person is not a mere sham for many members of society"[382], but also that such private property preserves and grants equitable access to nature's goods.

Second, Hegel's argument turns upon a particular interpretation that, in the encounter of the free personality in private property, we have the liberation of the human from nature that is, in turn, predicated upon the de-sacralisation of nature. Put in different terms, we have the affirmation of progress and the denial of the powers of nature. In the intervening period, neither of these assertions has gone unchallenged. In postnatural perspective, it is clearer that although through our machines there is an ever-increasing possibility of the manipulation of nature, the latter is not merely passive and instead engages human beings through a range of feedback mechanisms. Hegel is not wrong about this: claims of an Anthropocene are evidence of human success in this sphere but this liberation is not unambiguous. As I argued in chapter 3, Hegel's position undercuts natural law's construal of "nature" but nonetheless brings its own ambiguities. There is no liberation *from*

---

[381] Ritter (1982), 125.
[382] Wood (2010), 107.

nature – and it is difficult to establish with any confidence a different preposition.[383]

In earlier work, and searching for the correct preposition, I have considered the phrase "liberation *into*" – but that seems to invite a kind of immersion into nature. We need something like a liberation *alongside* nature that can be thought out by reference to the doctrine of creation. Additionally, in order to respect the continuing powers of nature, and their importance in the support and nurture of human beings in their habitat, we shall need to explore the matter of human beings recognizing themselves in nature. In other words, that human freedom is not a matter of alienation in which the free personality achieves important "objectivity" through private property. Instead, what is required is the acknowledgement that the human person is given or receives a certain sustaining "objectivity" from the universality of nature. I refer here to the air we breathe, the turning of day and night, and the autopoeitic processes that sustain us. These are indeed universal, in the sense with which Hegel speaks of the Abstract Right of property, and are central to the dignity of human beings. Yet these are also necessary, particular, and mediated in part by institutions. Nonetheless, this postnatural right seems to fit uneasily in Hegel's schema. For what has such postnatural right to do with the freedom of the will?

I want to argue, first, that nature can embody the self-determination of the human will, but that is not to say that the realisation of freedom is achieved in any straightforward sense. Nature is not passive; it does not *receive* the will; it may also be subject to processes of reification. I have tried to capture some of this by the development of a social-institutional framework for the consideration of nature. Second, nature has a certain (teleological) independence and cannot be understood simply as that which is other, as reified; it is other as beyond the human.[384]

In the first sense, nature is particular; in the second sense, nature is universal. Nature may, concretely, be moved between these senses in practice. The practical liberation of humanity from nature can therefore not be asserted as an historical *achievement*. *Philosophy of Right* §52 is crucial here: Hegel distinguishes between taking control and possession of the variety of natural objects and references taking a breath of air and a drink of water. This he contrasts with matter, which has a determinate form by which the person can take possession: in property, "the actuality of taking possession" is secured by the free will.

This seems a curious contrast at first glance. Of course, not all air and all water can be appropriated by human beings. However, that should make us cautious about the claim to securing exclusive possession to land. Moreover, just because it is not possible to appropriate all air or all water does not mean that proximate

---

[383] See Ritter (1982), 12.

[384] I am drawing here on a distinction Hegel makes between *Sache* and *Ding*: see translator's introduction to Ritter (1982), x.

sources of water or air cannot be tainted or spoiled. What Hegel calls the indi-
vidualizing of the elemental does not mean that the elemental cannot be spoiled.
Indeed, there might be an argument for holding the elemental as some form of
collective or common property precisely because the elemental *can* be spoiled.
We need to recover a concept of the thing that is not to be contrasted with the
person – that is, that does not simply receive the human will and thereby does not
simply function as a passive contrast to the human. What Hegel offers us is an
anthropocentric and de-mythologised version of Adam's naming of the animals.
We need a different sort of contrast between human/nature that includes the contrast person/thing but also includes both mutuality and reciprocity as well as the
alterity of nature. Thus, we need a concept of nature that receives the human will –
but not abstractly? – but also understands humanity and nature as co-inhabitants,
and nature as other, as subsisting, as independent. Freedom must incorporate these
aspects if a comprehensive account of right – postnatural right – is to be achieved.
The concept of institution is clearly vital to this part of my argument.

There are further difficulties in Hegel's approach. Beginning from Abstract Right – as Hegel calls it – validates private property and asserts the de-
sacralisation of nature; it is not clear how human freedom relates to nature. Also,
there is no agreement in Hegel studies whether what we are being offered is an
historical argument, a metaphysical argument, or an actualisation argument.[385] In
other words, are we supposed to read the *Philosophy of Right* as proposing an historical argument in which western institutions are steadily extending freedom as
part of an immanent development? Alternatively, are we being offered an account
with transcendent reference in which the divine Spirit seeks to actualise itself
directly, or through human freedom, in human life and institutions? Or, finally,
is Hegel's position best understood as an account of the actualisation of human
freedom that is dependent neither upon an historical nor a metaphysical narrative
but upon a human capacity for self-actualisation? As we enter this critical discussion, I shall continue to work with the trajectories of the social-institutional, the
historical-teleological, and the anthropological-eschatological.

It will be obvious that I am defending an account of the externality of right.
Yet, we may appreciate through this discussion of Hegel on Abstract Right that I
am concerned to develop an account based in the sociality of humanity and nature:
nature is not passive, is independent, and yet is for humanity. I have argued that
such interactivity is enacted in institutions of a greater society. Reference to will
and freedom refers us in turn to the anthropological and to praxis. Yet, as reference
to the social-institutional commends, this is no abstract praxis. What is important
is not to push the issue into some noumenal sphere and thereby to argue that the
interaction between the human and animal was once harmonious and might be
so once more. In the meantime, thereby, humans will act as if such harmony is

---

[385] Patten (1999), chapter 1.

not available: presently lost, and to be restored only by divine agency. This would be a deferred eschatology, of the type criticised by Gordon Kaufman and Sallie McFague and discussed in chapter 7 with reference to the miraculous.[386] Instead, what must be developed here is some account of postnatural – that is, mutual – interaction. For there to be the realisation of creaturely freedom, there will need to be productive *activity* – habitats are always transformed, as we have seen – but also an *acknowledgement* of ecological necessity.[387] Creaturely labour is always located labour; (re)production is always co-production.

In these remarks, I am trying to elucidate the basis of such a claim. This elucidation is important in that I am not arguing from the "fact" of the institutions of present societies. For I am not arguing either for the superior privilege of current arrangements or that truly postnatural institutions are presently to be found everywhere. Although postnatural right defeats historicism, it does not follow that certain institutions are to be deduced from it. The historical-teleological trajectory requires attention to the ideality of an open future. Mine is therefore not a project of reconciliation, in Hardimon's sense,[388] and I am not concerned to defend Hegel's organicism, as Alison Stone suggests we might.[389] Given the ambiguity of the concept of nature, presented most fully in chapter 2, I am not sure what overcoming alienation from nature might mean and nor whether we can be fully "at home" in institutions, even postnatural institutions.

8.4 SOCIAL FREEDOM

If Abstract Right directs us to the consideration of personal freedom, my emphasis on institutions raises the matter of social freedom. In this section, I seek to enlarge some of the discussion of chapter 5 where the focus was on the institution of Ecosystem Services. Yet the ethical demand of postnatural right is to enquire after the justification of institutions. Postnatural right provides criteria of evaluation. Moreover, to discuss institutions of a greater society raises the issue of how social freedom is to be considered in a postnatural context: what normative difference the greater extension of society makes to the present enquiry. Once more, we shall be following Hegel's *Philosophy of Right*. In that the present discussion encroaches on an enquiry into freedom and/in nature reserved for volume 2 of the present series, we shall not proceed too far, however. Nonetheless, some account of social freedom is required for we need a glimpse of how freedom is realised in postnatural institutions in ways that are constituted by encounter with the nonhuman.

---

[386] Kaufman, *Theology for a Nuclear Age* (1985); McFague (1987).

[387] Pannenberg (1981), 53.

[388] Hardimon (1994), 95. I have developed a theological account of being at home in this *oikos* in Scott (2015b), 155-167; and Scott (2014b), 115-135.

[389] Stone (2014), 105-122 (here 106).

We may approach this issue by recalling a reservation I offered in chapter 5 regarding the terminology of institution as this applies to nature. There I argued that despite the soundness of the argument for the incorporation of nature into a greater society, the warrant for making the same incorporative act regarding institutions seemed less secure. By way of conclusion, I suggested that it overstepped an epistemic limit to describe nature, at whatever scale and perspective, as an institution. I did not conclude from that, however, that nature was not present in institutions – emphatically it is, constitutively – nor that the presence of nature in institutions made no normative difference. Indeed, I hold that the social encompasses humanity and nature and thereby the institutional, whatever restrictions are in place regarding the use of this terminology, includes nature too. Moreover, such institutional inclusion makes a difference to ethical enquiry. At issue here is the nature of an institution and its relation to free will and the realisation of freedom. In this section, I explore this issue.

In the third part of *Philosophy of Right*, titled Ethical Life, Hegel discusses the social institutions of family, civil society and the state (PR §142 to the end). Hegel insists that freedom of the will is constitutive of Ethical Life.[390] As Stone puts it, for Hegel "individuals are free, or have free will".[391] Yet, that means the argument for postnatural right now finds itself in difficulty: we must think across Jameson's rift to consider how postnatural institutions encompass humanity and nature and yet are to be traced to the human self-determining will. If we are successful, we shall also have established the normative difference that a greater society makes. For we shall have established how an institution is founded in human willing but the ethical account of that willing is altered by its postnatural quality – that is, by human-nature encounters.

In chapter 5, I have already commented in a discussion of institutions in a postnatural condition that we need not be so restricted as to operate only on a society-wide scale. If nature is present to all human activities, we should expect to find many institutions, at a range of scales, featuring an encounter of nature and humanity. Relations of right need not be restricted to a handful of social institutions. In chapter 1, I called this a "plurality of social orders"; we might speak in addition of a "plurality of institutions". Such a plurality might encompass different scales: a zoo, a broiler chicken facility, and climate change operate at different scales but may be identified as institutions; moreover, they also overlap. We have additional criteria from chapter 5 for identifying an institution. Membership, as you recall, was one of these. To help us, we also have normative criteria, developed in my interpretation of postnatural right: universal, necessary, social, revolutionary and ideal. It is in and through institutions that we secure the realisation of freedom – that is, human freedom. So our concern is not to justify certain institu-

---

[390] Neuhouser (2003), 52.
[391] Stone (2014), 106.

tions but rather to indicate how the criteria work in securing a right order of life for an extensive membership that includes the non-human. What is a good social institution in a postnatural condition?

Following Neuhouser, we may pick up this discussion by noting the subjective and objective aspects of social freedom. If for Hegel the bare definition of freedom is "being-with-oneself-in-another", the sort of freedom that Hegel identifies as social is practical. It refers to freedom of the will and its real instantiation in a world; its aim, as we have seen, is related to reconciliation. Here I shall briefly explore what, in Neuhouser's interpretation, Hegel means by objective and subjective with reference to freedom, and the implications of this line of thought when considered from the five dimensions of postnatural right.

I begin by recalling the importance of freedom of the will. Back in chapter 5 I expressed a reservation about referring the terminology of institution to nature in that nature does not seem to have the requisite freedom for the description of nature-as-institution to be intelligible. It does not follow that nature is not present in institutions and cannot be encountered in institutions. It means instead that institutions cannot be the organised expression of nature for nature is not free in the required sense. A different way of putting this matter would be to draw on the contrast between the holistic and the individualistic, as proposed by Campbell.[392] In the contrast between the whole of society and the individual, the greater society proposes a postnatural holism: the meaning of society is extended to encompass nature; a greater society has a combinatory function. In the consideration of institutions, however, such holism is inappropriate – for reasons elaborated earlier in this section. Instead, we must take up a theme introduced in chapter 3 in which we noted that it is possible to see the "individual" as a social whole. On that holistic interpretation, the individual is the source of the willing of institutions. If we follow Hegel a little further in the distinction between objective freedom and subjective freedom, we shall see that this conclusion is not as momentous as first appears.

For Neuhouser, Hegel makes an important distinction between objective and subjective freedom. Here is Neuhouser's preliminary account of the difference: "The former he [Hegel] equates with the "laws and institutions of the rational social order... ; the latter is said to consist in the frame of mind, or "disposition" of individual social members".[393] The point here being, as I understand it, that if institutions are vehicles for the realisation of freedom that realisation must be *both* freeing for the individual *and* freely undertaken. If the direction is "being-with-oneself-in-another", then it should be possible to demonstrate that an institution makes an objective contribution to that aim and that the individual can appreciate said contribution from the perspective of the individual's own willing.

---

[392] Campbell (1991), 36-38.
[393] Neuhouser (2003), 53.

As will be evident, developing this line of enquiry in a postnatural condition raises a difficult issue. That is, "being-with-oneself-in-another" is articulated while open to the possibility that the other is a non-human other. That is, the realisation of freedom in postnatural institutions is not only an intrahuman matter. It is true that from the perspective of nature there is no "being-with-oneself-in-another"; this Hegelian definition of freedom does not apply to nature's powers, actions and agencies. However, that does not exclude the institutional presence of nature in freedom's realisation. Neuhouser argues that "objective" means for Hegel the reality or truth of existence in the external world, independently of any consciousness; in this account of the independence of institutions, nature, as the argument of chapters 2 and 5 has commended, is included. Indeed, this point about the independence of nature is fully in line with the argument of the otherness of nature, in one of its meanings, advanced in chapter 2. What more can be said about the objective aspect?

Institutions as the sites of objective realisation are, in this interpretation, objective embodiments of freedom. As such, "they realize a kind of freedom independently of whatever subjective relation (such as affirmation, rejection, or indifference) social members might have to their laws and institutions."[394] Objective conditions are required to make freedom possible and social institutions provide these conditions. Further, in a postnatural condition, there is no prospect of a free life except through the stability and support of non-human resources. Indeed, we noted in chapter 6 that a postnatural order has the features of self-integration, creativity and self-transcendence. Consistent with this, postnatural institutions need to provide these as conditions of the free fulfilment of human creatures. That is, the postnatural encounters of institutions exhibit the characteristics of life: integration, creativity, and self-transcendence. It may easily be appreciated that the institution of Ecosystem Services is one in which a certain sort of integration is being pressed upon the non-human, its creativity is being administered and its self-transcendence little thought of (referred to as infinity). As such, this is not a right-ful institution. Or, put differently, we might say that the institutional vision of such an institution should encompass the flourishing of all members of the institution, as far as is possible.

And what of subjective freedom? Recall that we are here concerned with the attitude or disposition of the human individual. In other words, that citizens participate freely in laws and institutions because of their confidence that these are sites of freedom's realisation; there is some subjective relationship between the individual and the institution, undertaken freely. As Neuhouser puts the matter, "the socially free individual *freely* and *effectively* wills the laws and social institutions that are the *real conditions of his or her own freedom . . .* ".[395] Given the analysis

---

[394] Neuhouser (2003), 82.

[395] Neuhouser (2003), 84.

of this book so far, a large question mark must be placed over whether the individual can freely will the conditions of institutions as it remains uncertain in what ways they contribute to a right order of life. Certainly, Ecosystem Services fared poorly in this analysis. This, however, points to the strength of postnatural right as a way of indicating why the free individual should not trust specific institutions. After all, right is a notion of defence and negation from the perspective of which authorities are challenged; right is antagonistic. Moreover, we saw in the discussion of the concept of society in chapter 1 that the term has both a descriptive and a normative aspect, etymologically and theologically. So postnatural right invites the posing of the question: why are these institutions the way they are, and how might they be changed? The freeway is open for different and alternative institutions. There is no requirement in my argument to accept that the "reality" of social institutions in their objectivity provides the conditions for freedom.

Drawing this section to a close, we may now note the normative difference that thinking ethically with the concept of a greater society makes. That is, the social inclusion of nature in a greater society – indeed, that society is co-constituted by nature – makes a difference to our ethical thinking. In line with our consideration of the meaning of society introduced in chapter 1, we are dealing with the normative as well as the descriptive. The *maior dissimilitudo* is once more operative: society encompasses humanity and nature – as does "institution", *but not in the same way*. If institutions are based in will, such organisation is properly to be traced back to the work of the human. The holistic and the individualistic function in a complicated way in our understanding of a greater society. Yet, despite this caution, from the perspective of the objectivity of social freedom we should judge the contribution of an institution to the conditions of human social freedom in a fashion that includes the contribution of nature. Thereby, although an institution is not instituted by nature yet nature makes an institutional contribution to the realisation of human freedom. Of Ecosystem Services we do not say that nature institutes these services; we do say that nature co-constitutes these services. If anthropogenic climate change is a postnatural institution – after all, is the weather not now joined to climate as a hybrid? – I am not arguing that such climate change is instituted by nature; once instituted, however, the institution is co-constituted by the climate. Additionally, this caution regarding the status of nature as institution also supports a hesitation as regards placing nature within a social contract. Such a contract invites the identification of nature as property and supports ideas such as "natural capital" (see section 5.9). A refusal to speak of nature as institution provides an epistemological break, if you will: a standpoint that transcends the standpoint of contract.[396]

From the perspective of the subjective aspect of social freedom, it is hard to see how the individual might freely will – that is, have a freely appropriate re-

---

[396] See Stone (2014), 111.

lationship with – institutions if these institutions are not ideal. The extension of society to a greater society thereby raises the issue of the good of social institutions and whether or not an individual may support them – *from the perspective of nature's contribution*. This is the difference in ethical thinking determined by a postnatural condition. It is not possible to will institutions freely nor see them as institutions of the realisation of freedom if such willing has severe ill effects on nature over the long term.

8.5 RIGHT AND THE GOOD

In the previous section, I considered the social freedom of a greater society. We are now in a position to ask: what of the condition for the *realisation* of creaturely freedom? My argument begins from an acceptance that the human transforms, and mixes itself with, nature; as I have argued elsewhere – and will not repeat here – nature is *in nobis, pro nobis* and *extra nos*.[397] We were never in a natural condition; we have always been hybrid.

Moreover, such a postnatural condition will be *teleological*: concerned with what is normative, with what is good. We may not be confident that any creaturely agent can secure or achieve this good. Instead, as Jenson puts it, "The good is what *ought* to be: that is to say, it is what may not be now and may never be, and is no less the good for all that."[398] In addition, precisely because of its elusive quality, this good is ideal: for if this good is not yet and indeed may never be, then it can only be anticipated: this reality is a good that may or may not be achieved. It is precisely an eschatological good. Nature accompanies the human, both for God, for itself and for the human. And as such indicates a good – precisely, a postnatural good.

As ideal, additionally, right is an activity that is, as postnatural, *social*. That is, it has built into it a free creativity and reference to the otherness and productivity of nature. So it is grounded in a postnature that is yet to come, and it is grounded in nature in the sense of a wider nature in which the human is placed – a greater society. In that it is ideal, postnatural right is *necessary* and *revolutionary*. It is necessary in the sense that it assumes ecological dependencies; it is revolutionary in the sense that it demands an equality of basic regard among creatures.

Right is an ecological, social and so historical *achievement*. Right develops by reference to the dynamic situatedness of the human and is thereby carried by institutions. It is a mixture of the actual and teleological. In addition, the *telos* encompasses the non-human and is oriented on God. Postnatural right therefore identifies the conditions of a right order of life and invites the *realisation* of a greater society based in these conditions. Postnatural right identifies both an ideal order and commends its realisation. We are enquiring after an account of right that

---

[397] Scott (2003), 180-87.
[398] Jenson (1995), 71.

will emerge out of present circumstances and will be useful towards the common advantage of the liberty and security of all creatures.

Postnatural right emerges as the effort to explore our capacities to act as human animals but also as participants in a *logos*, a pattern, a dynamic working of ecological relationships, a dis-order, an anti-rule for the realisation of freedom. The postnatural condition is then an effort to identify this reality and postnatural right is an effort to guide action. What is fundamental is the coalition of animals, human and non-human, in a wider natural context: the contrast human/natural must be refused in favour of a concept of *postnature* as a way of thinking about the re-institutionalising of humanity-nature.

The postnatural condition identifies the common good as discoverable, as intersubjective. The extension of freedom is then by way of this discoverability, and the creation of new institutions that permits new discoveries. Hegel avoids this conclusion by indicating that freedom is secured by private property, family, civil society and the state. Yet I argue that the externality of right – objective freedom – is secured differently. That is, such externality is secured through intersubjective encounter that is always institutionally mediated. Postnatural right redistributes our concern, re-patterns our encounters, and encourages new types of meeting.

At this point, it will I hope be clear that I am not proposing a transcendental deduction of postnatural right. This needs some articulation in that, arguably, Fichte attempts such a deduction and I have in earlier work made a transcendental argument to which this present argument is related. In *Foundations of Natural Right* Fichte is, I consider, making an argument that can be characterised as transcendental, in direct Kantian lineage. In his transcendental deduction, Fichte argues through the presentation of three theorems that self-consciousness is grounded in an awareness of the individual's free activity, that the presence of other such free individuals is required for me to come to realisation of my freedom, and therefore that I stand in what Fichte calls a "relation of right" to others.[399] Such an enquiry may be called "transcendental" in that Fichte transfers Kant's approach to the constituting of the individual through the act of knowing to an account of the self-consciousness of the free individual and the material world – including relations with others – that such an awareness of freedom requires. Thus if I understand myself by reference to a radical freedom, Fichte enquires after the conditions of such an awareness. There is some discussion as to whether the basis of this approach by Fichte is "theoretical" or "practical" but such concerns need not delay us here.[400]

In *A Political Theology of Nature*, I offered a transcendental enquiry that was not dependent on a Kantian approach. Instead, as reprised in chapter 1, I argued for four transcendentals as a way of characterising the "thinginess" of things

---

[399] Fichte (2000), 18ff.
[400] See Wood (2016b), 168-198.

rather than proposing the condition of an enquiry.[401] I then proceeded to develop such transcendentality into an ecosociality that privileged concepts of relation, encounter and interactivity.[402] My overall approach was closer to Plato than to Kant. In the *Republic*, Plato is concerned to distinguish between convention and nature in relation to justice.[403] In turn, this leads Plato to consider justice in the context of the city and justice in terms of the self.[404] There are clearly resonances between justice in the *Republic* and postnatural right: crucial is the matter of social organisation as the point of the emergence of, and education into, virtue. For Plato, however, moral psychology refers us to the comprehensiveness of virtue. For postnatural right a different concept of nature is in play: one that joins the human and the non-human. The matter at hand is thereby not the stability of the concept of justice but the attempt to include the non-human in moral enquiry as a pathway towards freedom in a greater society, a right order of life. We may now see why an account of virtue is deferred to volume 3 of the present series, which covers the topic of politics by reference to culture. For what needs elaboration is the greater ecclesiality in which virtue emerges and is learned: a pedagogy of attention. For example, which institutions – such as social movements – perform such virtues? We will therefore in volume 3 of the present enquiry be concerned with a moral culture – precisely, a politics.

What has been learned about postnatural right so far? Postnatural right emerges out of a discussion of the mutual yet asymmetrical dependencies that are performed among creatures. Moreover, I have extended the meaning of "social" to encompass the ecological. In other words, to develop a demand for a re-institutionalisation of nature in which the question is asked: "what form of polity best provides a rich, flourishing human life".[405] In our postnatural circumstance, we shall need to expand this question: what form of polity, we might say, provides for a rich, flourishing life for humans *and others*? What is required here, as John Ely suggests, is the re-thinking of a "way of life" in more comprehensive ways than heretofore: a move in thinking towards a postnatural way of life vested in an account of immanent right.[406] Postnatural right is *social* thereby.

I propose that postnatural right is a *universal* phenomenon. We have seen that the doctrine of creation is descriptive and normative, asking what and why questions. Yet its scope is universal. Although universal, such postnatural right is not only general. It has historical content: it assumes the ideal of production for ex-

---

[401] Scott (2003), chapter 2.

[402] These matters developed for an account of postnatural right are the central concern of volume 2 of the present series.

[403] Plato, *Republic*, I-IV.

[404] See Annas (1998).

[405] Ely (1996), 134-166 (here 134).

[406] Oakley (2005), 27. Oakley makes an important distinction between immanent and imposed laws. In the discussion in this section, we are exploring right as immanent.

change, and notes that this production makes greater wealth; and it is associated with a distributive pressure towards equality. In other words, our idea of right is not a-historical but changes and has changed over time. Right now includes productive activity and we now work from the principle that what we make is available to be redistributed. In my view, the labour and women's movements are part of this historical development – a "long revolution" (Raymond Williams) – in which what counts as morally considerable *and* significant *changes*. The meaning of right is altered – and *not* only extended – by reference to participation and control over production and reproduction. The basis of *Sittlichkeit* is not a static society or the state. Instead, *Sittlichkeit* is an historical development: a development in the west in which the emergence of civil society, and the labour, women's and animal liberation movements, are important. A moral culture emerges as an historical development and is an historical achievement.

I learned this historical sense from A. D. Lindsay's account of Marx's labour theory of value. In a very interesting analysis, Lindsay argues that: "The labour theory of value is the negation of the doctrine that some men [sic] have in themselves a right to more wealth than others, and seeks to point the way to an economic system where men co-operate in the production of wealth, and where each individually owns the wealth which his own labour has created and no more".[407] I shall not here pursue the details of the labour theory of value. Instead, I note the important historicising point that Lindsay makes: Marx is introducing into his economic theory a moral point about wealth and its production and distribution. Although theories of natural right often make assertions about some natural condition of humanity and other similar formulations, this is, as Lindsay pithily puts it, "good ethics under bad history". What is helpfully disclosed in this analysis is the moral loading that right bears.

Yet my position also notes a further historical development: all wealth making has an ecological component. This refers us to the *necessary* aspect of right. Value and nature are related in this historical development and change through the development. What postnatural right identifies and secures is a *necessary* notion of the free, eco-productive individual, living co-operatively in a determinate ecological circumstance. As *revolutionary*, postnatural right demands an equality of basic regard among creatures. What is required is what Kathryn Tanner calls "a vision of cosmic justice in which all beings are due equal consideration at some basic level of moral concern" as the moral outworking of a teleological postnature.[408] This, we might say, is what needs to be real-ized in our situation. The equality of human beings among themselves, and in relation to nature, is here an important matter: social equality invokes an equality of access to nature's goods. And sharing of the wealth of nature will require forms of co-operation. One way of

---

[407] Lindsay (1925), 60-61.
[408] Tanner (1994), 99-123 (here 118).

thinking about this is to think about wealth not in terms of its creation but instead in terms of its *making*. The good to which we aspire is the making of wealth in which nature is also acknowledged as a partner in this making. As *ideal*, a central task of the public sphere related to postnatural right will be a renewal of the debate of ends of the human and the ends of nature: to what *teloi* are these directed? "When we have been historically creative," Jenson argues, "it is because we have shared some look into the future, some metaphor of freedom and goodness or purity or mutuality, which could draw us forward through time."[409] Postnatural right provides freedom in institutions as historically creative. Of course, none of this can be thought except by reference to "this transcending facet of a teleological system was always firmly rooted in or concretely mediated by real political circumstances."[410] We also need a "theory of the institutions providing the good life" in support of a "form and nature of a *free and equal political mode of life*".[411] For, if I am right, there can be no free and equal political mode of life that is not also directed to what we can risk in not defending the human.

This may function as a reminder of the terms "societal" and "sociability" that I first presented in chapter 1 in the discussion of a greater society. There I argued that "societal" refers to the quality of the life of a society. For a greater society, we now begin to get some clues as to this quality, albeit understood in general way: various social movements, for example, that are part of a "long revolution", have contributed to this societal quality. On a smaller scale, we take up sociability, and remind ourselves of Williams' point that "society" once also had the sense of company or fellowship. The task before postnatural right is to provide ways forward, partly by attention to institutional vision, that imagine and promote social relationships that cohere more fully with the ideality of right and its demand to historicise, contextualise and socialise, in the name of fellowship.

What then is postnatural right? An identification of the conditions for the realisation of (e)(co)freedom: an external ordering of social life in which nature and the transcendence of nature are operative, in a greater society, and anchored in the immanence of right ordering by God – given in institutions and yet transcended. Such right is not founded on reason's categorical imperative (Kant) nor the self-consciousness of free activity (Fichte) nor the culture of a state (Hegel). Instead, it is founded on a basic equality – an external ordering with animals and others – that humans share with other citizens – and which is refounded in the new covenant of the resurrection of Jesus Christ. The point here is not to recover Eden's original right but to explore into the future the complexities of right in a postnatural condition. The complexification of society is not a *lapsus secundus*[412] but instead the deepening of certain tendencies already present in creation – in my

---

[409] Jenson (1995), 72.
[410] Ely (1996), 140-141.
[411] Ely (1996), 138.
[412] Scott (forthcoming).

social account these are related to the "deeper organizational principles operating throughout the history of life", for which Simon Conway Morris argues.[413]

8.6 CREATIO CONTINUA

Humans are bio-historical beings, operating in technological, social and political dynamics of constitutive significance. The human creature is not naked. First, the human creature presented in my argument is always already producing an order, embedded in institutions and working out of a contingent history. Human beings do not make their lives out of nothing but rather, as Marx opines, in circumstances not of their own choosing. Second, human beings are free but this freedom operates in a postnatural condition. That is, there are other creatures, powers and forces that are exercising their "freedom", powers and agency. Additionally, human action in our present circumstance is more circumscribed by the institutional infrastructure in which it takes place than is usually acknowledged. The temptation of nakedness is everywhere evident.

It is not enough to say we must theorise the human with its other creatures and attachments. Nor it is enough to say that we must grasp the human in its context. We must ask a normative question: in the present context, and as the present context moves into a future, what should co-operation between creatures, human and non-human, be? This is the realisation of postnatural right. History will not simply deliver it and nor should we seek to reconcile ourselves to present institutions. The search for freedom meets a new issue: encounters with the non-human. Freedom can no longer only mean the reduction of interference and the maximisation of the scope of human action without also paying attention to the ways in which human beings transform their contexts, especially in their use of non-renewable resources.

As I have said, humans are bio-historical beings, operating in technological, social and political dynamics of constitutive significance. These are, we might say, the relations of postnatural right: the human self only comes to be (in its fullness) in these constitutive relations that are social, historical and anthropological relations of right. In addition, these relations form as institutions, have an aim or end, and operate as distributive means of goodness. These relations of right are to be judged as universal, necessary, social, revolutionary, and ideal. As such, right is both the measure of the ratio, pattern or shape of a greater society and the measure of a right order of life. The marker of freedom and the recommendation of freedom, postnatural right affirms the dignity of creatures and criticises current social arrangements from the perspective of a larger creaturely "liberty".

We have already seen that a postnatural basis emerges out of a wider creatureliness and not simply by attention to the human. Moreover, the fact that the content of right can change suggests that postnatural right does not operate with

---

[413] Conway Morris (2010), 156.

a fixed account of natural structures that might be understood as transhistorical. In human-and-other-activity there is the distribution of goodness, and this distribution takes place in and through institutions. These are the relations of right in which creatures are placed. Yet this is not an argument that is concerned with the imposition of a particular order. Instead, we have seen that such right is historical – although not reductively so – and thereby proceeds by the addition of ends through institutional repetition.

Theologically speaking, this conclusion is a discussion of *creatio continua*. Some theologians dispute the importance of this concept. Jenson, for example, argues that a distinction between creation and preservation or initial and continuing creation obscures the prior theological point that "The world is no less dependent on God's creating word in any moment of its existence than it was at the beginning".[414] As a criteriological point, this is correct: the point of a doctrine of creation – that all that is (nature in sense 3) is always dependent on God's creative Yes – is maintained thereby. The difficulty, however, as we already have seen in chapter 3, is that if the distinction between *creatio originalis* and *creatio continua* is not maintained, difficulties in identifying and understanding historical change persist. Indeed, Moltmann argues that if we are adequately to grasp the "process of creation" then theological attention is to be paid to the traditional distinctions between *creatio ex nihilo*, *creatio continua* and eschatological consummation. Emphatically, for a theology of postnatural right, we need an account of what Moltmann calls *creatio mutabilis*: the directional irreversibility of creation as an ec-centrically designed open system; the contingency of *ex nihilo* is the source of the contingency of *continua* and points towards its completion.[415] From this perspective, *creatio continua* may be understood as God's preserving *and* innovating work. We are speaking then, as the next section will make clear, of entering into a new condition.

Recalling the discussion of ecstatic life in chapter 6, we should expect such preservative and innovative work to operate through all levels of life, from atoms to humanity, as Moltmann puts it. In the context of postnatural right, our focus has a specific scale: the right of social-institutional life. One more time, we encounter the conceptual force of "greater society": an answer to "What is going on?" must count in nature (sense 3). God's activity operates in and through the social-institutional activity of creatures; reformed by right, God acts with and out of institutions whose context and orientation is historical-teleological; the reform of institutions as the place of encounters between humanity and nature moves along an anthropological-eschatological trajectory.

---

414 Jenson (1999), 2, 9.
415 Moltmann (1985), 207-09.

8.7 CREATIO NOVA

As ideal, right offers a transcendent pattern: we are referred, ambiguously, to a future state. Right refers us to that which is *established* and yet not *determined* – that is, to new creation. Here a great deal depends on what is meant by reference to the resurrection of Jesus Christ. In *A Political Theology of Nature*, I made the argument that the resurrection of Jesus Christ requires us to think beyond the natural hiatus of death; and in *Anti-human Theology*, I reprised and extended this argument by amplifying my position that the sociality of humanity that is affirmed in the resurrection is also and always the sociality of humanity-nature. On this account of the transcendence of the Gospel, God re-secures the relationship between creatures by resurrection.

McCabe provides us with a relevant discussion of such resurrection transcendence. For McCabe, death is a matter of destruction only, except for the resurrection of Jesus Christ. In the light of the return of Jesus from death, we are presented with the "beginning of a new and unpredictable life". In a sense, this is no different from every revolution in which there is always a change in structures that in turn produces the new humanity. Yet, resurrection is not merely a change *in* structures but rather a change *of* structures by which we exist at all.[416] The resurrection is not about change and survival of the human body but its return through the hiatus of death. All other revolutions are less than this and so are "an image of, and preparation for, the resurrection of the dead". These are types of the resurrection, McCabe argues:

In a sense every revolution draws upon the powers that are not catered for in the preceding society, powers which therefore seem to be invisible because they transcend the terms of that society . . . The power and the spirit of every revolution thus comes from "outside" the society that is overthrown. The power and the spirit of the ultimate revolution, the resurrection, comes from "outside" man altogether. For the Christian, this is what divinity is: God is he who raised Jesus from the dead.[417]

Amplifying this McCabean clue, God is the one who raised Jesus from death, raised Israel out of Egypt, and raised a world out of nothing.[418] In this manner, God acts consistently, out of the unity of God's being. By such action, something is established if not yet determined. On the matters of establishment and determination, a great deal depends on what is meant by reference to the resurrection. That is, do I mean that postnatural right conforms in some deducible – that is, analogical – fashion to Jesus' resurrected body or that attention is to be paid to the transformation of matter that is Jesus' resurrection and the implications of that transformation?[419]

---

[416] As such, resurrection is not a "miracle" in the sense explored in chapter 7.
[417] McCabe (2003), 133-35.
[418] Scott (2010a), 131.
[419] See Pannenberg (1981), 32-33, for a framing along these lines.

Conformity is, I suspect, the route taken by O'Donovan in *Resurrection and Moral Order*. It is not a promising start when O'Donovan opines that Christian ethics springs from God's gift in Jesus Christ. "Springs from" seems to lack historical attentiveness. Still, and more promisingly, O'Donovan refuses to separate out an ethics of the Kingdom from an ethics of creation. Nonetheless, in beginning from the reality of resurrection, O'Donovan then finds himself obliged to provide a creaturely counterpart, one which – presumably – matches the humanity of Christ, and he promptly finds this in a claimed "thereness" of the natural order.[420]

By contrast, in the development of postnatural right, I have focused on the transformation of matter that the resurrection of Jesus Christ "inserts" into historical flow, following on from *ex nihilo* and exodus. What emerges is an account of postnatural right that is dynamic, stresses historicity and human praxis, and future *telos*. Yet, with reference to nature, order and technology, I have retained an account of the independence of nature, argued against the subsumption of natural ends, and stressed the supernatural end of humanity and nature. In this manner, I argue for the transforming of matter in the light of the resurrection of Jesus Christ and in turn argue that postnatural right is better aligned to this transformation than other options critically evaluated in earlier chapters.[421]

I have said that postnatural right refers us to that which is *established* and yet not *determined* – that is, to new creation. To elaborate fully on these two points would take us beyond the scope of this volume. What is established takes us into the area of the metaphysical underpinning of right: precisely what are the patterns of encounter operative here, and how are these both material and spiritual? Such considerations are the subject of volume 2 of the present enquiry. The lack of determination suggests that there is an openness to the present order. The present order is always a moral order but it also can be reshaped in the light of the transformation that is the resurrection of Jesus Christ. To explore that further is the burden of volume 3 of the present enquiry, which will offer a politics of postnature by reference to a moral culture.

For the present, a theological and ethical exploration of a right order of life in a postnatural condition has been the aim. Linking nature, order and technology has provided the scope for the consideration of relations of right: what is required by social beings is to be in relation to others in an historical flow with specific

---

[420] O'Donovan (1994), 13, 17.

[421] Perhaps it is now clearer why I have found it so difficult to integrate Bloch (1986) into my argument for there is such a great divergence between how natural law has been interpreted by its own theorists and Bloch's interpretation of the same material. I have already noted in chapter 3 that substantive continuity in the interpretation of natural law is not warranted. Nonetheless, the effort by Bloch to understand natural law as anticipatory rather than given and comprehensive is warmly to be welcomed even as it gives the appearance of being an interpretation subject to great strain.

reference to the activity of human beings. Such right relations are secured institutionally, by reference to an ideal and by reference to goodness extended through the acknowledgement of right.

Such acknowledgement emerges from the truth of creation: what is established is universal, identifies creatures by necessity as placed, and as social; establishes all as regarded equally by God and as oriented on a future ideal. The future is postnatural and may be right-ful, towards a right order of life.

BIBLIOGRAPHY

Annas, Julia (1998), *An Introduction to Plato's Republic*, New York: Oxford University Press.

Antonaccio, Maria (2015), "Technology and the humanisation of nature: new resources for critical assessment", in Celia Deane-Drummond, Sigurd Bergmann and Bronislaw Szerszynski (eds.), *Technofutures, Nature and the Sacred*, Farnham: Ashgate, 31-46.

Aquinas, Thomas (2006), *Summa Theologiae* vol. 28, trans. Thomas Gilby, Cambridge: Cambridge University Press.

Arnhart, Larry (1998), *Darwinian Natural Right: The Biological Ethics of Human Nature*, Albany: SUNY.

Attfield, Robin (2014), *Environmental Ethics*, Cambridge: Polity, second edition.

Balthasar, Hans Urs von (1993), *The Theology of Karl Barth*, San Francisco, CA: Ignatius Press.

Barkham, Patrick (2013), *Badgerlands: The Twilight World of Britain's Most Enigmatic Animal,* London: Granta.

Bauman, Whitney (2003), *Theology, Creation and Environmental Ethics: From* Creatio ex nihilo *to* terra nullius, London & New York: Routledge.

Bergmann, Sigurd (2015), "'Millions of Machines are already Roaring': Fetishised Technology encountered by the Life-Giving Spirit", in Celia Deane-Drummond, Sigurd Bergmann and Bronislaw Szerszynski (eds.), *Technofutures, Nature and the Sacred*, Farnham: Ashgate, 115-37.

— (2016), Review of Christof Hardmeier and Konrad Ott, *Naturethik und biblische Schöpfungserzählung: Ein diskurstheoretischer und narrativ-hermeneutischer Brückenschlag*, Worldviews 20, 211–214.

Berlin, Isaiah (2000), *The Roots of Romanticism*, London: Pimlico.

Bloch, Ernst (1986), *Natural Law and Human Dignity*, Cambridge, MA: MIT Press.

Borgmann, Albert (1984), *Technology and the Character of Everyday Life,* Chicago: University of Chicago Press.

Boucher, David (2008), *The Limits of Ethics in International Relations,* Oxford: Oxford University Press.

Brock, Brian (2010), *Christian Ethics in a Technological Age,* Grand Rapids: Eerdmans.

Burdett, Michael S. (2015), *Eschatology and the Technological Future*, London & New York: Routledge.

Cahill, Lisa Sowle (2005), "Creation and Ethics", in: Gilbert Meilaender and William Werpehowski (eds), *The Oxford Handbook of Theological Ethics*, Oxford: Oxford University Press, 7-24.

— (2013), *Global Justice, Christology and Christian Ethics*, Cambridge: Cambridge University Press.

Campbell, Tom (1991), *Seven Theories of Human Society*, Oxford: Clarendon Press.

Catling, David C. (2013), *Astrobiology*, Oxford: Oxford University Press.

Cavanaugh, W. T. and Scott, P. M. (2019), "Introduction", in: Cavanaugh, W. T. and Scott, P. M. (eds), *Wiley-Blackwell Companion to Political Theology*, Oxford: Wiley-Blackwell, 2nd edn, 1-11.

Charles, J. Daryl (2008), *Retrieving the Natural Law: A Return to Moral First Things*, Grand Rapids & Cambridge: Eerdmans.

Cicero (1998), *The Republic and the Laws,* Oxford: Oxford University Press.

Clingerman, Forrest (2015), "Redeeming the climate: investigating a theological model of geoengineering", in: Celia Deane-Drummond, Sigurd Bergmann and Bronislaw Szerszynski (eds.), *Technofutures, Nature and the Sacred*, Farnham: Ashgate, 175-92.

Clingerman, Forrest and O'Brien, Kevin J. (eds) (2016), *Theological and Ethical Perspectives on Climate Engineering*, London: Lexington Books.

Conradie, Ernst M. (2005), *An Ecological Christian Anthropology: At home on the earth?*, Aldershot: Ashgate.

— (2015), *The Earth in God's Economy*, Zurich: LIT Verlag.

Conway Morris, Simon (2010), "Evolution and the inevitability of intelligent life", in: Peter Harrison (ed.), *The Cambridge Companion to Science and Religion*, Cambridge: Cambridge University Press, 148-72.

Cortez, Marc (2010), *Theological Anthropology*, London: Bloomsbury/T & T Clark.

Curran, Charles E. (1996), "Natural Law", in: P. B. Clarke and A. Linzey (eds), *Dictionary of Ethics, Theology and Society*, London: Routledge, 594-97.

Daston, Lorraine and Stolleis, Michael (eds) (2008), *Natural Law and Laws of Nature in Early Modern Europe*, Farnham: Ashgate.

Davaney, Sheila. G. (2006), *Historicism: The Once and Future Challenge for Theology*, Minneapolis: Fortress Press, 2006.

Deane-Drummond, Celia (2004), *The Ethics of Nature*, Oxford: Blackwell.

Deane-Drummond, Celia, Bergmann, Sigurd, and Szerszynski, Bronislaw (2015), "Introduction", in: Celia Deane-Drummond, Sigurd Bergmann and Bronislaw Szerszynski (eds.), *Technofutures, Nature and the Sacred*, Farnham: Ashgate, 1-13.

Demant, V. A. (1936), *Christian Polity*, London: Faber and Faber.

— (1948), *Theology and Society: More Essays in Christian Polity*, London: Faber and Faber.

— (1966 [1947]), *The Idea of a Natural Order*, Philadelphia: Fortress Press.

Demant, V. A. (1936), *Christian Polity*, London: Faber and Faber.

D'Entrèves, A. P. (1951), *Natural law: An Historical Survey*, New York: Harper Torchbooks.

De Vries, Hent (2006), "Introduction: Before, Around and Beyond the Theologico-political",in: Hent de Vries and Lawrence E. Sullivan (eds), *Political Theologies: Public Religions in a Post-secular World*, Fordham: Fordham University Press, 1-88.

Dickens, Peter (1992), *Society and Nature: Towards a Green Social Theory*, New York: Harvester Wheatsheaf.

Drummy, Michael F. (2000), *Being and Earth: Paul Tillich's Theology of Nature*, Lanham, Maryland: University Press of America.

Dulles, Avery (2002), *Models of the Church*, New York: Doubleday, expanded version.

Dupré, Louis (1993), *Passage to Modernity: An Essay in the Hermeneutics of Nature and Culture*, New Haven and London: Yale University Press.

Ellis, Fiona (2016), *God, Value and Nature*, Oxford: Oxford University Press.

Ely, John (1996), "Ernst Bloch, Natural Right and the Greens", in: David Macauley (ed.), *Minding Nature: The Philosophers of Ecology*, New York: Guilford, 134-166.

Fichte, J. G. (2000), *Foundations of Natural Right*, Cambridge: Cambridge University Press.

Finnis, John (2011), *Natural Law and Natural Rights*, New York: Oxford University Press, 2nd edn.

Francis I (2015), *Laudato Si': On Care for our Common Home,* Brooklyn and London: Melville House.

Gardiner, Stephen M. (2011), *A Perfect Moral Storm: the Ethical Tragedy of Climate Change*, New York: Oxford University Press.

Gardner, Sebastian (2013), "The Limits of Naturalism and the Metaphysics of German Idealism", in: Espen Hammer (ed.), *German Idealism: Contemporary Perspectives*, London and New York: Routledge, 19-49.

Gill, Robin (1977), *Theology and Social Structure*, Oxford and London: Mowbrays.

Graham, Gordon (2013), "Nature", in: N. Adams et. al. (eds), *The Oxford Handbook of Theology and Modern European Thought*, Oxford: Oxford University Press, 399-417.

Gregory, Eric (2010), *Politics and the Order of Love*, Chicago and London: Chicago University Press.

Grinspoon, David (2016), *Earth in Human Hands* (New York & Boston: Grand Central Publishing.

Guardini, Romano (1994), *Letters from Lake Como: Explorations in Technology and the Human Race*, Grand Rapids, MI: Eerdmans.

Habermas, Jürgen (1987), *Toward a Rational Society*, Cambridge: Polity Press.

— (1991), Communication *and the Evolution of Society,* Cambridge: Polity.

Hardimon, Michael O (1994), *Hegel's Social Philosophy: The Project of Reconciliation*, Cambridge: Cambridge University Press.

Hardy, Daniel W (1996a), "Creation", in: Paul Barry Clarke and Andrew Linzey (eds), *Dictionary of Ethics, Theology and Society*, London and New York: Routledge, 189-96.

Hardy, Daniel W. (1996b), *God's Ways with the World*, Edinburgh: T&T Clark.

Harvey, David (1989), *The Condition of Postmodernity*, Oxford: Blackwell.

Hegel, G. W. F. (1991), *Elements of the Philosophy of Right*, Cambridge: Cambridge University Press.

— (1999), *Political Writings*, Cambridge: Cambridge University Press.

— (2012), *Lectures On Natural Right And Political Science: The First Philosophy Of Right,* New York: OUP.

Heidegger, Martin (2013), *Nature, History, State 1933-34*, London: Bloomsbury.

Herzfeld, Noreen (2009), *Technology and Religion*, West Conshohocken, PA: Templeton Press.

HM Treasury UK (2009), *Building Britain's Future*, ‹www.hm-treasury.gov.uk/bud_bud 09_index.htm›, accessed 12 12 13

Hobbes, Thomas (1994), *Leviathan, With Selected Variants from the Latin Edition of 1668*, New York: Hackett.

Hodgson, Peter (1994), *Winds of the Spirit*, London: SCM Press.

Hooker, Thomas (1989), *Of the Laws of Ecclesiastical Polity*, Cambridge: Cambridge University Press.

Jameson, Fredric (2009), Valences *of the Dialectic,* London: Verso.

Jamieson, Dale (ed.) (2001), *Blackwell Companion to Environmental Philosophy* (Oxford: Blackwell.

Jenkins, Willis and Christopher Key Chapple (2011), "Religion and the Environment", in: *Annual Review of Environment and Resources* 36, 441-63.

Jenson, Robert W (1995), *Essays in the Theology of Culture,* Grand Rapids, MI: Eerdmans, 67-75.

— (1999), Systematic *Theology,* volume 2: *The Works of God*, New York, Oxford University Press.

Kaufman, Gordon (1972), "A Problem for Theology: The Concept of Nature", *Harvard Theological Review* 65(3), 337-366.

— (1985), *Theology for a Nuclear Age*, Manchester: Manchester University Press.

Kersting, Wolfgang (1992), "Politics, Freedom and Order: Kant's Political Philosophy", in: Paul Guyer (ed.), *The Cambridge Companion to Kant*, Cambridge: Cambridge University Press, 342-366.

Latour, Bruno (1993), *We have never been Modern*, London: Harvester Wheatsheaf.

LeVasseur, Todd and Anna Peterson (eds) (2016), *Religion and Ecological Crisis: The "Lynn White Thesis" at Fifty*, London: Routledge.

Lewis, C. S. (1967), *Studies in Words*, Cambridge: Cambridge University Press, 2nd edn.

Lindsay, A. D. (1925), *Karl Marx's Capital*, London: Oxford University Press.

MacIntyre, Alasdair (2007), *After Virtue*, London: Bloomsbury 3rd edition.

MacKinnon, D. M. (2011), *Philosophy and the Burden of Theological Honesty*, John McDowell (ed.), London: T&T Clark International.

Macpherson, C. B. (1962/2011), *The Political Theory of Possessive Individualism*, Oxford and New York: Oxford University Press.

Making Space for Nature (2010), ‹www.gov.uk/government/news/making-space-for-nature-a-review-of-englands-wildlife-sites-published-today›, accessed 12 12 13]

Marx, Karl (1973), *Grundrisse*, Harmondsworth: Pelican.

— (1975), "A contribution to the critique of Hegel"s *Philosophy of Right*, Introduction", Karl Marx, *Early Writings*, London: Penguin, 243-257.

McCabe, Herbert (2002), *God Still Matters*, London: Continuum.

— (2003), *Law, Love and Language*, London: Continuum.

McFague, Sallie (1987), *Models of God: Theology for an Ecological, Nuclear Age*, London: SCM Press.

McGrath, Alister E. (2001), *A Scientific Theology: Nature*, Grand Rapids: Eerdmans.

— (2004), *The Science of God*, London and New York: T&T Clark International.

— (2006), The *Order of Things: Explorations in Scientific Theology*, Oxford: Blackwell.

Metz, Johann Baptist (1970), "Political theology", in: K Rahner and A Darlap (eds), *Sacramentum Mundi* vol. V, New York: Herder and Herder, 34-38.

Midson, Scott (2018), *Cyborg Theology: Humans, Technology and God*, London: I B Tauris.

Milbank, John (1993), "Out of the Greenhouse", *New Blackfriars* 74: 867, 4-14.

Mill, J. S. (2008), *Three Essays on Religion*, New York: Cosimo.

Moe-Lobeda, Cynthia D. (2013), *Resisting Structural Evil: Love as Ecological-economic Vocation,* Minneapolis: Fortress Press.

Moltmann, Jürgen (1985), *God in Creation: An Ecological Doctrine of Creation*, London: SCM Press.

— (2015), "European Political Theology", in Craig Hovey and Elizabeth Philips (eds), *The Cambridge Companion to Political Theology*, Cambridge: Cambridge University Press, 3-22.

Natural Choice, The (2011), *Securing the Value of Nature*, London: The Stationery Office.

Neuhouser, Frederick (2003), *Foundations of Hegel's Social Theory: Actualizing Freedom*, Harvard: Harvard University Press.

Northcott, Michael. S. (1996), *The Environment and Christian Ethics*, Cambridge: Cambridge University Press.

Nuccetelli, Susana and Gary Seay (eds) (2012), *Ethical Naturalism: Current Debates*, Cambridge: Cambridge University Press.

Oakley, Francis (2005), *Natural Law, Laws of Nature, Natural Rights*, New York and London: Continuum.

O'Donovan, Oliver (1994), *Resurrection and Moral Order*, Leicester: Apollos, 2nd edn.

O'Donovan, Oliver (1996), *The Desire of the Nations*, Cambridge: Cambridge University Press.

Pannenberg, Wolfhart (1969), *Theology and the Kingdom of God* (Philadelphia, PA: Westminster Press.

— (1981), *Ethics*, London: Search Press.

— (1993), *Toward a Theology of Nature* (Louisville, KY: Westminster/John Knox Press.

— (2007), *The Historicity of Nature: Essays of Science and Theology* (West Conshohocken, PA: Templeton Foundation Press.

Parella, Frederick J. (2009), "Tillich's Theology of the Concrete Spirit", in: Russell Re Manning (ed.), *The Cambridge Companion to Paul Tillich*, Cambridge: Cambridge University Press, 74-90.

Patočka, Jan (2016), *The Natural World as a Philosophical Problem*, Evanston, Il.: Northwestern University Press.

Patten, Alan (1999), *Hegel's Idea of Freedom*, Oxford: Oxford University Press.

Pattison, George (2007), *Thinking about God in an Age of Technology*, Oxford: Oxford University Press.

Plant, Raymond (1973), *Hegel: An Introduction*, London: Routledge.

Plato, *Republic*, many editions.

Pope, Stephen J. (1994), *The evolution of altruism and the ordering of love*, Washington, DC: Georgetown University Press.

— (2005), "Reason and Natural Law", in: Gilbert Meilaender and William Werpehowski (eds), *The Oxford Handbook of Theological Ethics*, Oxford: Oxford University Press, 148-167.

— (2007), *Human Evolution and Christian Ethics*, Cambridge: Cambridge University Press.

Porter, Jean (1999), *Natural and Divine Law,* Grand Rapids MI., and Cambridge, UK: Eerdmans.

Prenter, Regin (1967), *Creation and Redemption*, Philadelphia: Fortress.

Rahner, Karl (ed.) (1975a), *Encyclopaedia of Theology: The Concise Sacramentum Mundi*, London: Burns & Oates.

— (1975b), "Order", in K. Rahner (ed.), *Encyclopaedia of Theology: The Concise Sacramentum Mundi* (Tunbridge Wells: Burns and Oates, 1975), 1110.

— (1993), The *Content of Faith* (New York: Crossroad).

Roberts, Richard H. (1996), "A Postmodern Church? Some Preliminary Reflections on Ecclesiology and Social Theory", in: David F. Ford and Dennis L. Stamps (eds), *Essentials of Christian Community*: Edinburgh: T & T Clark, 179-195.

Ritchie, David G. (1894), *Natural Rights*, London: George Allen & Unwin.

Ritter, Joachim (1982), Hegel *and the French Revolution: Essays on the Philosophy of Right*, Cambridge, MA: MIT Press.

Rodwell, John (2013), BESS Report *Aesthetic & Spiritual Responses to the Environ-ment*, ‹www.nerc-bess.net/index.php/documents/2-uncategorised/129-workshop-report--spiritual-responses-to-the-environment›, accessed 12 12 13

Ruether, R. R. (1981), *To Change the World: Christology and Cultural Criticism*, London: SCM Press.

— (2009), *Christianity and Social Systems*, Lanham: Rowman and Littlefield.

Schindler, David L. (2011), *Ordering Love: Liberal Societies and the Memory of God* (Grand Rapids, MI: Eerdmans.

Scott, P. M. (1994), *Theology, Ideology and Liberation*, Cambridge: Cambridge University Press.

— (1997), "Beyond Stewardship? Dietrich Bonhoeffer on nature", *Journal of Beliefs and Values* 18:2, 193-202.

— (2000), "The Future of Creation: Ecology and Eschatology", in: David Fergusson and Marcel Sarot (eds), *The Future as God's Gift*, Edinburgh: T & T Clark, 89-114.

— (2003), *A Political Theology of Nature*, Cambridge: Cambridge University Press.

— "Creation" (2004), in: Scott, P. M. and Cavanaugh, W. T., The *Blackwell Companion to Political Theology*, Oxford: Blackwell, 333-347.

— (2010a), *Anti-human Theology: Nature, Technology and the Postnatural*, London: SCM Press.

— (2010b), "Which nature? Whose justice? Shifting meanings of nature in recent ecotheology", in Peter Clarke and Tony Claydon (eds.), *God's Bounty: The Church and the Natural World*, Boydell and Brewer, 430-456.

— (2011a), "Right out of Time? Politics and Nature in a Postnatural Condition", in C. Deane-Drummond and H. Bedford-Strohm (eds), *Religion and Ecology in the Public Sphere*, London: T & T Clark, 57-75.

— (2011b), "Thinking like an Animal: Theological Materialism for a Changing Climate", *Studies in Christian Ethics* 24: 1, 50-66.

— (2014a), "Humanity", in: M. Northcott and P. M. Scott (eds), *Systematic Theology and Climate Change*, Abingdon: Routledge, 108-123.

— (2014b), "The re-homing of the human?", in: E. Conradie et. al. (eds), *Christian Faith and the Earth*, London: Bloomsbury, 125-130.

— (2015a), "Does nature pluralize? Towards a greater society", *Political Theology* 16:1, 5-19.

— (2015b), "Places as ungiven, memories as competitive?", in: Rodwell, J. and Scott, P. M. (eds*), At Home in the Future: Place and Belonging in a Changing Europe*, Zurich: LIT Verlag, 155-168.

— (2017), "Afterword: Whither Anglican Social Theology?", in Stephen Spencer (ed.), *Theology Reforming Society*, London: SCM Press, 167-75.

— "God's Work in the Emergence of Humanity", in: E. Conradie and H. Koster (eds), *T&T Clark Handbook on Christian Theology and Climate Change* (London: Bloomsbury: T & T Clark, forthcoming).

Soper, Kate (1995), *What is Nature? Culture, Politics and the Non-human*, Oxford: Blackwell.

Stone, Alison (2014), "Hegel on Law, Women and Contract", in: Maria Drakopoulou, *Feminist Encounters with Legal Philosophy*, London: Routledge, 105-122.

Strauss, Leo (1953), *Natural Right and History*, Chicago: University of Chicago Press.

Swimme, Brian (2014), *The Journey of the Universe*, Yale: Yale University Press, repr.

Tanner, Kathryn (1994), "Creation, Environmental Justice, and Ecological Justice", in: Rebecca Chopp and Mark Lewis Taylor (eds.), *Reconstructing Christian Theology*, Minneapolis: Fortress Press, 99-123.

Tillich, Paul (1963), *Systematic Theology*, volume III, University of Chicago Press.

— (1977), *The Socialist Decision*, New York: Harper & Row.

Turner, Denys (2008), *Faith and the Existence of God*, Cambridge: Cambridge University Press.

UK National Ecosystem Assessment: Synthesis of key findings (2011), UNEP-WCMC, Cambridge, ‹http://uknea.unep-wcmc.org/Resources/tabid/82/Default.aspx›, accessed 26 08 18

Welker, Michael (1999), *Creation and Reality*, Minneapolis: Fortress Press.

Weintraub, Jeff and Kumar, Krishan (eds.) (1997), *Public and Private in Thought and Practice: Perspectives on a Grand Dichotomy* (Chicago & London: University of Chicago Press.

White, Lynn (1967), "The Historical Roots of our Ecologic Crisis", *Science* 155, 1203-07.

Williams, Raymond (1980), *Problems in Materialism and Culture*, London: Verso Books.

— (2014 [1976, 1983]), *Keywords: a Vocabulary of Culture and Society*, London: Flamingo.

Williams, Rowan, (2016), *On Augustine*, London: Bloomsbury Continuum.

Wilson, E. O. (2016), *Half-Earth: Our Planet's Fight for Life*, London: Norton.

Wilson, Jonathan R. (2015), *God's Good World: Reclaiming the Doctrine of Creation* (Grand Rapids: Baker Academic.

Wirzba, Norman (2015), *From Nature to Creation*, Grand Rapids: Baker Academic.

Wood, Allen W. (2010), *Hegel's Ethical Thought*, Cambridge: Cambridge University Press.

Wood, Allen W. (2016a), *Fichte's Ethical Thought*, Oxford: Oxford University Press.

Wood, Allen W. (2016b), "Fichte's Philosophy of Right and Ethics", in: D. James and G. Zoller (eds), *The Cambridge Companion to Fichte* (Cambridge: Cambridge University Press, 168-198.

Woodfield, Andrew (1976), *Teleology*, Cambridge: Cambridge University Press.

Wordsworth, William (1995), *The Prelude – the four texts (1798, 1799, 1805, 1850)*, London: Penguin.

‹http://www.bbc.co.uk/news/uk-england-24459424›, accessed 30 12 13

‹http://www.bbc.co.uk/news/uk-25599249›, accessed 07 01 14

‹www.millenniumassessment.org›, accessed 1 07 14

INDEX

INDEX OF SUBJECTS

INDEX OF NAMES

Studies in Religion and the Environment / Studien zur Religion und Umwelt
published on behalf of the European Forum for the Study of Religion and the Environment
by Sigurd Bergmann

Panu Pihkala
Early Ecotheology and Joseph Sittler
vol. 12, 2017, 312 pp., 44,90 €, pb., ISBN 978-3-643-90837-7

John Rodwell, Peter Scott (Eds.)
At Home in the Future
Place & Belonging in a Changing Europe
vol. 11, 2016, 216 pp., 29,90 €, br., ISBN 978-3-643-90638-0

Ernst M. Conradie
The Earth in God's Economy
Creation, Salvation and Consummation in Ecological Perspective
vol. 10, 2015, 362 pp., 44,90 €, pb., ISBN 978-3-643-90625-0

Anders Melin
Living with Other Beings
A virtue-oriented approach to the ethics of species protection
vol. 9, 2013, 184 pp., 29,90 €, pb., ISBN 978-3-643-90420-1

Ernst M. Conradie
Saving the Earth?
The Legacy of Reformed Views on „Re-Creation"
vol. 8, 2013, 392 pp., 39,90 €, pb., ISBN 978-3-643-90304-4

Sigurd Bergmann; Irmgard Blindow; Konrad Ott (Eds.)
Aesth/Ethics in Environmental Change
Hiking through the arts, ecology, religion and ethics of the environment
vol. 7, 2013, 216 pp., 29,90 €, pb., ISBN 978-3-643-90292-4

Ernst M. Conradie (Ed.)
Creation and Salvation
Volume 2: A Companion on Recent Theological Movements
vol. 6, 2012, 416 pp., 29,90 €, pb., ISBN 978-3-643-90137-8

Ernst M. Conradie (Ed.)
Creation and Salvation
Volume 1: A Mosaic of Selected Classic Christian Theologies
vol. 5, 2012, 232 pp., 29,90 €, pb., ISBN 978-3-643-90136-1

Tarjei Rønnow
Saving Nature
Religion as Environmentalism, Environmentalism as Religion
vol. 4, 2011, 288 pp., 29,90 €, pb., ISBN 978-3-643-11052-7

Sigurd Bergmann; Heather Eaton (Eds.)
Ecological Awareness
Exploring Religion, Ethics and Aesthetics
vol. 3, 2011, 272 pp., 29,90 €, pb., ISBN 978-3-8258-1950-7

Sigurd Bergmann; Dieter Gerten (Eds.)
Religion and Dangerous Environmental Change
Transdisciplinary Perspectives on the Ethics of Climate and Sustainability
vol. 2, 2010, 256 pp., 29,90 €, pb., ISBN 978-3-643-10093-1

LIT Verlag Berlin – Münster – Wien – Zürich – London
Auslieferung Deutschland / Österreich / Schweiz: siehe Impressumsseite